LEPIDUS

LEPIDUS

The Tarnished Triumvir

Richard D. Weigel

London and New York

First published 1992
by Routledge
11 New Fetter Lane, London EC4P 4EE

Simultaneously published in the USA and Canada
by Routledge
a division of Routledge, Chapman and Hall, Inc.
29 West 35th Street, New York, NY 10001

Typeset in 10 on 12 point Baskerville by
Falcon Typographic Art Ltd, Fife, Scotland
Printed and bound in Great Britain by
TJ Press (Padstow) Ltd, Padstow, Cornwall

British Library Cataloguing in Publication Data
Weigel, Richard D.
Lepidus; the tarnished triumvir.
I. Title.
937.07092

Library of Congress Cataloging in Publication Data
Weigel, Richard D.
Lepidus: the tarnished triumvir / Richard D. Weigel.
p. cm.
Includes bibliographical references and index.
1. Lepidus, Marcus Aemilius, d. 13 B.C. 2. Rome – History – 53–44
B.C. 3. Rome – History – Civil War, 43–31 B.C. 4. Statesman – Rome –
Biography. 5. Generals – Biography. I. Title.
DG260.L48W45   1992
937′.05′092 – dc20   91–45971   CIP

ISBN 0–415–07680–3

This book is dedicated to my parents, Russell and Welthy, and to Leslie and Lauren, all of whom have been a constant source of support, and to my mentor, Professor Evelyn Clift (1910–86)

CONTENTS

ACKNOWLEDGMENTS

I want to acknowledge the excellent advice and guidance on my dissertation with which Professor E. H. Clift provided me. She was an outstanding mentor. I would also like to thank Western Kentucky University for two summer research grants and a sabbatical leave that supported my Lepidus project. In addition, I want to express my appreciation to Susan Knight Gore and her Interlibrary Loan staff at Western Kentucky University and to the University of Cincinnati's Blegen Library for providing me with so many source materials.

1

AN INTRODUCTION TO
THE PROBLEM

Marcus Aemilius Lepidus was a major figure in Roman affairs during the last years of the Republic. As a close associate of Julius Caesar and later as pontifex maximus and as a member of the Second Triumvirate, Lepidus was a significant force in Roman political, religious, and military activities. Although he merits mention in virtually every historical account of that period, he is frequently dismissed quickly, made sport of, or bitterly attacked. In the prevalent view, Lepidus is caricatured as weak, indecisive, fickle, disloyal, and incompetent. Many commentators treat him with scorn and derision, chiefly, in my view, because he aroused Cicero's ire and because he dared challenge the authority of a young man who would later become *Divus Augustus*.

Certain quotes from antiquity have directly contributed to the proliferation of this extremely negative image of Lepidus. Cicero referred to him as 'lacking in principle and consistency, and . . . chronically ill-disposed to the free state' (*levitatem et inconstantiam animumque semper inimicum rei publicae*).[1] The orator also placed Lepidus and Mark Antony in the class of *sceleratos cives* and blamed the resumption of the war after Mutina on Lepidus' 'wickedness and sheer folly' (*scelere et amentia*).[2] Decimus Brutus branded Lepidus as 'that weathercock of a fellow' (*homo ventosissimus*).[3] Velleius Paterculus claimed that all Roman commanders were better than Lepidus and also called him 'the most fickle of mankind' (*vir omnium vanissimus*).[4]

Such accusations of incompetence, vanity, fickleness, and disloyalty appear to be very strong indictments of the man's ability and character until one considers carefully the sources and the specific situations that provoked the comments. Then one might agree that the testimony clearly lacks objectivity. And yet, the general tone of the bitter attacks continues to color the common perception of

Lepidus and the interpretation of his place in history. In literature, for example, we can see it in William Shakespeare's *Julius Caesar* and *Antony and Cleopatra*. In the former, Antony says to Octavian of Lepidus:

> This is a slight unmeritable man, meet to be sent on errands . . . though we lay these honors on this man, to ease ourselves of divers slanderous loads, he shall but bear them as the ass bears gold, to groan and sweat under the business, either led or driven, as we point the way; and having brought our treasure where we will, then take we down his load and turn him off, like to the empty ass, to shake his ears, and graze in commons.[5]

Although Octavian points out that Lepidus was 'a tried and valiant soldier,' Antony continues:

> So is my horse . . . Lepidus . . . must be taught and train'd and bid go forth; a barren-spirited fellow; one that feeds on objects, orts and imitations, which, out of use and staled by other men, begin his fashion: do not talk of him, but as a property.[6]

The Baron de Montesquieu, a great admirer of Cicero, condemned Lepidus as 'the most evil citizen who existed in the Republic' (*le plus méchant citoyen qui fût dans la république*).[7] In the modern historical novel *Three's Company*, which focuses on Lepidus' career, Alfred Duggan makes sport of the protagonist, picturing him as cowardly, stupid, shying away from combat, dominated by women, and longing for someone to give him orders. Duggan has Fulvia entice him, then slap him down and call him a 'fat miserable slug.'[8]

In modern historical scholarship, Lepidus has fared little better. W. W. Heitland described Lepidus as 'weak and shifty.'[9] Frank B. Marsh claimed that: 'Lepidus was not a man of much ability or energy.'[10] Sir Ronald Syme pictures him as a 'flimsy character,' as a 'cipher,' as 'ambiguous,' and as 'perfidious and despised.'[11] Ernst Hohl referred to Lepidus as 'a notorious simpleton' (*ein notorischer Schwachkopf*).[12] Erich Gruen sees him as 'absorbed in vanity and idleness.'[13]

The roots of the negativism that surrounds Lepidus' character seem to reach back to three specific incidents in the man's career. The first of these was the joining of the forces of Lepidus and Mark Antony in May of 43 BC, an event that stirred up fervent anger in Cicero. Although one can assume that Lepidus' close association with Julius Caesar would have caused Cicero to view Lepidus as one of the opposition, their relations prior to 43 do not appear to have been unfriendly. However, Lepidus' position in that year as provincial governor of Narbonese Gaul and Hither Spain gave him a strategic role in determining the outcome of the struggle between Cicero's senatorial forces and those following the outlaw, Antony. Cicero made a valiant effort to secure Lepidus' support through heaping piles of oratorical praise on him and even voting him an equestrian statue on the Rostra. The orator saw Lepidus' subsequent merger with Antony after Mutina as a betrayal that had snatched imminent victory from the Senate and reignited the Caesarian cause. His frustration and anger poured forth in a torrent of abuse against the man whom he had so recently praised. The effect of this bitter attack has lasted long beyond Cicero's lifetime.

The second source of negativism came from the proscriptions following the creation of the Second Triumvirate in November of 43. The executions and property confiscations naturally caused a negative response against all three triumvirs, but the inclusion on the list of Lepidus' brother, L. Aemilius Paullus (cos. 50), and of Antony's uncle, L. Caesar (cos. 64), aroused especially negative comment from historians who wanted to moralize on the betrayal of family ties. It mattered not that the two proscribed relatives had led the effort to declare Lepidus and Antony public enemies nor that both men survived the proscriptions, Paullus apparently because his brother had permitted him to escape.[14] The inclusion of relatives of Lepidus, Antony, Plancus, and Pollio, plus that of a reported former tutor of Octavian, was probably a symbolic gesture to demonstrate the toughness and will of the new regime. Although one cannot excuse the evils of the proscriptions in general, the particular charge against Lepidus for proscribing his brother is weakened somewhat by these circumstances, especially by testimony connecting the triumvir to Paullus' escape.

The third root of negativism stems from the humiliating deposition of Lepidus from the triumvirate in 36 BC. Putting aside for the moment the questions of the suspect loyalty of Lepidus' troops and of whether or not Lepidus was justified in challenging Octavian over possession of Sicily, the humiliation itself gave Julio-Claudian and later imperial historians a perfect opportunity to make fun of Lepidus for losing control of his legions to the young Caesar. It unfortunately seems to be human nature to mock a public official who has stumbled or fallen from power. In the laughter aroused by portraying Lepidus kneeling at Octavian's feet, people would probably forget that the man had once been Octavian's equal in power and had even received a better share in the initial triumviral distribution.

Through a careful examination of the three specific incidents contributing to the general negative perception of Lepidus, one can see that a large part of that judgment was politically motivated and far from objective. Although I cannot hope to reverse completely the general impression of Lepidus that has prevailed in the past, I believe that a more objective analysis of the man's life can expose the roots of negativism and show that there is reason to consider other interpretations of his ability, his character, and his role in history. I have no intention of glossing over Lepidus' failings, but I expect to show that he was competent and, on the whole, successful both as soldier and administrator. I shall dispute the usual characterization of Lepidus as a foolish nonentity and in my evaluation try to put aside the passions of the period that led to his eventual condemnation. Through a careful analysis of Lepidus' life and a close examination of all available sources, this 'tarnished triumvir' can be better understood and seen as a typical Roman noble who pursued a policy that was consistent with his past and that appeared to him to be the more secure option, rather than as some comical yet despised stereotype who has no place in a history of Rome.

2

THE AEMILII LEPIDI

A man's life is generally influenced or even determined, at least to some degree, by the lives led by his ancestors. This was even more characteristic of Republican Rome than of most societies. A Roman noble grew up very much in the shadow of his paternal ancestors. A family's future was closely tied with its past and the young noble was constantly reminded of his heritage through seeing his ancestors' portrait busts on display around the atrium or in procession at a funeral, reading inscriptions that recorded the public offices they had held, or hearing stories told about their lives, often repeated from detailed family histories. It was natural for Roman nobles to cultivate in their sons a driving ambition to imitate or even surpass the political and military achievements of their forefathers. Romans elected to the position of moneyer (*triumvir monetalis*) frequently chose coin-types that commemorated ancestors' accomplishments. They were certainly aware that this kind of 'public filial piety' would reflect glory on their own names and help them gain public recognition and political success. In many ways then, the past continued to live and affect developments and lives in the present.

Marcus Aemilius Lepidus was born around 89 or 88 BC into a tradition of distinguished public service in Rome. Many ancestors of the same name had held the major political, military, and religious posts of the state. As an Aemilius, young Lepidus was born with a special advantage, that of being included in one of the six *gentes maiores* that had flourished since the regal period. As a child he must have heard the story about the 'founder' of the Aemilian *gens*, a Mamercus Aemilius, a son of Numa Pompilius, Rome's second king (traditional dates, 715–673 BC), or, in another version, a son of the philosopher Pythagoras.[1] The Aemilian *gens* was also connected with the very founding of the city through the variant legend telling of an Aemilia, the daughter of Aeneas and Lavinia, who gave birth to Romulus by the god Mars.[2] Another family legend made an Aemilius the grandson of Aeneas through Ascanius and still another tied the founder to Jupiter.[3] Many Roman noble families associated their origins with the gods and kings, but that should not diminish the distinction attached to the Aemilian family as one of the oldest and finest in Rome.

L. Aemilius Mamercus [96][4] in 484 BC became the first family member to reach the consulship. Of seven major branches of the *gens* (Mamercus/Mamercinus, Papus, Barbula, Paullus, Lepidus, Regillus, and Scaurus), the Aemilii Lepidi were the fifth to appear in the consular lists, with a M. Aemilius Lepidus [65] in 285 BC. Although the Aemilii Paulli may have received more attention in history books, the Aemilii Lepidi lasted for the longest period and produced the most magistrates known to us. The Lepidi apparently split into two branches around the mid-third century BC. One group, including Lepidus' direct ancestors, generally named their eldest sons 'Marcus' and younger sons 'Lucius' or 'Quintus,' while the other preferred the *praenomen* 'Manius,' but also used 'Marcus' occasionally.

The ancestors who were most likely the *exempla* for young Lepidus and other Aemilii to model themselves after include M. Aemilius Paullus [118], the tragic hero who fell as consul at Cannae in 216, and his son Lucius [114], the victor at Pydna in 168.[5] These 'cousins' loomed so large in family annals that Lepidus' brother Lucius received the name 'Paullus' as a *cognomen* and passed it on to his son as a *praenomen*. One can be sure that young nobles of the Aemilian *gens* could recite the story of M. Aemilius Paullus choosing to die honorably with his fallen soldiers at Cannae rather than to flee and secure his own life. His daughter married the great Scipio Africanus and his son grew up not only to conquer Perseus at Pydna, but also to become augur, censor, twice consul, and three times *triumphator*. The son, Lucius, however, suffered the great misfortune of having witnessed the end of his family line. After he had allowed his two older sons, one of whom became Scipio Aemilianus, to be adopted into other families, his two remaining sons died young.[6]

Other ancestors revered by the Aemilii were Mamercus Aemilius [97], who as dictator three times in the late fifth century had defeated the Etruscans, L. Aemilius Privernas [101], twice consul and twice dictator, who, a century later, won major victories over the Gauls and Etruscans, the M. Aemilius Paullus [117] who, as consul in 255, erected a *columna rostrata* on the Capitoline after a naval victory in the First Punic War, and L. Aemilius Regillus [127], who defeated the fleet of Antiochus in 190.[7] Even the Aemilian women had their model, the vestal virgin Aemilia [150b], who had preserved the sacred fire in Vesta's temple by throwing her veil on the dying embers, thus magically reigniting them.[8]

Within the Lepidus branch of the family there were also several models for young nobles to imitate. These include M. Aemilius Lepidus [66], consul in 232 and augur, whose death in 216 was marked by funeral games for three days and the rare exhibition of twenty-two pairs of gladiators fighting in the Forum.[9] Another is the praetor M. Aemilius [19, 67] who defended Lilybaeum and the western Sicilian coast against Carthaginian attack in 218.[10] It is likely that the triumvir Lepidus later recalled that particular deed when he besieged the forces of Sextus Pompey defending that same seaport in 36 BC. Another distinguished family member is the M. Aemilius Lepidus [69] who rallied a group of retreating soldiers and contributed markedly to the Roman victory over Antiochus III at Magnesia in 190.[11] M. Aemilius Lepidus Porcina [83], consul of 137 and augur, earned a reputation as a great orator.[12]

There is one ancestor, however, who clearly stands out as a model for the future triumvir Lepidus. This is his great-grandfather, M. Aemilius Lepidus [68], who was twice consul, pontifex maximus, *triumphator*, censor, and six times *princeps senatus*. When the future triumvir became moneyer around 61 BC he chose this man's career for commemoration on all three of his coin designs.[13] This famous Lepidus left behind him giant tracks for any Aemilius to live up to and attached the family name to monuments such as the Pons Aemilius, the Basilica Aemilia, and the Porticus Aemilia, to the Aemiliana district in Rome, to the great road across northern Italy, the Via Aemilia, and to the region surrounding that highway, still today called Emilia.

This Lepidus was born around 230 BC. It was most likely he, and not another relative of the same name, who performed a valorous act in battle at the age of 15. Killing an enemy and saving the life of a citizen, probably in one of the battles following Cannae in the Second Punic War, earned the young man an equestrian statue built on the Capitoline at the direction of the Senate.[14] This statue and the courageous act it symbolized were important enough to the future triumvir Lepidus to be commemorated on one of his coins. A second coin-type honored the service of his ancestor in 201 BC. In that year

Lepidus negotiated for Rome with Philip V of Macedon prior to the outbreak of the Second Macedonian War and, in the scene portrayed on the coin, acted as guardian for the young Ptolemy V Epiphanes of Egypt.[15]

As curule aedile in 193 with his kinsman L. Aemilius Paullus, Lepidus built two Porticus Aemiliae.[16] While praetor in 191 he defended Sicily against invasion and saw to the transport of grain to the troops fighting Antiochus III in Greece.[17] As consul in 187 Lepidus defeated various tribes in Liguria and built the Via Aemilia from Placentia to Ariminum.[18] In 183 he was chief colonial commissioner for the establishment of the colonies of Mutina and Parma along the new road. He was most likely the patron for the families settling these colonies, thus establishing a strong tie with this region which would last for several generations.[19]

In 180 BC Lepidus was elected pontifex maximus and in the following year he capped his career by becoming censor. In one of the public reconciliation scenes that the Romans loved, Lepidus and his colleague as censor, M. Fulvius Nobilior, agreed to bury their personal enmities for the good of the state.[20] As censor Lepidus dedicated temples he had vowed in battle during his first consulship to Diana and to Juno Regina and another one vowed by his kinsman L. Aemilius Regillus to the Lares Permarini.[21] Although his colleague had actually contracted for the basilica, that building later became known as the Basilica Aemilia and the Aemilii Lepidi took a major interest in its maintenance.[22] The third of the future triumvir's coin-types pictures a building that is generally identified as the Basilica Aemilia, but it could instead represent one of his Porticus Aemiliae.[23] A second consulship in 175 was rewarded with a triumph for victories in the north.[24] Lepidus had become one of the senior statesmen of the Republic and his status was recognized by the six consecutive pairs of censors who named him *princeps senatus*.

This famous Lepidus had served Rome well during a public career of over sixty years. He proved himself to be an effective administrator, a good general, and a capable diplomat. His long tenancy of the treasured post of pontifex maximus distinguished him from most other nobles who had had successful careers. Lepidus personified the master Roman *nobilis* in almost everything he did. He accomplished with a particular style each task that he assumed. As a young legate he stood up against King Philip V of Macedon, his consulships were marked by military success, and his censorship and even his aedileship were distinguished. Lepidus also spoke out against the poor treatment that Perseus received in Roman captivity after his defeat at Pydna.[25] As *patronus* to many *clientelae* in Liguria and Cisalpine Gaul he built a lasting relationship between these areas and his family.[26] Foreign envoys coming to Rome sought out his counsel.[27] Even in death his nobility stood out. He had instructed his sons on the simplicity he desired for his funeral because real distinction for him came not from expense, but from the display of ancestor busts.[28] In many ways this man was his own ancestor. He left his mark on Rome and Italy and was an outstanding model for his descendants. The high standards that he set for his family, however, could prove to be very frustrating for those who found his great success unattainable.

That young Lepidus, the future triumvir, knew the stories told about the achievements of his great-grandfather and the other ancestors mentioned above one can hardly doubt. He may have stopped regularly by the equestrian statue on the Capitoline and dreamed that one day he too would merit such a statue. Lepidus as a young boy probably could have recited the names and deeds of each ancestor whose portrait bust stared at him from the atrium of his house. These men continued to live in a very real sense with their descendants. They served not only as models, but actually decided to some extent the future careers of their namesakes. A Roman noble could himself be a political success simply because he possessed such ancestors. His training and even his character were to a great degree determined by those who had gone before him. A large part of young Lepidus' destiny was to be fashioned by shadowy figures from earlier pages in the annals of the Aemilii Lepidi.

Lepidus may have been born into one of the finest of Roman noble houses, but the time of his birth was inauspicious both for the Republic and for his individual family. The glorious days of the half-century following the Second Punic War, when Rome was expanding, the economy flourishing, the city building new roads, public buildings, aqueducts, and so on, were now past and a period of political and social turmoil portended an uncertain future. It is somewhat ironic that Rome's success abroad brought on internal crises that threatened the very stability of the state. In a sense, at the same time that Rome was conquering peoples in all directions and extending Roman dominion over them, she herself was being consumed internally by these alien elements and overwhelmed by problems new to her and to her constitution.

The age immediately preceding Lepidus' birth around 89 or 88

BC[29] had seen the civil disruption and violence occasioned by the reforms of the Gracchi brothers and the opposition they met, the Jugurthine War and the political corruption it exposed to public view, and the foreign threat presented by the Cimbri and Teutones. Also included were the 'new army' and Marius' unprecedented run of consulships, the schemes of Saturninus and Glaucia, and the rebellion of the Italian Allies in the Social War. In many ways, Republican traditions were being challenged and discarded and the basic fabric of the constitution was being torn in the process.

The situation that Rome faced at Lepidus' birth was bleak. Unfortunately, things would only get worse. It is ironic that as the children of Lepidus' generation matured, the state became almost progressively less stable. This generation of Romans would preside over the death-throes of the Republic that their ancestors had fought so hard to build and protect. To a certain degree they cannot be blamed, for the end seemed almost inevitable. Some individuals, however, did more than their share to hasten that destruction.

3

LIKE FATHER, LIKE SON?

During the period from the late third to the late second century BC the Aemilii Lepidi had achieved repeated victories in contests for public office in Rome. The great pontifex maximus had firmly established his name both in the annals and on the map and would remain an impressive model for any young Aemilius Lepidus to emulate. However, in the late second century political success for the family abated somewhat and the new lights failed to attain the brilliance of those they replaced from previous generations. It is true that our sources for much of this period are not extensive and that could account in part for the decline in our knowledge of the family's political fortune. Still, the consuls of 158 and 126 BC are little more than names in the *fasti* and the consul of 137, M. Aemilius Lepidus Porcina[83], although a famous orator, ended up the object of derision for the failure of his siege of Pallantia in Spain.[1] Between 126 and 78 BC not a single family member reached the consulship.

A sudden gap of almost fifty years between consulships for the Aemilii Lepidi is not easy to explain, but it almost certainly had a decisive effect on the course taken by the next successful family member, the consul of 78 BC, M. Aemilius Lepidus[72]. There is some indication that political factionalism caused personal attacks on Lepidus Porcina, and Cicero's testimony that Tiberius Gracchus was a devoted listener to Porcina's oratory could indicate that this Lepidus was associated with the Gracchan reform movement and its ultimate disaster.[2] Without additional information, these points can only suggest some possible causes for the family's political difficulties. The suggestion of a Gracchan connection is especially interesting, however, in light of the association of some of the Aemilii Lepidi with 'popular' causes in the following century.

Quintus Aemilius Lepidus[78], the father of the future consul of

11

78 BC, is known to history only through his son's 'Q.f.' filiation. It is of course possible, given the incomplete nature of our sources for the period of his life, that he held offices as high as the praetorship. However, his failure to win the consulship must have given his son Marcus a tremendous incentive to achieve power once again for his family and also for himself. After all, growing up under a father whose career had not lived up to his political 'birthright' could easily have made life rather unpleasant for the son, as well as for the father. Such a situation could help explain, at least to some extent, the son's excessive ambition and impetuosity.

The M. Aemilius Lepidus who would finally restore his family to the consulship in 78 BC was probably born around 120, just after the second Gracchan experiment had ended in violence with the death of its author. As a young *nobilis* whose immediate family had recently experienced some lean political years, this Lepidus had something in common with Sulla, Catiline, and Julius Caesar, all of whom lusted for power and used extraordinary methods to acquire it. Lepidus grew up in the years that saw the introduction of the volunteer army and several consecutive consulships for its initiator, Marius. Lepidus also witnessed the increased use of force in politics, particularly by Glaucia and Saturninus, by M. Livius Drusus, and by Sulpicius Rufus in support of their radical measures. Political opposition too often found its expression in acts of violence. The tremendous power that a general with an army loyal to him personally or a tribune advocating 'popular' legislation could wield must have impressed a young noble with a burning ambition to live up to or exceed the deeds of his ancestors.

Our sources are too fragmented to allow any kind of clear picture of the early career of the future consul of 78 BC to emerge. Many historians have assumed that because Lepidus was supposed to have married an Appuleia he must have been associated as a young man with the faction of L. Appuleius Saturninus, Glaucia, and Marius.[3] Such a tie to the great war hero and repetitive consul Marius is not unlikely given Lepidus' family's recent political difficulties, and it could have benefited both sides. His noble name and his need for quick political success would have made Lepidus a natural target for recruitment and an association with Marius' great popularity and patronage would have been tempting for any noble who saw the normal route to power blocked. However, by the time of the faction's final showdown with the Senate in 100 BC Lepidus was counted among the defenders of the state.[4] Such a rapid turnaround would not be impossible because even Marius had deserted his colleagues by that time, but the whole involvement of Lepidus with this group could just as likely have never taken place at all. In fact, Sir Ronald Syme recently rejected the only evidence for a marriage to an Appuleia so the alleged connection to the Saturninus faction appears now to lack any substance.[5]

There is inscriptional evidence indicating pretty conclusively that Lepidus served in the Social War on the staff of Pompeius Strabo at Asculum in 89 BC.[6] How long he served is not clear, but his later friendship with the younger Pompey may have developed from this connection with the father. However, even if it is granted that Lepidus' eldest son being named 'Scipio' suggests adoption into the family of L. Cornelius Scipio Asiagenus, the consul of 83 and a supporter of Cinna, it does not follow automatically that Lepidus also supported the 'democratic' regime of Cinna.[7] It is difficult to believe that Lepidus could have benefited from the Sullan proscriptions and served as praetor, propraetor, and consul during Sulla's lifetime if there had been any kind of strong association with Cinna.[8] He more probably would have joined Sulla's proscription lists, instead of receiving political rewards from him.

There may indeed have been no family connection with Scipio Asiagenus. Lepidus, with his usual flair for the dramatic, may simply have given his first three sons *cognomina* commemorating famous individuals from the line of the Aemilii. The eldest was apparently Scipio, named in honor of the 'former Aemilius' Scipio Aemilianus, the second Regillus, in memory of the L. Aemilius Regillus who had defeated the fleet of Antiochus in 190 BC, and the third L. Paullus, evoking the image of the conqueror at Pydna.[9] This reconstruction cannot be proven, given our lack of sources on the first two sons, but the *Scipio, Lepidi filius* of Orosius (5.22) and the *Regillus, Lepidi filius* of Cicero (*Att.* 12.24.2) do suggest some consistency and such an unusual naming system would be quite in character for a man who would import Numidian marble just to grace the threshold of his elegant home. This man also honored his ancestors by placing portrait shields of them both in the Basilica Aemilia and in his house, which was reputed to be the finest in Rome.[10] Lepidus' naming one son 'L. Aemilius Paullus' is unusual in itself, but can be clearly documented. If this reconstruction is accepted, the major argument for a connection with Cinna's regime disappears.

As to Lepidus' enrichment from the proscriptions, there is only Sallust's questionable testimony in a speech put in the mouth of

Lepidus.[11] This reference cannot be rejected, particularly in light of Lepidus' ostentatious elegance in the decoration of his home, which does reflect a significant amount of wealth. Sallust's speech raises some serious doubts about validity, but Lepidus may very well have profited from the proscriptions, especially if his job as praetor involved judgments regarding the proscribed or overseeing the confiscation of their property.

Appian reports that an Aemilius Lepidus was instrumental in taking Norba, one of the last strongholds of resistance to Sulla.[12] Some historians have identified this Lepidus as the future consul of 77 BC, Mam. Aemilius Lepidus Livianus [80], because of his military experience and Sullan affiliations.[13] However, it seems more likely that Appian would have identified the conqueror of Norba as Mamercus Aemilius or Mamercus Livianus if he had meant the consul of 77. The description of the victor as Aemilius Lepidus would seem to indicate that Lepidus, the consul of 78, took Norba.

Lepidus apparently served as praetor in 81 and nothing is known about his service in this position, aside from the assertion that he profited from some role associated with the proscriptions. The fact that Lepidus received the praetorship and then followed that with the administration of Sicily as propraetor in 80 BC indicates that the man must have had the support of the dictator Sulla, at least at this particular time.

In his misgovernment of Sicily, where two of his ancestors had served effectively as praetors, Lepidus revealed the negative aspects of his character. It is not so much the fact that the Metelli brothers prosecuted him for maladministration upon his return to Rome; this charge was soon dropped, possibly after the intervention of Pompey, and in any case such a suit could have had a political motivation.[14] It is Cicero's testimony in his second speech against Verres that mentions Lepidus' abuse of the Sicilians only as a point of comparison for Verres' extortion in the same area.[15] It is a particularly damning comment because the orator appears to make it in an offhand, almost documentary manner. Cicero had no reason to exaggerate Lepidus' abuses here and he went on to state that even Lepidus did not levy sums of money in place of the necessary grain.[16] Exactly what Lepidus did do as propraetor we do not know, but the Sicilians apparently suffered during his governorship.

The details of Lepidus' consulship in 78 BC and its aftermath are very confused and our few sources charged with emotion and political bias. Plutarch portrays the consul as an enemy of Sulla and has the dictator warn Pompey that his assistance to Lepidus' election had strengthened a future enemy.[17] The foresight that Plutarch gives Sulla can very probably be ascribed to the biographer's own hindsight, looking back at the changes Lepidus probably proposed only after the dictator's death. Plutarch also has Sulla make a prophetic statement about the young Julius Caesar.[18]

Sulla at the time of the consular elections must have had enough power and influence to block the candidacy of a really outspoken opponent of his regime. Surely Pompey would not have risked openly supporting the election of such a man! Robin Seager's suggestion that Pompey may have backed Lepidus' candidacy because Lepidus was likely to cause trouble and create a situation that would further Pompey's career is slightly fantastic.[19] Pompey and Lepidus had a natural connection through their joint service on Pompey's father's staff and that alone is enough cause to explain the political support. It is quite possible, however, that Sulla disapproved of Pompey's backing Lepidus for reasons other than that Lepidus had already proposed radical changes to the Sullan constitution. Sulla may have been upset by Lepidus' propraetorship in Sicily and he may have been suspicious of the man's growing wealth and ostentatious behavior. Sulla could also have preferred the election of Mamercus Aemilius Lepidus Livianus to the patrician consulship, but this does not mean that he was dead-set against Lepidus' candidacy from the start.[20] Lepidus is more believable as a lesser luminary among the Sullan leadership rather than a Cinnan radical in disguise, inexplicably rewarded by his bitter political opponents. His increasing wealth and flamboyant behavior may have raised some questions about his priorities, but it is doubtful that Lepidus' colleagues viewed him on the eve of his consulship as a potential leader of rebellion.

There existed a strong mutual dislike between Lepidus and his consular colleague, Q. Lutatius Catulus.[21] This personal quarrel may be largely responsible for the frustrations, hostility, and polarization of views that characterized the consular activities in 78. Catulus' chagrin over coming in second in the consular voting, the disagreements between the consuls over the selection of an urban prefect to conduct the Latin Festival and over the issue of providing Sulla with a state funeral, and possible competition over public building projects helped create an atmosphere of hostility and inflexibility between the men who were supposed to be working together in the interests of the whole Roman state.[22] When seen in the light of this continuing personal feud, some of Lepidus' acts, although still not fully justified, appear to be less revolutionary in motivation and more the moves of a politician trying to forge a successful coalition.

Recent historical scholarship on Lepidus' rebellion in 78 BC has moderated somewhat the extreme interpretations of previous accounts.[23] Rather than being an evil man determined from the start to lead a revolution of the discontented masses, Lepidus is better understood as a more moderate leader who was involved in a power struggle with Catulus and who progressed by steps through a reform program which finally, though not inevitably, led to open revolt in his march on Rome. This view does not ignore Lepidus' ambition, his desire to reestablish his family in a position of leadership in Rome, his opportunism, or his ultimate resort to violence. It does, however, moderate the attacks of other historians who classify Roman leaders of this period as either 'good guys' or 'bad guys' and in so doing distort the historical picture.

Lepidus' attempt to block the public funeral for Sulla first marked him as a spokesman for those elements in the population who, for various reasons, were discontented with life under Sulla's regime. These would have included large numbers of people evicted from their lands and replaced by Sullan veterans, the hungry and unemployed in the cities who depended on a restoration of the grain dole, and citizens of the equestrian and lower classes who had been stripped of much of the political power to which they had become accustomed. It may be that because his break with the Sullan leadership naturally attracted to him some remaining followers of Marius and Cinna this association later convinced historians that Lepidus had always been a radical *popularis*. Although Lepidus' public stance against a state funeral may have been taken just to secure the following of these alienated groups, Léonie Hayne points out that the proposed funeral and burial in the Campus Martius may also have violated Sulla's own sumptuary law limiting funeral expenses and that Lepidus may in addition have wanted to avoid the violence likely to attend a procession through Italy and major state ceremony honoring Sulla.[24]

Catulus' support for the elaborate funeral naturally positioned him as leader of the more conservative senatorial group who had benefited from Sulla's rule and constitutional changes and who stood to lose the most from altering that system. Perhaps already at this point both men were locked into a collision course between their rival groups. If they wanted to remain the leaders of their factions, they had to say and do certain things to rally their supporters and attack their enemies.

There were certain aspects of Lepidus' political program that were well intentioned and not revolutionary in nature. His law providing for the distribution of five *modii* of grain each month was in direct violation of Sulla's ban and certainly gained him substantial support. However, the measure must also have met an immediate need because, if we can believe the testimony of Granius Licinianus, it passed *nullo resistente*.[25] Lepidus' success here must have further fueled the ire of Catulus and his followers. The *Lex Aemilia* to ration food is another indication of the serious problems facing Rome and it also demonstrates that Lepidus was concerned with something more than just currying the favor of the discontented because this would not have been a very popular measure.[26]

Lepidus' bill to recall those still in exile from Sulla's proscriptions also passed.[27] This was self-serving, but it should not be viewed as a revolutionary measure. However, the recall must have made those who had helped initiate the proscriptions a little uneasy. Lepidus also resisted at first the call for a restoration of the powers of the tribunes.[28] He later changed his mind, but his early stance once again supports the more moderate interpretation of his consulship.

The disturbance in Etruria at Faesulae, where evicted citizens banded together to attack the Sullan veterans who had replaced them as landowners, seems to have been the key turning-point for Lepidus. Although our scanty and biased sources often give the impression that he openly advocated rebellion from the beginning, it is hard to believe that the Senate would have trusted Lepidus with an army if it was already known that he advocated the same redistribution of land favored by the rebels in Etruria. The Senate sent the consuls to put down the disturbance, requiring both men to take an oath that they would maintain the peace.[29]

The mission to Faesulae gave Lepidus the opportunity to witness the full extent of the economic, social, and political discontent in Italy and to assess the potential for organizing the opposition into a powerful force. He must have decided to build up his military support and become the champion of the oppressed, the future savior of Rome. Earlier reformers had seen the need for change, but had lacked the control of armies necessary to effect it. Marius, Cinna, and Sulla had used military strength to further their political careers and Lepidus believed that he could do the same. After all, Lepidus had little to look forward to beyond his proconsulship because he was not fully accepted by the power structure in the Senate. He chose to forge a new coalition and let it carry him to greater heights, while at the same time addressing some of the serious economic and social problems plaguing Rome and Italy.

The details are confused and unclear, but Lepidus apparently picked up the support of many malcontents and adventure-seekers in the area of Faesulae and set up a base of power in his proconsular province of Cisalpine Gaul, where his name was magic to the descendants of *clientelae* settled there by his famous ancestor in the previous century. The area had also served as a recruiting-ground for Carbo against Sulla and would continue to be a source of senatorial opposition later in the first century.[30]

Lepidus must have introduced at this point his more extreme measures, which called for the restoration of land to those dispossessed by Sulla's veterans and for the return of the powers of the tribunate. These proposals presented a far more serious and immediate threat to the established order. They conjured up fears and memories of civil war and a repetition of the violence that had accompanied the programs of the Gracchi, Sulpicius, and Drusus or even a reignition of the Social War.

Once Lepidus decided to rally the discontented elements in Etruria and elsewhere behind his standard, his personal conflict with Catulus assumed the character of an insurrection. His march on Rome with an army and his demand for another consulship, even though he had recent precedent for such acts, cast Lepidus in the mold of a Marius, Cinna, or Sulla. Catulus and his senatorial supporters could legitimately label Lepidus an enemy of the state and proceed against him militarily. Pompey came to the defense of the state against his former friend and defeated the enemy forces in Cisalpine Gaul, which resulted in the deaths of Lepidus' chief lieutenant, M. Brutus, and Lepidus' eldest son, called Scipio.[31] After Catulus repelled the attack of Lepidus' troops on Rome, Pompey prevented their regrouping by beating them near Cosa.[32] Lepidus departed for Sardinia and died there soon afterwards, while the remnants of his army went on to Spain to join Sertorius.[33]

Lepidus' ambition and overconfidence led him to acts he would probably have never contemplated in a less turbulent period. He saw the discontent and anger in Italy and felt he could channel it into a coalition that would give him great power in Rome.

However, the movement carried him far beyond his initial goals and raised too severe a challenge to the established order in the Roman state. Recent studies have correctly interpreted Lepidus as a more moderate reformer who gradually turned or was pushed to revolution. The nature of our sources unfortunately will not allow a more complete reassessment of his career. The abuses of his propraetorship in Sicily remain as a blot on his reputation. In addition, despite the personal nature of his initial quarrel with Catulus and the positive aspects of his consulship, Lepidus, for whatever reasons, chose the route of power and war over the path of peace and accommodation and he must be held accountable for that choice.

What is most important for our purposes here is to determine what effect the father's failure and death in disgrace had on the son, the future triumvir. At about age 11 or 12, the young M. Aemilius Lepidus experienced the glory of seeing his father inaugurated as consul. This emotional peak was soon followed by the traumatic events of having to watch his father being branded as a public enemy and driven from Rome by force. The sudden deaths of his father and oldest brother and the shame and humiliation associated with his father's revolt must have made a lasting impression on young Lepidus. Was the son to be like the father? Not really, because he would instead learn to work with others and his route to power was tied to the careers of his colleagues, especially Julius Caesar, who had declined the invitation to join Lepidus' father. Although both men suffered the indignity of condemnation as public enemies and fell from power in disgrace, these similar experiences do not tell the complete story. The future triumvir would choose a path very different from that of his father and his skills of arbitration and administration, as well as his noble name, would bring him greater and longer-lasting success, even if also eventually leading to his undoing.

4

THE FIRST TRIUMVIRATE

The death of Lepidus as a disgraced outlaw in 77 BC must have left a major void in the lives of his two surviving sons. Lucius was about 15 or 16 at the time and Marcus 11 or 12. Although it seems unusual for the youngest son to receive his father's *praenomen*, it is quite possible that the eldest son had been called 'Marcus' before becoming 'Scipio' or that the future triumvir received the name only after the deaths of his father and oldest brother. This does not explain why Lucius Paullus was not renamed 'Marcus' in preference to his younger brother, but he may of course have chosen to keep his distinguished name.

The divergent paths followed by the two surviving brothers should give pause to prosopographers who assume that members of a family can generally be grouped together in the same political faction. Both of them would, however, choose the more common political route of association with more powerful men over the more individualistic, rabble-rousing approach that had caused their father's downfall. Lucius would generally side with Cicero and the defenders of the Republic, while Marcus would join Caesar's inner circle of assistants.

Whether or not their mother retained an influence over her two sons is not clear. Pliny the Elder's statement that Lepidus had divorced her seems no longer to be relevant.[1] She may have married someone who could have assisted her sons' development and later careers or they could have been looked after by other family members. The only other Aemilii Lepidi known to us from this period are two stalwart optimates, Mamercus Aemilius Lepidus Livianus [80], the consul of 77 BC, and Manius Aemilius Lepidus [62], consul in 66.[2] There is probably no connection with the young men's eventual choices of leaders, but it is interesting to note that

Mamercus was in some way related to Caesar, on whose behalf he intervened with Sulla when Caesar was proposed for proscription.[3] Manius Lepidus, on the other hand, was a close friend of Cicero.[4]

The two young men grew up during the decade of the 70s BC, when Sulla's arrangements were systematically dismantled and a new generation of leaders, including Cicero, Pompey, Crassus, and Julius Caesar, began to dominate affairs in Rome. Some of their father's 'revolutionary' proposals became law, but fundamental economic and social problems continued to threaten the Republic.

The period from 60 to 50 BC is influenced to a great degree by the power bloc known as the First Triumvirate. By joining forces, Caesar, Pompey, and Crassus found that they could better advance their individual political interests. While Caesar received the consulship and built up glory, wealth, and soldiers' loyalty during his extensive military operations in Gaul, Pompey and Crassus were able to satisfy their supporters and also receive second consulships and their own lucrative provincial commands, in Spain and Syria respectively. Cicero's position of power declined somewhat from its peak during his consulship in 63, as his exile and subsequent relatively muted criticism show. Still, the orator had many senatorial allies and substantial support. The triumvirs were far from being in total control of the situation in Rome and the turmoil caused by riots and by the gang activities of Milo and Clodius were only a prelude to the horrors of the Civil War that would follow.[5]

It is in the midst of this volatile political situation that Lucius Paullus and Marcus Lepidus began to play individual roles. Despite the ignominy associated with their father, the young men possessed several advantages, including the Aemilian tradition and substantial family ties and inherited support.[6]

Lucius first appears in our sources in 63 BC when he indicted Catiline for violating the *Lex Plautia* concerning public violence.[7] This act helped set the stage for Cicero's subsequent first 'Catilinarian' oration to the Senate, which exposed the plot to seize power in Rome. In 57 BC Lucius also helped sponsor the bill that brought about Cicero's recall from exile.[8] Lucius' career would continue to follow the interests of the optimates for the most part, with the marked exception of his consulship in 50 BC, when Caesar succeeded in purchasing his neutrality.

Marcus, or Lepidus, as we may now call him without causing too much confusion with his relatives, joined the College of Pontiffs at a fairly young age. This would be a significant achievement for him, both as a major step in imitation of the outstanding career of his 'model ancestor' and for the later role he would play as pontifex maximus. If Lily Ross Taylor's suggested emendation of Macrobius' list of pontiffs (*Saturnalia* 3. 13. 11) is correct, then young Lepidus probably succeeded his relative, Mamercus Aemilius Lepidus Livianus, as pontiff in the late 60s BC.[9] Why Marcus received this opportunity over his older brother is not clear, but a combination of factors, including his name, his politics, and the support of the new pontifex maximus, Julius Caesar, was probably involved here.

The office of moneyer, or *triumvir monetalis*, in the first century BC gave its occupants substantial freedom to commemorate an individual family's accomplishments and thus provided a very effective form of free advertising for their own future political careers.[10] Lepidus' tenure of this position occurred roughly in the period between 62 and 58 BC and he issued three distinct coin-types honoring the achievements of the famous M. Lepidus of the second century.[11] The coin proclaiming Lepidus' position as *tutor* for King Ptolemy V of Egypt might seem to be a rather obscure choice from the numerous events of the pontifex maximus' extensive career. However, the Egypt Bill of 65 BC and renewed Roman interest in Egyptian affairs made this special relationship between the Aemilii Lepidi and Egypt something young Lepidus would definitely want to bring to people's attention.[12] The equestrian statue earned for bravery in battle as a youth and a building associated with his censorship in 179 were also honored on coins.[13] The pontifical symbols used on some of the issues and the name M. LEPIDVS boldly inscribed on each coin could refer to both the ancestor and to the moneyer. The implied message to Romans is something like: 'Vote for Marcus Lepidus, whose name has brought Rome such glories in the past!'

Erich Gruen and Léonie Hayne have suggested that Lepidus and especially his brother L. Paullus pursued some kind of inherited blood feud against Pompey because of that man's desertion from and ultimate defeat of their father.[14] The evidence cited in support of this alleged *inimicitia* is circumstantial and difficult to accept in light of the fact that the brothers Lepidi both successfully negotiated with Sextus Pompey.[15] Would the Senate have selected L. Paullus as one of its three representatives to deal with Sextus if such a state of hostility had really existed between the two families?

Caesar makes no reference to Lepidus having served in the Gallic campaigns. This may seem strange in light of the close relationship between the two men in the next decade, but Lepidus may already have been managing Caesar's interests in Rome during this period, as he would later. Lepidus probably held the quaestorship sometime between 60 and 57 BC, since it was a prerequisite to his later magistracies, but there is no evidence recording his service in that position. In 57 BC, Lepidus is included in Cicero's list of pontiffs who ruled against Clodius' attempt to dedicate a shrine of Libertas on the site of Cicero's house.[16]

During Cicero's exile Clodius had declared the orator's property on the Palatine sacred ground and torn down his house, hoping to prevent Cicero from relocating there upon his return. Lepidus' vote in support of Cicero's position here need not have any particular political meaning since the decision was unanimous, with the pontifex maximus, Caesar, absent because of his campaigns in Gaul. Clodius' shenanigans were an outrage even to some of the supporters of the triumvirate and the restoration of Cicero's house was a relatively minor concession to make, especially in view of the overwhelming popular support that had attended the orator's recent return from exile.

The established view that one had to have held a curule magistracy prior to being chosen *interrex*, which Lepidus supposedly became in 52 BC, indicates that Lepidus must have been curule aedile around 53 BC.[17] There is no record of such service, although Lepidus as aedile could conceivably have been involved in his brother's rebuilding of the Basilica Aemilia during that period.[18] The aedileship was an office where ambitious politicians would spend a great deal of money on constructing buildings and presenting public games, all with an eye towards currying support for future campaigns.

By 53 BC whatever stability had resulted from the uniting of Pompey, Caesar, and Crassus in the First Triumvirate had been shattered by the loss of Julia in childbirth and by the death of Crassus in the disaster at Carrhae; civil war loomed on the horizon. Electoral corruption, political trials, and violence increased. The consuls of 53 BC had not been elected until July and the following year also began without consuls. The clashes between the rival gangs of Milo and Clodius had increased in frequency because in the election campaign Milo was seeking the consulship and Clodius the praetorship. Violence had prevented the elections for 52 from being held and the murder of Clodius in mid-January and the subsequent uproar and burning of the Curia only escalated the chaos. It was in the midst of this turmoil that the Senate selected M.

Lepidus as the first *interrex*, but Clodian supporters besieged him in his house throughout the five days of his term and he was unable to hold the elections. Return volleys of arrows drove back the attackers from both Lepidus' and Milo's houses, but turbulence continued to plague Rome.[19]

The selection of Lepidus as *interrex* is somewhat unusual because he had not yet been praetor, but his family name and his experience as pontifex, and perhaps the impression that he was relatively neutral in this particular election campaign, may have singled him out for the appointment. E.S. Staveley has suggested that the few patricians qualified to serve as *interrex* had already held the difficult job during the previous year and that they welcomed the chance to appoint Lepidus, newly eligible through having completed his curule magistracy.[20] It is not known whom he chose as his successor, but after a long period Ser. Sulpicius Rufus presided over the election of Pompey as sole consul.[21]

Although Asconius says that Lepidus' wife at the time of his service as *interrex* was a Cornelia, his statement is generally rejected because all other sources attest to the fact that Iunia, Brutus' half-sister, was married to Lepidus and that she was the mother of his presumed first child, Marcus. For this son to have been engaged to Antony's daughter in 44 and married to a Servilia before his insurrection against Octavian in 30, he must have been born as early as 58 BC. This would place Lepidus' marriage to Iunia around 60 or 59 at the latest.[22]

The marriage to Iunia is important, incidentally, not only for the ties that it established between Lepidus and Brutus, Cassius, and P. Servilius Isauricus. This marriage connection is also only one of several political or social ties between the Aemilii Lepidi and the Iunii Bruti. The most recent example of these bonds before the marriage can be seen in the service of Brutus' father as a legate under Lepidus' father in the rebellion of 78–7 BC.[23]

Although there is very little evidence on Lepidus' early life, it is still interesting to note that there is no indication in these years that he leaned at all in the direction of the *populares* leaders who opposed the conservative senatorial majority, perhaps because his father had died in shame for taking such a path. It is possible that his election as pontifex when Caesar was pontifex maximus, when seen in light of his later closeness to Caesar, indicates that he was already an agent for Caesar in Rome while the campaigns were going on in Gaul. There is nothing in the sources, however, that confirms or even suggests such activity. Lepidus' concurrence with the unanimous pontifical ruling on Cicero's house, his selection by the Senate as *interrex* in a period of turmoil, and the attacks on his house by the followers of Clodius all indicate that to this point he was, if anything, a senatorial stalwart.

It is possible that the selection as *interrex* and the house siege refer not to M. Lepidus, the future triumvir, but to M' Lepidus, the consul of 66 BC. This interpretation would require shifting M. to M' in a few texts, but it would resolve the problems of explaining how such a young man who had not yet served as praetor could receive the office of *interrex* and Asconius' statement that Lepidus' wife was a Cornelia when all other sources suggest that he must have already been married to Iunia. There is not enough evidence to conclusively reject the idea that M. Lepidus held the position of *interrex*, and the curule aedileship that would therefore be a prerequisite, but M' Lepidus would have been a more likely candidate, given his consulship.[24]

M. Lepidus' brother, L. Paullus, had even stronger credentials as a supporter of the optimate cause than did Marcus. Lucius had indicted Catiline and assisted Cicero's prosecution of Cethegus, was falsely accused by Vettius of leading a group planning to assassinate Pompey, had helped sponsor the bill to secure Cicero's return from exile, had testified as one of Cicero's witnesses in defense of M. Scaurus, and had been considered such a powerful opponent for the praetorship in 53 BC that Clodius postponed his own candidacy by one year.[25] Cicero had praised L. Paullus as 'a man born for the purpose of preserving the Republic' (*hominem ad conservandam rem publicam natum*).[26]

Lucius' election as consul for 50 BC was seen as a great success by the optimates, who had fought hard to elect men they could trust to deal with the thorny task of terminating Caesar's command.[27] However, the effort to replace Caesar in Gaul and bring him back to Rome before he could win another consulship and escape trial by his opponents would still fail. It appears that L. Paullus and the tribune C. Scribonius Curio, both elected as optimate candidates, managed to maneuver and block proceedings sufficiently to delay action against him without actually supporting Caesar openly.[28] Paullus' apparent defection to the Caesarian cause is generally attributed to a bribe of 1500 talents, paid from Gallic booty, with which the consul was able to complete his magnificent rebuilding of the Basilica Aemilia.[29]

Lepidus may well have played a role in securing his brother's 'benevolent neutrality' for Caesar, but our meager sources do not offer any insight into this situation. The elections for 49 BC returned two anti-Caesarian consuls, but Lepidus won the praetorship and M. Antony became tribune.[30] The fact that Lepidus was to serve as *praetor urbanus*, regardless of whether he was elected to that task or just given that important assignment under Caesar, indicates that at least by this time he was an active agent for Caesar in Rome. It is not likely that he would have been trusted with such a post if he had been newly converted to the cause in the midst of the Civil War.

The year 49 BC began with the stage set for the conflict between the two surviving colleagues of the First Triumvirate, Caesar and Pompey. Although the agreement to work together may have satisfied Pompey's immediate needs and brought him some additional commands, in the long run it was Caesar who had benefited the most from the arrangement. The past decade had seen Caesar rise dramatically in power and Pompey was at least partially responsible for that success. Now Caesar would be able to use his seasoned troops against the senatorial forces raised by his former colleague.

In the early months of 49 BC, after crossing the provincial boundary of the Rubicon river with his troops, Caesar systematically gained control of so much of Italy that Pompey was forced to withdraw with his army and senatorial supporters and try to regroup in Greece. Caesar decided to go to Spain to defeat the forces under Pompey's legates there before pursuing his opponents to the east. First, he stopped off in Rome, seizing the treasury reserved for defense against the Gauls and leaving Lepidus in charge of the city as praetor and Antony with troops to defend Italy.[31]

With the consuls gone to support Pompey, Lepidus, if he was *praetor urbanus*, would have governed Rome anyway. If he was one of the other praetors, and the original *praetor urbanus* had fled Italy with Pompey, then he performed the job unofficially. In either case, the selection of Lepidus to be in charge of the city is a statement of Caesar's confidence in the man, as well as an effort to keep the Caesarian administration as close to constitutionality as feasible.

Aside from governing Rome in Caesar's absence, Lepidus' only other known act as praetor was securing the appointment of Caesar as dictator. As early as March Caesar had asked for Cicero's opinion as to the constitutionality of a praetor holding the consular elections or naming a dictator. Caesar wanted to find a method to elect himself consul for 48 and probably had Lepidus in mind as the best candidate to hold those elections. Cicero was opposed to the whole idea, but could not justify Sulla's appointment as dictator by an *interrex* either.[32] Caesar probably decided that the dictatorship would be his most legal route to a consulship and so instructed Lepidus.

While Caesar was at Massilia (Marseilles) on his way back from Spain, he learned of his selection as dictator through a law secured by Lepidus as praetor.[33] Caesar came to Rome and assumed this dictatorship for eleven days to conduct the elections which, to no one's surprise, gave him the consulship for 48 BC. With the assistance of unidentified praetors and tribunes, almost certainly including Lepidus, who introduced motions to the tribal assembly, the dictator secured the restoration of rights for a large group of people who had been exiled for bribery by Pompey. After holding the Latin festival, Caesar resigned his dictatorship and left Rome for Brundisium.[34]

Before departing for Greece Caesar had arranged for Lepidus to become proconsul in Hither Spain for the year 48 BC. This appointment can be interpreted both as a reward for Lepidus' service as praetor in 49 and as part of Caesar's effort to place governors loyal to him in the provinces.[35] Again the appointment reflects Caesar's confidence in Lepidus' abilities because the opposition in Spain had only just been reduced and to place an incompetent governor there would have been too great a risk when Caesar was leaving for Greece. There is no recorded opposition to Lepidus' receiving a provincial governorship in violation of Pompey's law requiring a five-year interval between a man's magistracy and his command. None should really be expected in a time of civil war and those who would have objected most strenuously were all removed from the center of power, awaiting the outcome which would be decided at Pharsalus.

During 48 and 47 BC, while Caesar was engaged in defeating Pompey in Thessaly and in carrying on operations in Egypt and in Asia Minor, Lepidus governed Hither Spain as proconsul. Although he saw little military action, he did play a vital role in keeping the peace in a land ripe for revolt. This was particularly important because of Caesar's military commitments elsewhere. Caesar counted on Lepidus to maintain control in Spain during this crucial period and Lepidus performed his task admirably. The extent of the danger can be better understood when one considers the violent opposition that developed in Spain in 46 and 45 BC, causing

Caesar to return and crush the rebellion at Munda. Caesar granted Lepidus a triumph for preventing that kind of revolt from breaking out when it could least be handled, although some may mock this military honor accorded for preserving the peace. [36]

The situation for which Lepidus earned his triumph actually occurred outside his province in Farther Spain, where Q. Cassius Longinus had been serving Caesar as governor with propraetorian authority since 49 BC. Cassius had abused both the provincials and the soldiers under his command and was faced with several attempts at assassination and finally with a mutiny among his troops which raised his quaestor, M. Claudius Marcellus Aeserninus, as its commander.[37] In an effort to regain control, Cassius appealed for help in Caesar's name from King Bogud in Mauretania, just across the straits in Africa, and from Lepidus, the new proconsul of Hither Spain. He requested that aid be sent as soon as possible both for the defense of the province and for his personal safety.[38] Bogud did send help to Cassius, but the struggle between Cassius and Marcellus, which had shifted from Corduba to Ulia, continued until the arrival of Lepidus.

Lepidus brought with him to Ulia a force including thirty-five legionary cohorts and a large contingent of cavalry and auxiliary troops. Despite the fact that Cassius had called for Lepidus' help, the proconsul clearly responded as an impartial third party intending to end the dispute, rather than as a supporter of Cassius. Marcellus wisely submitted himself to Lepidus' judgment.

Lepidus set up his camp at Ulia and invited Cassius to visit him under a guarantee of personal safety. Cassius, probably fully aware that Lepidus knew of his guilt and seeing no chance to gain anything through arbitration, apparently spurned this offer. Lepidus had forbidden any fighting and Cassius knew that his forces were not strong enough to resist the combined troops of Lepidus and Marcellus, even if he could count on Bogud's support. Cassius must also have anticipated his imminent replacement and, aware of Caesar's recent victory over Pompey at Pharsalus, seen that the end to his independent exploitation of the area was near in any case. He chose to make the best of the situation and escape with his life and his extorted wealth.

Lepidus apparently succeeded in arranging a truce to allow for the destruction of entrenchments and Cassius' withdrawal from the area, but a surprise attack on Marcellus' camp by Bogud's auxiliary troops was only defeated by the swift arrival of Lepidus' soldiers. Lepidus and Marcellus soon joined forces and marched towards Corduba. Cassius fled towards Carmo and later perished on his way back to Rome, after having been replaced by C. Trebonius.[39]

Lepidus was successful in ending the immediate threat to the peace caused by the abuses of Cassius. The incident may seem trivial, but it was important for Caesar to keep a unified control over his forces and to promote peace in the provinces at a time when there was still a threat from the remaining Pompeian opposition, especially in Spain.

Nothing else is known about Lepidus' proconsulship in Spain during 48 and 47 BC. It is possible that it was during this period that he founded the Roman colony that assumed his name, Colonia Victrix Julia Lepida. This site was located in the north-east, near the Ebro River. The colony, better known as Celsa, could also have been an accomplishment of Lepidus' second governorship of Hither Spain around 44 to 42 BC.[40]

It was Lepidus' valuable service in quieting a potentially dangerous rebellion and in reinforcing Caesarian control in Spain that caused Caesar to honor Lepidus with a triumph and reward him with the offices of consul and *magister equitum* for the year 46 BC. Lepidus had now reached the pinnacle of a Roman noble's political career and could be quite proud that he had replicated the achievements of his famous model ancestor to a great degree. It probably did not trouble Lepidus too much that his success was to some extent a result of his loyal service to another man because that condition was becoming practically mandatory for the ambitious Roman noble of his time.

5

FRIEND OF CAESAR

Lepidus received in 46 BC the rewards for his loyal and important services performed in support of Julius Caesar over the previous several years. The glory of Lepidus' consulship was enhanced by the honor of serving in this consummate office of the Roman Republic with Caesar as his colleague. In addition, the dictator granted Lepidus a triumph for his handling of the struggle between Marcellus and Cassius in Farther Spain and, probably later in the year, named him as his *magister equitum*.

Caesar's selection of Lepidus to govern Rome once again during his absence, this time while the dictator went to war with the remaining Pompeian opposition in Africa, and the bestowal upon Lepidus of the two offices and of a triumph, can all be interpreted as political rewards for someone whose noble name was needed to bring Caesar's ersatz government greater legitimacy. However, although Lepidus' background was helpful and rewards were clearly involved, Caesar was also displaying through these acts his confidence that Lepidus would perform his important tasks ably. It is difficult to believe that a man as shrewd as Caesar would have entrusted an 'incompetent mediocrity' with such authority and yet this trust is often overlooked because of the prevailing interpretation of Lepidus common to so many historians.

Caesar's choice of Lepidus to administer Rome during his absence showed not only the dictator's faith in Lepidus' ability to govern, but also demonstrated at the same time his lack of trust in Antony and constituted a public rebuke for Antony's failure to keep Rome stable in 47 BC. Disapproval of Antony's bawdy lifestyle, riots over Dolabella's proposals for debt cancellation and remission of rents, and mutinous veteran soldiers all pointed to Antony's lack of control and convinced Caesar to return to Rome early to restore stability.[1] Caesar's dramatic address to the discontented troops was complemented by his replacement of Antony as Rome's administrator with Lepidus, who had served very well in that capacity as praetor in 49 BC. Caesar needed a non-controversial figure who could prevent another outbreak of violence in Rome at this particularly critical time. Lepidus was also elected Caesar's colleague as consul, a position for which he was then for the first time legally eligible. To further strengthen Lepidus' position, he must have been reintroduced to the city in triumph for his activities in Spain and also received Antony's position as master of horse. The triumph, a reward that Caesar did not confer freely upon others, probably occurred late in 47 as a prelude to Lepidus' inauguration as consul.[2]

Although Dio Cassius questioned the legitimacy of Lepidus' triumph and the lack of a precedent for his being simultaneously consul and *magister equitum*, there is no evidence that anyone found unusual what would seem to have been the most blatant departure from constitutional traditions, the election for the first time since 343 BC of two patrician consuls.[3] Caesar obviously desired to keep one consulship for himself and Lepidus surely wanted to become consul in his first year of eligibility, but instead of yielding one or the other position to avoid criticism, Caesar chose to forge ahead in total disregard for the constitutional provisions. This impulsive drive to get his own way, accompanied by his apparent scorn for tradition, would eventually lead to Caesar's assassination.

The consulship of Caesar and Lepidus in 46 BC began with the dictator in Africa, preparing for the next stage of his campaign against the remaining Pompeian opposition. Lepidus must have performed the inaugural duties expected of a consul. He was probably assisted in his task of administering Rome by six or eight city prefects, who assumed tasks normally carried out by the urban magistrates.[4] Two other Caesarian agents, L. Cornelius Balbus and C. Oppius, performed valuable service as lobbying agents for the dictator's programs. In the light of Lepidus' association with other building projects of Caesar later, it is plausible to suggest that he was also involved in 46 BC with supervising the construction of Caesar's new forum and its crowning jewel, the temple of Venus Genetrix. This work prepared well for Caesar's triumphant returns after both Thapsus and Munda and also provided jobs for the unemployed.

In the absence of Caesar, the pontifex maximus, Lepidus as his representative and as consul and later *magister equitum* probably played a leading role in the pontifical college. He was in a position to use religion as a political control if necessary, but there is no indication that the need ever arose. The pontiffs could have met to discuss expiation for the bad omens inaugurating the year.[5] If so, their prescription must have worked, because, from Caesar's point of view at least, things turned out very well. The dictator was able to defeat his opponents in Africa within a few months. After the victory at Thapsus the noble Cato took his life, thus removing from the struggle another leader of the Republican opposition.

Lepidus as consul must have directed the efforts to prepare for Caesar's triumphant return to Rome. Caesar was designated as dictator for the next ten years and received censorial powers of *cura morum* for three. Sacrifices for his victory were to be offered for forty days and a magnificent quadruple triumph was planned.[6]

It is difficult to speculate on how Lepidus must have felt privately about these and other excessive honors that he must have arranged to be lavished upon Caesar. On the one hand, Lepidus had tied his own fortune to Caesar's and had reaped within a few years most of the political rewards that a Roman noble could ever hope to achieve in an entire career. Lepidus may have viewed Caesar not just as a friend or patron, but as a kind of father-figure, a substitute for the father he had lost as a boy in a traumatic twist of fate and subsequent disgrace. Caesar must have filled that void to excess by providing security in the midst of chaos, by allowing his junior colleague to share in some of the reflected glory, and by helping to advance Lepidus' career just as his natural father might have done had he lived. Lepidus was devoted to Caesar and served him loyally. His desire for vengeance upon the dictator's murderers later would be prompted by real emotion and not merely by a hope for personal gain. Lepidus' wish to be pontifex maximus and his position as triumvir were influenced by the model of Caesar's splendid career. Unfortunately, the model was both flawed and ill suited to imitation.

At the same time, however, Lepidus must have winced at the excess of luxury and power demanded by Caesar and piled upon him by his fawning admirers. As consul, *magister equitum*, and loyal Caesarian, Lepidus had to foster and direct the cult of the leader, but he must have had doubts about the direction the dictator was taking. Here he differed from Antony, whose approach to life was more unconventional than that of the traditional Roman noble. Lepidus would have remembered the wisdom of his own model ancestor, who on his deathbed had advised his sons not to spend lavishly on his funeral because 'the dignity of the funerals of great men was properly enhanced not by expenditure, but by the parade of ancestral portraits' (*imaginum specie, non sumptibus nobilitari magnorum virorum funera solere*).[7] Although he would never openly break with his benefactor, Lepidus' personal feelings of anguish would later be apparent when Antony presented Caesar with the diadem during the celebration of the Lupercalia in 44 BC.[8]

In the summer of 46 BC Caesar returned to Rome from Africa to celebrate his four triumphs. His position of power by this time was virtually absolute and he used his authority to effect several reforms, including the establishment of the Julian calendar. Lepidus and the other pontiffs may have conferred with Caesar on this change, but the issue, although of major importance, was probably not that controversial. In order to coordinate the calendar and the solar year, Caesar as pontifex maximus and dictator extended the duration of the consulship of himself and Lepidus to 445 days.[9] This move should not be construed as an attempt to prolong the power of the consuls of 46 because there was no question as to whether or not Caesar would continue to be both dictator and consul. It was a valuable contribution intended to establish a more stable calendar and bring the religious festivals back into their proper relationship with the seasons of the year.

Other reforms that Caesar initiated in 46 probably included his reduction of the number of people receiving the grain dole from 320,000 to 150,000, his limitation of jury service to the senatorial and equestrian classes, his restriction of the length of the term of a propraetor to one year and of a proconsul to two consecutive years, and his *Lex Julia municipalis*, which set down rules for municipal administration.[10]

At some time during Lepidus' consulship, presumably when Caesar was absent, Cicero requested Lepidus' aid on behalf of one of the orator's best friends, his former quaestor L. Mescinius Rufus. Cicero wrote to Caesar's proconsul in Achaea, Ser. Sulpicius Rufus, asking him to settle Mescinius' local business affairs, which concerned his inheritance from his cousin, who had been a banker in Elis. To his own request Cicero added a letter from Lepidus to Sulpicius to strengthen further the recommendation of favorable treatment of Mescinius' case.[11] Lepidus' compliance with Cicero's request to write to Sulpicius on this matter shows not only the existence of a positive relationship between Cicero and Lepidus at this time, but also indicates a desire to cater to the orator's personal wishes to help keep the opposition quiet in Rome. Antony might not have performed that task so well.

There is some confusion about when Caesar first designated Lepidus as his *magister equitum*. Eutropius dates the event to 47 BC, the year before their joint consulship.[12] The Fasti Capitolini include the honor for 45 and 44 BC, but not for 46. Its absence in 46 is not conclusive, however, because a dictatorship for Caesar is also not listed for that year.[13] Dio places the office in 46 and complains that Lepidus had violated tradition by making himself *magister equitum* while still consul.[14] The suggestion is that it was done in Caesar's absence, but as consul in 46. If Antony's replacement by Lepidus was intended as a rebuke for Antony's mishandling of affairs in 47, then it should have occurred relatively soon after that.

Dio may of course have been mistaken, but the fact that he commented on the conflict involved in holding the two offices simultaneously, even though there was some precedent for that, appears to be the strongest evidence available. Lepidus as consul probably read in public the dictator's edict appointing him as *magister equitum*, perhaps late in the year 46, when he held the election creating Caesar's sole consulship for 45.[15] This would make sense in view of Caesar's plans because the dictator would want Lepidus to have the authority of some office so that he could 'legitimately' govern Rome during the campaign in Spain. Lepidus had been praetor while performing the duties in 49 and consul when repeating the job in 46. The office of *magister equitum* could give him the justification for officially being in charge during Caesar's absence in 45.

The Pompeian opposition had been regrouping in Spain where it found substantial support and was able to fuel the discontent left by the maladministration of Q. Cassius Longinus. Late in 46 Caesar decided that swift action was needed and he left Rome again, leaving Lepidus in charge with six or eight prefects to aid him in administering affairs.[16] Lepidus soon afterward used his consular authority to convoke an assembly to elect Caesar as sole consul for 45. He probably also read publicly an edict from the dictator proclaiming Lepidus as *magister equitum*.[17]

Caesar was occupied for the first eight months of the year 45 in winning a hard-fought victory over the Pompeian forces at Munda, near Corduba, and in reestablishing his control in Spain.[18] It was probably during this period that Lepidus directed some building projects which seem to have been part of Caesar's master plan to reconstruct Rome. One of these was the erection in the Campus

Martius of a permanent voting place to be used by the centuriate and tribal assemblies. Cicero had mentioned Caesar's intention to construct a marble building for assembly voting, surrounded by a porticus of a mile in circumference, as early as 54 BC.[19] Caesar may have begun the construction of the Saepta Iulia, but Dio Cassius credits Lepidus with the building, including an encircling porticus, and says that Agrippa further adorned the structure and dedicated it in 26 BC.[20]

The idea of a permanent polling place fits in well with the dictator's plans for an extensive building program to provide jobs and make Rome glisten as a shining example of Caesar's magnificence. The Saepta Iulia was very large and is thought to have been situated just east of the later site of the Pantheon, extending quite a distance to the south. The interior divisions for the tribes probably ran lengthwise in the rectangular structure, proceeding from an entrance in the north to exits on the south. The Diribitorium, where the votes were counted, was most likely attached to the southern end. This section may have been added by Agrippa.[21] Lepidus' direction of the project probably took place in 45, but it may have continued as late as 40 BC, when he left Rome for the last time with any real power.

A second structure associated with Lepidus was a temple of Felicitas, the goddess of good fortune. This temple was erected in the Forum on the site of the Curia Hostilia, the old Senate house burned in 52 BC by the funeral pyre of Clodius. According to Dio Cassius, it was completed by Lepidus when he was *magister equitum*.[22] This reference seems to indicate that it was finished in 45 or very early in 44. A letter of Cicero to Atticus may help date this more precisely. Cicero mentions in December of 45 that Lepidus had requested his presence and the orator speculates that augurs were needed to consecrate a temple.[23] This letter may very well refer to the consecration of the temple of Felicitas, since it is the only one known to have been built about this time.

Dio Cassius says that the recently repaired Curia Hostilia was destroyed, according to the official version, to make room for the temple to Felicitas.[24] Actually, however, the restorations of the Curia Hostilia by Sulla in 80 and by his son Faustus after 52 BC would have naturally associated the Senate house with the Cornelian family, and more specifically with Sulla. Dio says that Caesar preferred to construct a new Senate house and have that revered building associated with his own family by calling it the Curia Iulia.

35

Lepidus' temple to Felicitas thus gave Caesar an excuse to destroy the Sullan structure and a chance to add to his own glory by building a new meeting place in his own name to house a Senate that would be, hopefully, under his control. The temple was probably intended to honor the good fortune of Caesar, who had destroyed most of his opposition and was then at the peak of his power. The Saepta Iulia and the Felicitas temple were probably paid for from the public treasury, supplemented by Caesar's booty from Gaul or from the taxes and fines he had arranged after his various campaigns. Lepidus may also have used some of his own wealth, as his brother had done for the restoration of the Basilica Aemilia.

Two of Cicero's letters written during the summer of 45 BC give some insight into Lepidus' activities and the state of his wealth. At the end of August in 45, Lepidus requested Cicero's presence at an upcoming meeting of the Senate and mentioned that it would be a favor both to himself and to Caesar if the orator would attend. At the time of the request Lepidus was at Antium, south of Rome on the coast of Latium, living on an estate formerly owned by Cicero.[25] In a letter written a few weeks earlier, Cicero had referred to an estate in Lanuvium which Lepidus had obtained from Balbus.[26] It was natural, of course, for Roman nobles to escape the summer heat of Rome by visiting their estates, particularly those located along the coast or in the hills.

Lepidus must have been reasonably wealthy to have owned estates in Antium, Lanuvium, and presumably also in Circeii, where he would be exiled later, in addition to his home in Rome. Cicero considered Lepidus to be rich, but it is impossible to compare the extent of his wealth to that of other nobles of his time just by counting estates.[27] If he were unusually wealthy, one would expect to find references to his using money to gain power or position, as we have with Crassus, for example. However, there is no evidence of Lepidus' being extravagant, a characteristic recorded for his father, or of his using bribes to secure political advantage.

In the letter of late July in 45 BC concerning Lepidus' request that he attend the Senate, Cicero told Atticus that he did not feel that the matter could be of any importance because Oppius had not said anything about it to Atticus. Balbus, who normally would have discussed important issues with Atticus, was ill at the time. Cicero seems to view messages from Balbus and Oppius as vital, while contacts from Lepidus may have been more ceremonial or official.[28] This seems to indicate that while Lepidus was in overall charge of affairs in Rome, calling meetings of the Senate and Assembly to pass legislation and presiding at state functions, Balbus and Oppius carried out the details of day-to-day activities as something like Caesarian lobbyists.

Caesar's return to Rome in October of 45, marked by a glorious triumph over Roman citizens, began the final stage of his course to autocracy, which would soon lead instead to his assassination and further turmoil. The Senate continued to grant him honors and powers that were superfluous to his absolute rule. His ivory statue was even to be carried in the processions at the games with the images of the gods.[29] The Senate, although providing Caesar with the power and majesty of a king and virtually decreeing his deification, carefully avoided mention of the despised title of *rex*.[30]

In preparation for his campaign against the Parthians, Caesar received from the Senate the power to choose magistrates for the next three years in advance, the expected duration of that struggle. Lepidus was to govern the provinces of Narbonese Gaul and Hither Spain as proconsul and was chosen once again as *magister equitum*, at least until his departure for his provinces. Lepidus would hold the latter post for the early months of 44 BC and help Caesar prepare for the Parthian expedition. When Caesar left, Lepidus could also leave for his provinces. He would no longer need the position and Caesar had already named two men, C. Octavius and Cn. Domitius Calvinus, to replace him.[31]

Lepidus sent ahead friends as legates to govern Hither Spain and Narbonese Gaul in his name until his arrival.[32] Lepidus was a natural choice to govern Hither Spain because of his successful experience there in 48–7 BC and, after all, Caesar had just recently returned from pacifying the area. The dictator's choice of Lepidus, however, should not just be dismissed lightly as some easy assignment that anyone could handle. Caesar expected to be campaigning in the east for two to three years. Spain had been a habitual trouble spot in the past and if Spain and Narbonese Gaul were to fall to an enemy, Italy itself would be in danger. Caesar also knew that Sextus Pompey could find Spain once again to be a productive area for recruitment. It is difficult to believe that Caesar would have taken the risk of entrusting these provinces to an incompetent general. The dictator had trusted Lepidus' ability to control this potentially dangerous situation and that faith was well placed.

Caesar's selection of his *magister equitum* for 44 BC has aroused some interesting discussion.[33] Dio Cassius mentions Lepidus as holding the office again in 44, then says later that Caesar had designated two men, one of whom was the future Octavian, to receive it during the next two years.[34] Dio goes on to say that the two men replacing Lepidus were to act separately, seeming to suggest that both occupied the office simultaneously.[35] Appian, whose confused chronology has Lepidus first replacing Antony as *magister equitum* in 44, mentions that Octavian had been appointed for one year to the office which Caesar handed around among his friends.[36]

The Fasti Capitolini, unfortunately fragmentary at this point, do support the view that Lepidus was designated *magister equitum* in 44 to serve until he assumed his command. The name of the man who was to replace him is broken off, but the name of Cn. Domitius Calvinus is included as being appointed to serve *in insequentem ann[um]*.[37] The fasti, then, support Dio although making it clear that the two men were to hold the office in consecutive years. The text makes sense when reconstructed, in light of the other known evidence, to include Octavius as the man intended to replace Lepidus in 44 BC.

Pliny the Elder, in discussing the ups and downs of Augustus' fortune, included Caesar's preference of Lepidus for the office of *magister equitum* over Octavius as one of the downpoints.[38] Although Pliny's reversal of fortune here probably refers more to Octavian's ultimate conquest over Lepidus rather than to his receiving the post of *magister equitum* after Lepidus, his statement seems plausible.

It seems then that Caesar decided to keep Lepidus as his *magister equitum* for the beginning months of 44. The dictator sent Octavius to Apollonia to study and prepare to join him for the Parthian expedition scheduled to pass through that city on the Illyrian coast later in the year.[39] Lepidus having departed by that time to assume his provincial command, Octavius was to become *magister equitum* on the campaign and serve for the remainder of the year. Domitius Calvinus would replace Octavius in the position in 43. Calvinus was perhaps intended to use the title, as Lepidus had earlier, to govern Rome in 43 after Antony's consulship had ended.

This intricate network of relationships involving the post of *magister equitum* is particularly interesting for two reasons. First of all, Caesar preferred to stay with Lepidus, even to the point of temporarily rejecting the plea of his intended heir, so that Lepidus could leave the office with his dignity intact and not suffer the rebuke that had been attached to Antony's replacement earlier. Second, to bring Octavius into office as a kind of 'suffect' *magister equitum* serving for only part of the year, and while on campaign away from Rome, would lessen the impact of charges that Octavius was too young for the office and give him the experience of command and title for a limited period of time. The prior designation of a successor for 43 would allow Caesar to control and judge Octavius and avoid the humiliating situation of having to remove him from office. Caesar was both concerned about his treatment of Lepidus and interested in grooming Octavius properly and introducing the prospective heir at a calculated pace to positions of power.

In the last week of January in 44 BC, Lepidus as *magister equitum* must have assisted Caesar in the celebration of the Feriae Latinae on the Alban Mount and in the *ovatio* which the Senate had decreed for the dictator to mark his return to Rome. The associations with monarchy were particularly strong in Caesar's performance of the Alban rites, in his *ovatio* procession, in the adornment with diadems of his statues on the Rostra, and in his acclamation as *rex*.[40] Lepidus surely accompanied the dictator and witnessed these events, but, although his loyalty to Caesar is beyond question, one suspects that internally Lepidus must have found it difficult to watch his friend assume oriental trappings and act in a manner unbecoming a Roman.[41]

Lepidus' displeasure with the impending approach of monarchy was to be publicly evident, at least to Cicero, on February 15 at the celebration of the festival of the Lupercalia. Lepidus as *magister equitum* was probably seated next to the dictator on the Rostra, from where they could view the near-naked Luperci running part of their course around the Palatine and stopping frequently to strike women with their thongs of fertility. Caesar wore his purple toga and gold wreath and sat on his golden chair. Antony, Caesar's colleague as consul and a runner, was carried up to the Rostra and placed a diadem on the dictator's head. The crowd alternated its disapproval and approval as Antony would offer and Caesar reject the diadem. Finally, the dictator ordered that the diadem be dedicated in the temple of Capitoline Jupiter and that his refusal of the crown offered him by the 'Roman people' be recorded in the public records.[42] The sending of the diadem to Jupiter Optimus Maximus was very appropriate, incidentally, since *coronae aureae* had been dedicated there regularly for centuries.[43]

The Lupercalia incident has been subject to various interpretations and no clear pattern of Caesar's intentions can really emerge.[44] In some ways the scene appears to be a testing of the crowd to see if there was sufficient support to make Caesar a Roman king. On the other hand, the dictator's dramatic refusal and his determination that this act be forever recorded and the diadem dedicated to Jupiter suggest a decision to forego the title of *rex*, at least for some time, because he already had regal powers and honors and his act would allay fears of a kingship and encourage greater acceptance of his unconstitutional position. There is also the possibility that Caesar was concerned with preparations for a kind of Hellenistic monarchy to facilitate his conquest of the Parthians and the creation of a world empire after the model of Alexander the Great. Whatever his intentions, Cicero viewed the Lupercalia incident as a direct cause of Caesar's assassination and therefore held Antony responsible for the murder.[45]

Cicero also claims that Lepidus expressed publicly on the Rostra his disapproval of Antony's placing the diadem on Caesar's head by turning away, groaning, and displaying tears.[46] This is quite a statement considering that Lepidus was a loyal friend of Caesar and still his *magister equitum*, but the moment was powerful, even overwhelming, and not easy to accept for a man who had been raised on stories of various Aemilii defending Rome against foreign kings.

It is true, of course, that Cicero's testimony comes only in two of his *Philippics*, in which the orator is attempting to keep Antony and Lepidus apart and to convince Lepidus that the proper course is for him to side with the Senate. These speeches are naturally highly flattering to Lepidus, but one cannot therefore simply throw out their evidence because Cicero would hardly say something totally untrue about Lepidus' part in the Lupercalia incident, lest it offend him and work against all of Cicero's efforts. The orator's praise of Lepidus' conduct during the diadem episode would, however, offer Lepidus an outlet from his position between Antony and the Senate and help him to choose the 'right' course by communicating the message that the Senate trusted and accepted him. Although the degree of public disapproval may have been exaggerated, it is quite understandable that Lepidus as a *nobilis* of *nobiles* would shudder at the sight of a Roman consul, practically naked and in the forum, fawning before his colleague and offering a crown!

The acclamation at the Feriae Latinae, the *ovatio*, the Lupercalia incident and other appearances of diadems, the image of Caesar on coins, the dictator's remaining seated when a group of senators met with him before the temple of Venus Genetrix, the assumption of the title *dictator perpetuus*, and the seemingly endless arrogation of power and honors in one man's hands all combined to convince many Roman nobles, including some of Caesar's most trusted appointees, that the Republic was in the grip of a tyrant who must be killed.[47] These men believed that action had to be taken before the anticipated assumption of the kingship and Caesar's victorious return from still another military campaign might make the dictator even more invincible.

The two leading conspirators were M. Brutus and C. Cassius Longinus, both former Pompeians who had been pardoned by Caesar and who were currently serving by his appointment as praetors. Brutus was the son of the man who had died as the chief lieutenant of Lepidus' father in the rebellion of 78–7 BC. The Aemilii Lepidi and the Iunii Bruti had worked together several times in the past, in fact, and the conspirator Brutus was the half-brother of Lepidus' wife Junia. Lepidus was then brother-in-law to both Brutus and Cassius.[48]

The impending departure for the Parthian expedition and the rumor that the guardians of the Sibylline Books planned to announce at the next meeting of the Senate the discovery of an oracle to the effect that the Parthians could only be conquered by a king prompted the conspirators to plan to assassinate Caesar in the Senate on March 15.[49] The specific date of the assassination may have been chosen for symbolic reasons because until the mid-second century the Ides of March had been the traditional day for the commencement of a new consular year. On the Ides, the Senate would meet on the Capitoline and watch the new consuls take their vows before Jupiter himself. The conspirators may therefore have selected this day because it was sacred to Rome's chief god and because it symbolized the senatorial government of a pre-Gracchan Republic.[50]

According to Dio Cassius, the conspirators originally intended to murder both Mark Antony and Lepidus as well as the dictator.[51] It is difficult to speculate about how differently events might have turned out if the conspirators had succeeded in killing both consuls and the *magister equitum*. Without these two natural successors to Caesarian leadership, there would not have been the immediate stability provided by Lepidus' troops or the control over events held by Antony as surviving consul, and the results of the conspiracy might have been radically different, at least in the short run. The real imponderables are whether or not some other Caesarian leader or leaders would have emerged in place of Antony and Lepidus, whether or not the soldiers would have followed someone with whom they were unfamiliar, whether or not the 'liberators' might have found greater acceptance in Rome had the opposition not been so well organized, and whether or not Octavius would have risen to the top so quickly in such an altered set of circumstances. In any case, the conspirators chose, apparently at the insistence of Brutus, to kill only Caesar, so their deed would be perceived as a noble strike to save the Republic from a tyrant and not as a bloody massacre of political opponents to secure personal power.[52]

On the night of March 14 Caesar dined at Lepidus' house. Decimus Iunius Brutus Albinus, one of Caesar's close friends, but still a conspirator against him, was also present. While the men were drinking wine and the dictator was signing letters after dinner, the conversation turned to the question of what manner of demise was most desirable. Caesar expressed his preference for a sudden and unexpected death.[53] This ominous conversation could of course have been fabricated later as another portent of Caesar's assassination, but the fact that the final dinner took place at Lepidus' house need not be doubted. Such meals involving Caesar and his close friends and advisors probably took place regularly.

The Ides of March dawned with Caesar practically convinced by his wife Calpurnia to stay home and not attend the Senate that day because of illness and the ominous warnings they had received. Decimus Brutus convinced the dictator of the importance of his attending the meeting, however, and escorted him to his prearranged confrontation with death. Lepidus was apparently working that day outside the city with Caesar's troops and did not witness his friend's murder. Had he been there he could have done very little to interfere with fate, considering the large number of conspirators.

The assassination of Julius Caesar, intended to restore the stability of Republican government, resulted instead in reopening a power struggle that would end only after another bloody civil war. As the conspirators' daggers ended Caesar's life, they also recast the lives of many Roman nobles, and especially those of Mark Antony and Lepidus, his close friends and colleagues. Lepidus was now in his mid-forties and up until this point in his life he had owed much of the success in his career to his relationship with Caesar. With that tie violently severed, Lepidus was suddenly on his own. In some ways, it was like the period of his life when his father and oldest brother were taken away suddenly, but this time so much more was expected of him individually. The security and stability that he had grown accustomed to were now threatened and Lepidus was forced to rely on his own resources for the future. His noble name and his connections with Caesar's followers and soldiers would continue to ensure his preeminence, but Lepidus may have had too much confidence in their powers and thereby underestimated the capabilities of his opponents in the next struggle to rule Rome. He would rely on tradition and bonds of *amicitia* to keep him at the center of power, only to discover too late that he had been set adrift in an uncertain world where strength, cunning, and ruthlessness held sway.

To this point in Lepidus' career, there is no evidence of the vanity, fickleness, or incompetence that have dominated later descriptions of the man. We see instead a successful Roman noble whom Julius Caesar entrusted with several important tasks, including especially the administration of Rome itself on three occasions and of the volatile area of Spain twice. These assignments demanded leadership, competence, and – in Spain at least – decisive action. Lepidus performed them effectively in a critical period of unrest when a false step could have led to disaster for Caesar's interests. Lepidus' personal weaknesses and failures, and their distortion through history, all lay in the future.

6

PONTIFEX MAXIMUS –
AND *HOSTIS PUBLICUS*

Lepidus' activities at the time of Caesar's assassination on the Ides of March are not entirely clear. Plutarch believed that both Lepidus and Mark Antony were present at the Senate meeting in the Theater of Pompey and that they fled for protection to friends' houses when they witnessed the murder, naturally fearing for their own lives.[1] Although Antony's presence is attested to by other sources, which state that the conspirators purposely stationed Trebonius outside the entrance to detain him in conversation while the deed was committed, both Dio Cassius and Appian place Lepidus away from the scene. Dio reports that Lepidus was conducting military drills in the suburbs at the time of the murder.[2] Appian says that Lepidus was in the forum when he learned of the incident.[3] These accounts sound more plausible because Lepidus as *magister equitum* could quite naturally have been drilling troops in preparation for the dictator's imminent departure for Parthia. Lepidus would then have been informed of the murder upon his return to the city. Both Dio Cassius and Appian credit Lepidus with decisive action at this critical point. Appian says that Lepidus reacted by going immediately to the Tiber island, where he had a legion stationed, and transferring these soldiers to the Campus Martius, where they were instructed to await further orders.[4] Dio reports that Lepidus occupied the forum that night with his soldiers.[5] Lepidus' movement of troops into strategic areas played a vital role in stabilizing a chaotic situation and in determining its ultimate outcome.

Great uncertainty characterized the hours and days following Caesar's murder and this would ultimately play into the hands of Antony and Lepidus. The conspirators marched up to the Capitol and took possession of it with a group of gladiators for protection. They saw themselves as liberators and expected approval of their act, at least by the governing class. The Capitoline hill provided the security of a citadel that could be held by their small group of armed men. It also held the great temple of Jupiter where Brutus and his colleagues hoped to sanctify their deed of impiety and, at least symbolically, secure approval by Rome's gods. The site would also be the natural location for the inauguration of Dolabella as Caesar's successor as consul. Cicero would later anguish over the failure of the conspirators to take his advice to summon a session of the Senate *in Capitolio* immediately following the assassination.[6]

The conspirators correctly feared the potential opposition of Caesar's closest assistants, Antony and Lepidus, and with hindsight it is clear that Brutus's insistence on limiting the plot to one victim was shortsighted, although noble.[7] Antony's powers as consul were considerable and his leadership of the Senate and expressed willingness to work with his opponents were very effective. Lepidus had stabilized the situation by moving in his soldiers and, although he apparently favored gaining vengeance for Caesar's death, he agreed to support the consul's plan and would later join in negotiations with the conspirators. Time was on the side of the Caesarians.

On the morning of March 16 Lepidus gave a speech in the forum attacking the murderers holed up on the Capitol.[8] He presumably was addressing not only the soldiers under his command, but also veterans of Caesar's campaigns and the general populace, many of whom had been shocked by the assassination, but who had no understanding of the motives behind it, of its immediate impact on them, or of how they should respond to it. Lepidus' close association with Julius Caesar would quite naturally have caused him to desire revenge, but he must also have been aware that public advocacy of vengeance would help him inherit Caesar's supporters, particularly those among the legions. At the same time, however, Brutus was his brother-in-law. Lepidus decided to defer to Antony's plan to negotiate and await the turn of events in the Senate.

Brutus and Cassius sent a group of their friends as envoys to persuade Lepidus and Antony to work together with the conspirators for the future good of the state, instead of opening another chapter in Rome's bloody civil wars. Antony, uncertain of the mood of the Senate and wary of the powerful army of Decimus Brutus in Cisalpine Gaul, answered that although he and Lepidus felt bound by their oaths to avenge Caesar's death they would accept the decision of the Senate as to what should be done.[9]

On the morning of the 17th, Antony summoned the Senate to meet at the temple of Tellus, near his house in the Carinae district. As the senators were assembling there, an incident occurred involving the praetor L. Cornelius Cinna. This man, who was the brother of Caesar's first wife, had declared his support of the assassination and cast off his robe of office because it had been received from Caesar. When the praetor appeared for the Senate meeting once again wearing his robe, his disloyalty to Caesar and his apparent hypocrisy caused a group of people to attack him with stones and chase him into hiding. The angry crowd was ready to set fire to the house where he had sought refuge when Lepidus and a group of soldiers put a stop to the violence.[10]

When the Senate met, a large number of its members seemed to be in favor of condemning Caesar and honoring the murderers for their act. As consul Antony skillfully addressed the body, reminding many who sat there that they owed their present or future offices to Caesar's designation. This tactic struck home with many who had violently opposed Caesar moments earlier and they decided not to hold new elections for all those offices.

While the discussion was going on, Antony and Lepidus left to address a crowd that had assembled nearby. Many in the group demanded revenge for the murder, while the majority asked for peace. Antony, ever the politician, said things to please both sections of the crowd so that he might gain a broader base of support. Those urging revenge on the assassins turned to Lepidus and asked him to lead their cause. He was requested to come down into the forum so that everyone could hear him better and he mounted the Rostra to speak, visibly sad at remembering a recent appearance with Caesar on the same platform. Lepidus followed Antony's line of attack and tried to satisfy both sides. He praised Caesar, but said that vengeance for his murder would lead to further disruption of the state. He too left the question in the hands of the Senate. Those demanding peace, many of whom had been bribed by the conspirators, praised Lepidus and talked of his becoming pontifex maximus in place of Caesar. This naturally pleased Lepidus because that office suited his heritage and, although he postponed further discussion of the matter until later, the prospect of succeeding to the honored post once held by his model ancestor probably helped convince him to return to the Senate and work for peace.[11]

Antony decided to speak to the Senate again and he urged the members not to prosecute Caesar's murderers, but, on the other hand, to confirm the dictator's acts and decrees. Cicero was apparently the dominant force in persuading the Senate to grant amnesty to the assassins. Caesar's actions were also to stay in force.[12] The action of the Senate to bring about peace within the state was successful in calming down the fears that had arisen on all sides after the murder. The veterans in the city no longer feared a cancellation of the rewards granted to them by Caesar, magistrates felt more secure in their positions, the conspirators felt safe from prosecution, and the people in general must have felt relief at the relaxation of tension. Lepidus sent his son, presumably Marcus, and Antony sent his as hostages to the assassins so that they might feel that it was safe to descend from the Capitol. When they came down, Cassius was symbolically entertained by Antony and Brutus by his brother-in-law, Lepidus.[13] The conspirators may have breathed a sigh of relief, but the Senate's compromise had in reality given Antony just the kind of official sanction that he needed. Over the next several months Antony would abuse the spirit of this accommodation by using Caesar's notebooks and treasury to achieve purposes quite different from what the conspirators had envisioned for Rome.

The apparent reconciliation between Caesar's followers and his murderers did not last long. The public reading of Caesar's will and his state funeral served as catalysts to stir up public opinion and violence against the assassins. The will, which formally adopted Octavian as Caesar's heir, also made the dictator's gardens a public park and granted each inhabitant of Rome a sum of money. The secondary adoption by Caesar of Decimus Brutus further aroused the passions of the people against that particular conspirator and against the assassins in general. At the public funeral Antony presented a speech that recounted Caesar's exploits and the honors and oaths of loyalty given to him, climaxing with the display of the dictator's body and his blood-stained cloak. In reaction to the emotions awakened by the funeral, people ran madly through the streets and burned the Senate chamber in the Theater of Pompey, which had been the site of the murder, and the houses of several conspirators. Caesar's murderers, realizing that they were no longer safe in Rome, fled the city.[14]

Antony, with the conspirators out of Rome, proceeded to consolidate his control by establishing a closer alliance with Lepidus, whose name and military position he still had to take into consideration. First of all, the consul arranged for a marriage between his daughter and Lepidus' son. The son in question was probably the eldest and is presumably the same child who had been sent as a hostage to Brutus and Cassius. He was most likely the Marcus who later rose in rebellion against Octavian in 31 or 30 BC. Although the children were engaged, marriage does not seem to have ever taken place, at least before 37, when Antony sent his freedman Callias to Lepidus in Africa to complete the arrangements.[15] By 31 the boy was married to a Servilia.

Antony's second act in 44 to secure Lepidus' loyalty was to help him secure Caesar's revered position as pontifex maximus. Among the many honors accorded to Caesar before his death was a decree of the Senate that his son or adopted son would be appointed pontifex maximus.[16] This blatantly monarchical provision was ignored by Antony, as was the proper procedure of having an Assembly election, presided over by a pontifex and choosing from a list of candidates provided by the pontifical college. The consul restored the right of the college itself to select its leader, as the process had apparently functioned much earlier in the Republic. Lepidus would have been a prime candidate for the office even without Antony's help because of his long service as pontifex and because of the tradition connected with his ancestor's service in the same position. Octavian, although also a pontifex, appeared too young to assume the revered office and had not yet asserted himself in Rome. Dio thought that Antony could have given the position to himself, but Antony was not a pontifex and the blatant seizure of Rome's chief priesthood by someone unqualified would not make good political sense, especially in the charged atmosphere following the assassination.[17]

Although Brutus and Cn. Domitius Calvinus might have been potential rivals for the chief priesthood, Lepidus apparently held substantial seniority as a pontifex over both. The only pontifex at the time of Caesar's death known to have served longer on the college than Lepidus, P. Servilius Vatia Isauricus, died at an advanced age in the early summer of 44, quite possibly before Lepidus' selection.[18] The questionable way in which Lepidus gained the office of chief priest has sullied his reputation unnecessarily. The idea that he had usurped the honor illegally in the midst of political chaos persisted, even though he probably would have been the most likely candidate if a fair election had been held in the proper manner.[19] The charge would naturally have appealed to Augustus and the imperial historians because they believed that the emperor had been cheated out of his inheritance. The heritability of the chief priesthood, even with the Senate's flimsy approval, is so un-Republican that it is difficult to believe that Augustus would even make such a claim. It is worth noting, of course, that the emperor never pressed his case in the courts and that he patiently waited over twenty years until Lepidus' death opened up the office that Augustus had assumed was his by right of inheritance.

It was also shortly after Caesar's assassination that Lepidus' brother Paullus, who had dropped from our sources since his consulship in 50 BC, reappeared, once again a close friend of Cicero. The orator reports a meeting with Paullus in the Latin town of Caieta.[20] This place was very close to Formiae, where Cicero and M.' Lepidus had villas, and to Tarracina and Circeii, where other estates are known to have been owned by Aemilii Lepidi. It is quite likely then that Paullus also held property in this area, at Caieta.

In their meeting on April 14, Paullus reported to Cicero on the situation in Rome. He mentioned the arrest and execution of the false Marius by Antony and also showed Cicero a letter from his brother that told of a plot against Lepidus' life.[21] This news disturbed both Paullus and Cicero. It is very interesting to find such evidence of a close relationship between the brothers at this point, in view of their conflict in the following year. The proximity in the timing between Lepidus' letter to Paullus and one of Cicero's letters mentioning a conspiracy involving Caesar's freedmen suggests that they could be referring to the same plot.[22] It is quite possible that the dictator's freedmen had targeted Lepidus for his failure to carry out his pledge to avenge Caesar's death.

It is not clear exactly when Lepidus was inaugurated as pontifex maximus. Dio says that Antony as consul performed the ceremony with the pontifical college, observing few, if any, of the customary rites.[23] It seems most likely that the consecration took place in late March or early April, for soon afterwards Lepidus departed Rome to assume direct control of his provinces, Narbonese Gaul and Hither Spain, and to deal with the danger presented by Sextus Pompey. After all, there was no reason to delay Lepidus' inauguration as chief priest and in fact there was an urgency to make his position official as soon as possible. It does not appear that Lepidus returned to Rome again until after the formation of the Second Triumvirate and it seems unlikely that he would have left the city without having received full confirmation in his honored office.[24]

The main reason that Lepidus left Rome so soon after the assassination was that his presence was desperately needed in Spain. Sextus Pompey posed a serious threat to the delicate balance of power presided over by Antony in Rome. Sextus had recovered from the loss at Munda and, after defeating the provincial governor of Farther Spain, C. Asinius Pollio, he now controlled that province and presented an immediate danger to Hither Spain, then governed by subordinates for Lepidus.[25] Antony, fearing a loss of all of Spain, hurried Lepidus off to negotiate a settlement with Sextus. Lepidus, with previous experience in the province and as its current governor, was the natural choice to deal with the situation, but the consul in addition must have realized that Lepidus' withdrawal from Rome also increased his own control of the Caesarian interests in the city.

The Senate had earlier confirmed Sextus' pardon and voted a restoration to him of the money taken by the treasury from his family estate.[26] In order to give Lepidus more bargaining power, Antony now proposed that the Senate recall Sextus from Spain, pay him the sum of 50 million denarii from the treasury in compensation for his confiscated property, and appoint him as commander of the fleet. The Senate approved the consul's motion and applauded this friendly gesture toward the son of Pompey the Great.[27] Lepidus was already in his province when the decree was passed. Sextus Pompey was most interested in recovering his father's estate, or being adequately compensated for it, and it was on this point that Lepidus concluded an agreement with him to cease hostilities.[28] This accord was probably reached late in June.[29]

For his part in ending the threat of a full-scale war in Spain and in bringing Sextus Pompey back into the tenuous peace that then prevailed, the Senate voted Lepidus a *supplicatio*, or public thanksgiving. Antony proposed this measure on November 28, but the Senate adopted it without the customary speeches of praise because the consul considered it necessary to leave immediately when he heard that the Fourth Legion had gone over to Octavian's side.[30] Cicero's letter of November 5, stating that Balbus had informed him that Lepidus' holidays would last until November 29, may refer either to an anticipation on Balbus' part of when the *supplicatio* might be held or to other festivities proclaimed in honor of his new role as pontifex maximus.[31]

Cicero also sponsored a Senate decree honoring Lepidus for his settlement with Sextus Pompey and for other deeds. This was included in his fifth *Philippic* oration, delivered on January 1, 43 BC, and should be understood as an attempt on Cicero's part to keep Lepidus on the Senate's side in the growing struggle with Antony. To please Lepidus even further, Cicero caused the Senate to erect a gilt equestrian statue on the Rostra in his honor.[32] This act must have been particularly meaningful to Lepidus because the Senate had set up a similar statue on the Capitoline to honor his model ancestor. Cicero was certainly aware of the connection since Lepidus had even commemorated the monument on his coins. Lepidus' success with Sextus Pompey also earned him the title of *imperator* for the second time and he later celebrated a triumph for his deeds in Spain on December 31, 43 BC, after he had joined the Second Triumvirate and on the eve of his second consulship.[33]

From the time of his departure from Rome in April or May of 44 BC until he joined forces with Antony a little more than a year later Lepidus governed his provinces of Hither Spain and Narbonese Gaul. In many ways, these would prove to be his finest days. He was finally on his own, no longer acting for Caesar. He had already served as consul. He was pontifex maximus. He had just negotiated peace for Rome, even if it would prove to be only temporary, and he was in charge of two of Rome's greatest provinces. He was also in a strategic position where he could use his troops to determine the future of Rome if necessary.

It was probably during his stay in Spain after concluding his agreements with Sextus Pompey that Lepidus established the colony of Colonia Victrix Julia Lepida, generally identified with Celsa on the Ebro River.[34] Although Lepidus may have founded this colony during his earlier stay in Spain, the issue of coins and the temporary naming of the colony after Lepidus support this later date because it is doubtful that he would have used his own name and commemorated it on a coin when he was still governing at Caesar's will. The founding of colonies, of course, had been another of the achievements of Lepidus' model ancestor and the establishment of Celsa thus provides one more reason why Lepidus had cause to be proud and satisfied with his current position.

While back in Narbonese Gaul Lepidus issued additional coins, presumably to pay his soldiers, in the cities of Antipolis (Antibes) and Cabellio (Cavaillon). The coin-types were local, but both contained references to Lepidus' *cognomen*.[35] Lepidus very probably spent some time in the vicinity of Antipolis and he probably appreciated the lovely scenery of this location, with its wooded hills overlooking the sparkling sea, because of its similarity to the Italian vistas at Tarracina and Circeii, where his family owned property.

In the months following his negotiations with Sextus Pompey,

Lepidus probably consolidated control of his two provinces. Once he had settled the situation in Spain and arranged for the government of his Spanish province, Lepidus presumably spent most of his time in Narbonese Gaul during the last months of 44 and the early part of 43 BC. From this strategic position, he could move more quickly with his troops into the critical area of Cisalpine Gaul, where Decimus Brutus' control would soon be challenged by Antony. Although it is possible that Lepidus returned to Rome for the public celebrations in his honor in November of 44, this is highly unlikely for three reasons: there is no mention of such a visit in our ample sources for this period; Lepidus waited until over a year later to celebrate his triumph (it would have been highly irregular for a provincial governor to come to the city during his term of office); and it would have been both foolhardy and dangerous for Lepidus to have removed himself so far from his troops.

In Rome during this same period, a conflict was developing between Mark Antony and Octavian. Antony as consul was becoming unpopular because of his inaction in avenging Caesar's death and because he had forced the passage of legislation that benefited him, supported only by the explanation that it had been provided for in Caesar's papers, now conveniently in the consul's possession. Octavian was able to raise troops and also pick up two additional legions that had revolted against Antony late in November. Caesar's heir now owned a name that was magic to the soldiers and the young man was also more generous in dispensing donatives than was Antony.

Antony soon departed Rome for Cisalpine Gaul, which had been granted to him by a vote of the Assembly, so that he could attempt to dislodge the forces of the conspirator Decimus Brutus. The stage was now set for a struggle between Cicero, his supporters in the Senate, and the troops of Octavian on the one side and Mark Antony and his soldiers on the other side. The former were held together tenuously by opposition to Antony and the dream of a restoration of an aristocratic Republic, while the latter desired to avenge Caesar's death and restore the dictator's control of Rome in the person of Antony.[36] Personal ambition or self-interest also motivated the individual actions of both sides to some degree. The issue would be decided by the forces under the control of the provincial governors, particularly Lepidus, and by Octavian's ultimate desertion of the Republican cause.

Cicero realized that the support of the provincial governors would be a virtual necessity in order for the Republican coalition to defeat Antony. As long as they remained loyal to the Senate, the provincial governors could restrict Antony's movements and impede his escape from Italy, while at the same time depriving Antony of additional soldiers that might potentially rally to the support of someone claiming to avenge Caesar's assassination. At the same time that Cicero led the attack on Antony with his *Philippic* orations, the orator also had to campaign to hold on to the support of the provincial governors by regularly praising their devotion to the Republic through personal letters and public honors.

Lepidus was in the strongest position of the governors of the western provinces. The location of his troops allowed him to seal off support from C. Asinius Pollio in Farther Spain and from L. Munatius Plancus in the rest of Gaul. Lepidus could also bring help quickly, to either side, in Cisalpine Gaul or in Italy. Because these governors had been appointed by Caesar, Cicero had doubts about their loyalty to the Republic and had to work even harder to secure it.

Although Cicero may have hoped that he could convince Lepidus to side with the Senate against Antony, his extant correspondence reveals that he was skeptical all along of the chances of success. The orator resorted to high praise and extreme flattery to secure Lepidus' allegiance, but the memory of this hyperbole would only serve to heighten Cicero's bitterness when Lepidus finally came to Antony's rescue.

In December of 44 Mark Antony marched his troops to Cisalpine Gaul and demanded that Decimus Brutus leave the province in accordance with the legislation passed by the Assembly. Decimus refused to give in and to defend himself he retired with his men to the city of Mutina (Modena) and prepared for the anticipated siege by Antony.[37] It was Antony's siege of Mutina that caused the Senate to take action against him. On January 1 of 43 BC, Cicero urged the body to declare Antony a public enemy and send a force to raise the siege. The Senate was more cautious, however, and it voted only to send envoys to warn Antony to withdraw from Mutina and from the entire province of Cisalpine Gaul. Antony naturally refused the order and the Senate soon afterwards declared him a public enemy and in addition decreed that those soldiers under his command who did not desert him would also be branded as enemies of the state. The new consuls and Octavian were entrusted with the prosecution of the war against Antony. Lepidus and Plancus, as provincial governors in Gaul, were ordered to render assistance in the struggle.[38]

The impending civil war caused Cicero to increase his efforts to secure the active participation of Lepidus, Plancus, and Pollio on the Republican side. Late in December of 44, Cicero had referred to Lepidus in the third *Philippic* as *vir clarissimus*.[39] On the first of January in 43, after Hirtius and Pansa had assumed their consular offices, Cicero delivered his fifth *Philippic*, in which he branded Antony as a public enemy and increased his praise of Lepidus. It was in this speech that Cicero reminded the Senate of Lepidus' displeasure at the Lupercalia 'crowning' and proposed honors for the man whom he characterized as having an *odium servitutis* and displaying *moderatio, sapientia, clementia*, and *humanitas*.[40] The orator then introduced a decree praising Lepidus for his services to the state, especially for his peaceful accommodation with Sextus Pompey, and ordering the erection of a gilded equestrian statue in his honor.[41]

In March Cicero wrote Lepidus to express his disappointment that Lepidus had not thanked the Senate for bestowing such high honors upon him and to warn him against seeking peace with Antony.[42] C. Asinius Pollio wrote Cicero about the same time to inform him that Lepidus' guards were intercepting messages sent by land to Farther Spain and that it might be difficult to bring his legions through Lepidus' provinces because Lepidus had made it known that he would side with Antony. Pollio naturally reassured Cicero of his own continuing support.[43] This letter provides an early forecast of what Lepidus' policy would be: to the Senate he would maintain a neutral stand by claiming continued loyalty and calling for peace, while at the same time he would surreptitiously aid Antony by slowing down or blocking off forces attempting to join the opposition. Lepidus would only make a clean break with the Senate when his open support was absolutely necessary to carry on the Caesarian cause. Lepidus was no more fooled by the Senate's offers of empty honors than Cicero was by Lepidus' promises of loyalty. Both sides knew where their real interests lay and that each would only support the other so long as it was useful to do so. Both, however, had to carry on the charade as long as it prolonged the utility of the relationship.

Late in March Lepidus wrote to the Senate declaring his support for the negotiation of a peace settlement with Mark Antony and with hindsight one can say that things might have worked out better for all concerned if the senators had considered Lepidus' request more seriously. Cicero responded to this letter early in April in the thirteenth *Philippic*. His attitude toward Lepidus was quite different from that expressed in his speech at the beginning of January. The orator approved of Servilius' motion that the Senate should vote Lepidus its thanks for his letter and he reiterated his praise for Lepidus' past services to the state, for his noble family, for his revered position as pontifex maximus, and especially for his opposition to Antony's attempted crowning of Caesar at the Lupercalia and his peace agreement with Sextus Pompey. However, among all the sweet words of respect for Lepidus, Cicero expresses his distrust of the man's intentions by questioning his judgment in advocating peace with such a monster as Antony. Cicero also read from a letter of Antony which included a passage that expressed Antony's intent to live up to his alliance with Lepidus. The orator said that this statement was intended to fool the Senate into thinking that such a good citizen as Lepidus was either disloyal or insane, but the simple association of the two names and the expressed idea that Lepidus must have been mistaken in advocating peace negotiations with such an evil man show that Cicero was aware of Lepidus' friendship toward Antony, despite his vain hope that Lepidus could still be brought around to the Republican side. Cicero brought up Lepidus' model ancestor and his family traditions and made it very clear that Lepidus' armies were not his own, but belonged to the Senate and Roman people and should be deployed in their interests and definitely not against them. Cicero avoided any reference to the one ancestor whom he probably felt Lepidus was in danger of imitating, Lepidus' own father, the rebellious consul of 78 BC. It is quite likely that when Cicero expressed in early February in letters to two of the conspirators the view that had he been invited to the 'banquet' on the Ides of March there would have been no left-overs, he was already considering Lepidus as one of the *reliquiarum nihil*.[44]

On April 11 Cicero expressed his distrust and dislike of Lepidus in a personal letter to Brutus, Lepidus' brother-in-law. Cicero mentioned Lepidus' hatred for his own brother, Paullus, and for his in-laws, and described him as 'lacking in principle and consistency and . . . chronically ill-disposed to the free state'.[45] The startling contrast between the orator's public and private opinions on Lepidus' character might strike one as being similarly unprincipled and inconsistent, although it is true that Cicero was sincere in his devotion to the Republic and was willing to try anything to save it.

While Cicero was in control for the moment of the situation in

Rome, the joint forces of Hirtius, Pansa, and Octavian were advancing towards Mutina to raise the siege before the famine-weakened troops of Decimus Brutus would have to surrender to Antony. It was probably early in April that Lepidus sent reinforcements to Antony in the form of a praetorian cohort under the command of M. Iunius Silanus, aided by Q. Terentius Culleo. Lepidus had apparently sent this force to Mutina without explicit orders concerning which side Silanus was to assist, or at least under instructions to pretend that was the case. This arrangement allowed Lepidus to preserve the fiction that he had sent troops to aid Decimus Brutus, when he was actually helping the public enemy Antony. Silanus provided assistance to Antony in the preliminary battle fought in the marshes near the plain of Forum Gallorum as well as in the major conflict at Mutina.[46] Hirtius and Octavian won a decisive victory in the main battle, but Hirtius was killed while breaking into the enemy camp and Pansa died soon afterwards from wounds received at Forum Gallorum. Antony's advisers told him to continue the siege, but, fearing another attack or encirclement by Octavian, he decided to withdraw his forces toward the Alps, hoping for reinforcements from Lepidus or Plancus.[47]

Upon receiving word of Antony's defeat at Mutina, the Senate approved a *supplicatio* of fifty days, the longest 'thanksgiving' ever voted, in response to a proposal by Cicero.[48] It appeared that total victory was imminent and the consular armies were turned over to Decimus Brutus as sole commander in the war in the expectation that he would deliver the death blow. The Senate also sent letters to Lepidus, Plancus, and Pollio, instructing them to continue the war against Antony.[49] Cicero and the Senate had made a fatal error in pushing Octavian aside after the victories and rewarding Decimus Brutus instead. Octavian could see that he had been used by the Republican side and he must have been particularly irritated when Decimus, who had been on the point of surrender and who was also one of Caesar's murderers, received all the glory for victories that Octavian had been instrumental in bringing about. In failing to secure Octavian's allegiance, the Senate contributed greatly to its own eventual defeat.

After Mutina, Lepidus was quick to claim that Silanus had joined Antony in complete disregard of orders. Silanus and Culleo were spared execution, but Lepidus said they were kept outside his camp and not put in command of any operation.[50] However, the actions of Silanus caused the Senate to fear that the full forces of

Lepidus and Plancus, which had been summoned to Italy to help the Republican cause, might in a similar fashion join Antony. For this reason, according to Dio Cassius, the Senate wrote Lepidus and Plancus to tell them that they were no longer needed and that they should remain in their provinces. As a diversion the two governors were ordered to found a colony of those people who had been driven out of Vienne by the Allobroges and who were then settled north of Vienne, near the conjunction of the Rhone and Arar rivers. This area lay near the border between the provinces of the two governors. The Roman colony of Lugdunum (Lyons) was founded in Plancus' territory in accordance with the Senate's wishes.[51]

During late April and May Lepidus was still in a position where he could join whichever side appeared to him as the eventual winner. This waiting-and-watching posture, remaining technically in compliance with the Senate's orders while preparing to aid Antony openly if Antony's forces were still viable, would later brand Lepidus in the eyes of history as indecisive. However, Lepidus knew that he, as one of Caesar's closest assistants, could never expect more than empty honors from the Senate leadership. Their continued open support for Caesar's murderers made the Senate's position very clear. As Cicero reportedly said about Octavian: 'The young man is to be praised, honored, and removed.'[52] A successful future for Lepidus clearly lay only with Antony. If Antony's forces were no longer strong enough to compete, however, Lepidus must negotiate the best deal for himself and for his troops. Octavian remained the wild card at this point. Lepidus and Antony were quite naturally skeptical about his viability and even jealous of his sudden rise to power among troops they considered to be rightfully theirs. However, time would soon convince all three men that their futures lay not with the Senate, but in working together, at least for a while.

During this same period of waiting Cicero kept up an active correspondence with Decimus Brutus and Plancus regarding the war with Antony. Towards the end of April Plancus advised the orator that the troops of Lepidus might receive Antony as their friend. He also noted quite candidly that even some of his own soldiers favored Antony and he raised the possibility that Lepidus might block his path should he make a move toward Mutina. In addition, Plancus promised Cicero that he would make every effort to convince Lepidus to remain on the side of the Republicans. The orator replied by praising Plancus' deeds and expressing the hope that the attempt to secure the aid of Lepidus would be successful.[53]

Decimus Brutus also wrote Cicero during this period to urge him to contact Lepidus and prevent him from joining Antony. Decimus knew that Lepidus was not likely to support the Republicans, but he thought that it was an absolute necessity, as it later proved to be, to keep the legions of Lepidus, and those of Plancus and Pollio as well, from reviving Antony.[54] On May 6 Decimus reported that Antony was marching in the direction of Lepidus' forces. He also told Cicero that he had captured notebooks of Antony which listed the names of men that Antony had sent to Lepidus, Pollio, and Plancus, presumably to negotiate an agreement with them.[55]

Plancus did not mention any contacts from Antony in his letters to Cicero. Early in May he informed Cicero that he was working out an arrangement to keep Lepidus on the Republican side. Plancus said that he had sent messengers to Lepidus' camp and, with the assistance of M. Iuventius Laterensis, one of Lepidus' legates, Plancus had received a pledge to attack Antony if an attempt were made to enter Narbonese Gaul. Lepidus had even proposed that he and Plancus join their forces to better defend Gaul against Antony because while Lepidus' troops were weak in cavalry, that was Antony's strongest point. Plancus also expressed the hope that by uniting with Lepidus he could control those elements in the latter's army most likely to aid Antony.[56]

By mid-May, however, Plancus' letters were sounding increasingly doubtful of Lepidus' trustworthiness. Even Lepidus' own legate, Laterensis, was questioning his loyalty and his soldiers were openly declaring that they would not fight for either side and they were receiving no punishment for such traitorous statements. The fact that Laterensis, a dedicated Republican who soon afterwards would commit suicide in protest against the merger with Antony, was still in authority and negotiating with Plancus at this late date indicates the very fine line Lepidus was trying to straddle even with his own troops. There must have been more division of opinion on the issue of Antony among his soldiers than was readily apparent later. Plancus also reported that Lepidus was camped at Forum Voconii (Le Canet), only 24 miles from Antony's camp at Forum Iulii (Fréjus). Lepidus still wanted Plancus to join forces with him and he sent a certain Apella as a hostage to prove his faith to Plancus.[57]

In mid-May Lepidus sent Cicero two letters which still survive. They were mailed from his camp at Pons Argenteus, near Forum Voconii. In the first letter Lepidus said that he had arrived at the camp after several forced marches and that he was determined to defend his province against Antony. He went on to declare that he would not fail in his duty to the Senate and the Republic. The second letter, written on May 22, proclaimed his devotion once again, particularly in response to the false rumors he said his detractors were circulating about him.[58]

Although as late as May 23 Decimus Brutus found Lepidus' attitude to be satisfactory, perhaps on the strength of an earlier letter from Plancus reporting that Lepidus was not receiving Antony well, during this same period reports began to come in to Cicero of an agreement between Antony and Lepidus.[59] Asinius Pollio, noting that Lepidus had detained for nine days Pollio's messenger, who was bringing him the news from Mutina, reported to Cicero that Lepidus' public speeches delivered at Narbo and his letters both placed his loyalty to the Republic in question.[60] Decimus Brutus informed Cicero that Mark Antony in a public speech had referred to his having reached agreement with Lepidus.[61] Lepidus himself sent a letter to the Senate which Cicero described as *frigidus* and *inconstans*.[62]

There are several accounts of the actual union between the forces of Antony and those of Lepidus. Although Lepidus wanted it to appear as if his men had forced this action upon him – he certainly took great pains to make things look this way – it is most likely that the two men had secretly been in contact all along. They had seemed to be close friends following Caesar's death or they at least were working in close conjunction with one another. Antony had helped Lepidus secure the post of pontifex maximus, the two had set up a marriage alliance, and they had coordinated their efforts to calm the Spanish front by arranging an agreement with Sextus Pompey. Both men shared a desire for revenge against the murderers of Caesar and both knew that the senatorial forces that supported those same assassins could never trust the two former sidekicks of the dictator. The union of Lepidus and Mark Antony was therefore the natural outcome of the two men's earlier careers. Lepidus had no reason to despise Antony or consider him an enemy. Lepidus naturally had to avoid open fraternization with a *hostis publicus* so that he would not be branded with the same label. He had to keep his options with the Senate open as long as possible because if Antony had been finished off at Mutina it would be best for him and his troops to try to salvage some deal with the victors, but no real position of authority would come to either man through accommodation with the Senate.

After Antony's defeats at Mutina he withdrew his men from the scene and headed for the Alps. Had Decimus Brutus or Octavian pursued him immediately, a final defeat might well have taken place. By retreating across the Alps Antony hoped to pick up, and probably had reason to count on getting, reinforcements from the legions of Lepidus and Plancus and from P. Ventidius Bassus, a Caesarian who had raised three legions in Gaul.[63] The region might also have been considered a good one for recruiting additional soldiers. Q. Terentius Culleo, whom Lepidus had stationed to guard the passage over the Alps, allowed Antony to pass. According to Appian, Antony marched his forces to the river where Lepidus was situated and set up his own camp without a surrounding palisade and ditch, thus giving a sign that he was camping by a friend.[64] This description accords well with Plancus' report that Antony set up camp at Forum Iulii on May 15, 24 miles from Lepidus' camp at Forum Voconii, near the river Argenteus.[65]

Although messengers constantly went back and forth between the two camps, most sources indicate that Lepidus was cool to Antony's proposals for a joint effort and that he remained loyal to the Senate.[66] Lepidus' initial aloofness here can easily be explained by his need first to ascertain whether or not Antony could indeed be saved at all and then to try to strike the best bargain in return for his valuable aid. Dio Cassius claims that Lepidus would not hold a conference with Antony, but that instead he wrote to the Senate his accusations against Antony and received in return both praise and the command of the war against the outlaw.[67] High praise is attested elsewhere, but it is inconceivable that the Senate would have even considered replacing Decimus Brutus with Lepidus, especially after Mutina.

Several sources explain the joining of the forces of Lepidus and Antony as an action forced upon Lepidus by his own soldiers, who felt a natural kinship with Antony's troops. Appian says that the soldiers of the two camps began to fraternize, despite the orders of the tribunes banning such action, and that they built a bridge of boats across the river to facilitate communication. He also says that the Tenth Legion, which had originally enlisted under Antony but now served Lepidus, arranged for Antony's entry into Lepidus' camp. The legate M. Iuventius Laterensis warned Lepidus of what was going on and advised him to test his army's fidelity. Lepidus then divided his men into three groups and sent them out on a mission to protect some approaching convoys. According to Appian, the soldiers armed themselves for the march, took over control of the camp, and opened the gates to Antony, who went straight to Lepidus' tent and concluded an agreement with him.[68] Laterensis, after failing to persuade Lepidus to resist Antony's overtures, committed suicide with his sword in front of his fellow-soldiers. The legate was honored posthumously by the Senate with eulogies, a statue, and a public funeral.[69]

Velleius Paterculus agrees with Appian that Lepidus' soldiers admitted Antony into his camp, stating specifically that he entered through a breach they had made in the fortifications in the rear of the camp.[70] Plutarch, in an echo of accounts of Octavian's takeover of Lepidus' camp in 36 BC, portrays Antony dramatically walking up to Lepidus' camp and talking with his soldiers. Lepidus' order to drown out the speech with the sound of trumpets only made his men more sympathetic to Antony. Plutarch says that some even offered to kill Lepidus and that the soldiers tore down their ramparts to admit Antony and his troops.[71] This more dramatic version is more appropriate for a biography of Antony, but it probably contains little truth.

It is quite possible that Lepidus pretended to resist Antony so that his soldiers would 'force' him into union with the public enemy and absolve him of responsibility for deserting his professed allegiance to the Senate. In a letter sent to that body from Pons Argenteus on May 30, Lepidus explained that he had been compelled by a mutiny of his army to reach accommodation with Antony, although that name is not specifically mentioned. Lepidus advised the Senate to disregard private feuds and to work for the good of the state as a whole.[72]

Eutropius preserves a different tradition, perhaps from Livy, by mentioning no resistance and simply stating that Antony was well received by Lepidus after Mutina.[73] Dio Cassius says that Lepidus did not make a move to accept Antony until he heard of a compact between Octavian and Antony, but other sources credit Lepidus with bringing those two together at a later date.[74] The fact that Antony and Lepidus worked closely together both before and after their union, the early reports of an alliance between the two men, the assistance that Lepidus gave to Antony even before Mutina, and the questionable story of Antony's takeover of Lepidus' troops all point to the conclusion that resistance was a mere pretense carried out to defend Lepidus against the charge that he had sold out the Republic and openly disobeyed the orders of the Senate. Lepidus had to be careful about those of his soldiers who had enlisted in support of the senatorial cause, but the clear majority must have leaned in the other direction or else no merger would have taken place.

According to Appian, Lepidus brought to his alliance with Antony seven legions, many auxiliary troops, and a large quantity of military supplies. Lepidus' main weakness was in cavalry and this happened to be Antony's point of strength because their relative inactivity at Mutina had left them almost intact.[75]

The reaction of the Senate to word of the agreement between Lepidus and Antony was to declare Lepidus a public enemy (*hostis publicus*) and order that his equestrian statue be removed from the Rostra. His followers were also charged to desert him before September 1 or be considered enemies of the state. The Senate's action was unanimously voted on June 30, according to Cicero.[76] The lapse of one month before this vote allowed time to confirm the union of Antony and Lepidus and to ascertain whether or not Lepidus might again reverse his position. Plancus had reported on June 6 to Cicero that the alliance had taken place on May 29. He requested that Octavian's army be sent so that together they could resist the joint forces of Antony and Lepidus.[77] In letters written in mid-June, Cicero condemned Lepidus' fickleness for having placed the Republic in a difficult position. With all hope of Lepidus' assistance dashed, the orator could finally vent his anger.

The bitter invective that flowed from Cicero's pen in this period has totally engulfed Lepidus' reputation and branded him permanently before the bench of history. In letters written to Lepidus' brother-in-law, Brutus, Cicero attacked Lepidus' *levitas, inconstantia,* and *amentia*, grouped him with the *sceleratos cives*, and said that he was *animumque semper inimicum rei publicae* and *instrumentum regni*.[78] The harshness of these labels shows how strongly the orator believed that Lepidus had betrayed the *patria*.

During the latter part of 44 BC Cicero in *De Officiis* had outlined the Stoic principles of individual moral obligations and his judgment of Lepidus is quite consistent with these standards. Cicero divided the world into the *boni* and the *improbi*, allowing no room for refuge in between these opposite poles. The *boni* share a fortitude of character that directs them to pursue the path of honor, morality, and justice automatically, while also performing duties to family and state.[79] Those who choose the way of personal advantage and expediency, who lust for military commands, individual fame, and power over others, or who even hesitate in deciding to follow the route of virtue are *improbi*.[80] These are destroying the Republic and committing *parricidium patriae*.[81] The man who, as Lepidus had done, pretends to be doing one thing while pursuing the opposite course is held up for particular scorn.[82] From Cicero's perspective the *improbi* merited removal from society and he wanted to make sure that they suffered the punishment that their immoral choices had earned for them.[83] In addition to feeling intense anger at Lepidus' juncture with Antony, Cicero also realized that the war was not yet near a conclusion, as it had appeared to be immediately after Mutina.[84]

A very important factor in the outcome of this struggle would be Octavian's chosen path of action. The Senate had erred by bestowing on Decimus Brutus the honors that Octavian had both expected and deserved after Mutina. When Caesar's heir realized that the Senate was using him, without any intention of rewarding his efforts in a serious way, he must have had second thoughts about his opposition to Antony. The Senate was after all actively protecting and honoring the murderers of his adoptive father and, if Antony were removed from the scene, the chances were very slim that other Caesarians, such as himself and Lepidus, would last long without meeting a similar fate. Octavian, according to Appian, let the word reach Antony that conciliation was possible. He also wrote to Lepidus and to Asinius Pollio, expressing both his irritation at the way the Senate had treated him and his fears of future mistreatment of Caesarian leaders and advising the two governors in hope of finding common ground for negotiation with Antony.[85]

The union of Lepidus and Antony late in May caused the Senate once more to turn, however hesitantly, to Octavian for help and in return it became more responsive to his demands. Dio's contention that Octavian had already secretly made an agreement with Antony and that Lepidus joined Antony only after hearing of this compact does not seem likely because it appears that Lepidus was the mediator through whom Octavian and Antony resolved their differences.[86]

Octavian's acceptance of the command in the war against Antony and Lepidus was, according to Dio Cassius, calculated as a move toward getting the consulship. Both consular positions had been vacated with the deaths of Hirtius and Pansa and Octavian was even willing to accept Cicero as his colleague in order to be chosen. When the Senate still delayed in granting Octavian this honor, the young man made preparations for the war, but influenced his soldiers to take an oath not to fight against any of Caesar's former legions, which naturally made up the bulk of the forces of Antony and Lepidus.[87] After further argument back and forth between Octavian and the Senate over pay for his troops and his desire for the consular office, he sent centurions from his legions to demand the position for their commander. When the Senate still hesitated, Octavian marched his troops to Rome, in imitation of Sulla, took control of the city, paid his soldiers from the public funds, and arranged for his election to the consulship with Q. Pedius as his colleague.[88]

Cicero's correspondence during July, just prior to the takeover of Rome by Octavian, reveals the great frustration he felt over the actions of Lepidus, who in his opinion had wrecked the Republican cause by saving Antony from total defeat and rekindling the war anew. Although the orator had correctly gauged Lepidus' true feelings, despite the professions of loyalty in his letters, Cicero saw in Lepidus' agreement with Antony a major setback for the chances of a Republican victory. He therefore condemned Lepidus for being fickle and a traitor and obviously did not accept the story of the alleged mutiny of Lepidus' soldiers. Cicero also believed that it was absolutely necessary to bring Brutus and his legions back from Macedonia to Italy for the defense of the Republic.[89]

The condemnation of Lepidus as a public enemy caused Brutus to express an uncle's personal concern for the safety of Lepidus' children. Brutus apparently reproached Cicero concerning the treatment of Lepidus, presumably for the toppling of Lepidus' equestrian statue, and probably counselled caution until more specific details of Lepidus' intentions were known. He also requested Cicero to do all that he could do to protect his half-sister's sons and perhaps also a daughter. The Senate's declaration of Lepidus as a public enemy exposed Iunia and the children to confiscation of property and to the threat of being used as hostages for negotiation with Lepidus. Cicero told Brutus that, despite the pleas of his half-sister and mother, Lepidus' case could not be considered as separate from that of Antony. He reiterated his belief in Lepidus' guilt for causing great difficulties for the Republic and he blamed Lepidus for putting his children in peril through his own actions against the state. Despite all of his objections, however, Cicero promised as a favor to Brutus to do all in his power to protect the children.[90]

During this same period the Republican cause was temporarily bolstered by the union of Plancus' forces with those of Decimus Brutus. Plancus wrote later in July that if Octavian's assistance had come to him as promised, the war would easily have been ended or at least pushed into Spain. While Plancus and Decimus might carry on the war for some time, the forces of Antony and Lepidus were still formidable and Cicero, not yet aware of the danger that

Octavian might join the opposition, held out the hope that Brutus and Cassius would return to Italy to fight them.[91]

In August of 43 BC events began to point toward the conclusion of an agreement between Antony, Lepidus, and Octavian. Letters concerning a peaceful settlement and an arrangement for working in unison had most likely been circulating between Octavian and the other two men since the beginning of summer.[92] Octavian, in full control of Rome with his troops, had his adoption by Caesar officially ratified and passed a law to punish the murderers of his adoptive father. In one day he presided over a trial in which all of the conspirators, and several other enemies, were judged by default.[93] This was intended to shift legality and legitimacy, through force, to the Caesarian cause, but was also a portent of future proscriptions.

After arranging affairs in Rome, Octavian marched off with his soldiers, most likely proclaiming his intention to carry on the war against Antony and Lepidus, but in reality anticipating a union with them to avenge Caesar's death and to rule the state together. After all, Octavian knew that his future did not lie with the Republican cause, and time, the fanatic loyalty of Caesarian troops to Caesar's name, and success at Mutina had demonstrated to Antony and Lepidus that Octavian, despite his youth, was a serious force to be reckoned with. After Octavian's departure from Rome, his colleague, Q. Pedius, almost certainly on the direct order of Octavian, persuaded the Senate to repeal its decrees declaring Antony, Lepidus, and their followers' public enemies and to substitute instead an edict granting them amnesty and restoration of their property. Octavian was still in a position to deny responsibility for this act, but he must have been secretly pleased that a major obstacle blocking his union with Antony and Lepidus had been removed.[94]

Decimus Brutus remained the chief block to Caesarian dominance of the West. Plancus had joined Decimus early in the summer of 43 BC, but Asinius Pollio then persuaded Plancus to go over with him to the side of Antony and Lepidus. Now all three of the provincial governors who had earlier responded to Cicero's courting with effusive promises of loyalty had chosen the opposition. Decimus, left alone, did not want to risk a battle with his stronger opponents. He withdrew in hope of joining Brutus in Macedonia, but, because of a difficult journey and pursuit by Antony and Lepidus, his ten legions soon dwindled to a small band through desertion. According to Appian,

Decimus Brutus was captured by a Gallic tribe and executed on the orders of Antony.[95] With his death the Caesarian leaders had gained vengeance on one of the chief conspirators and had cleared the west of all active opposition to their common cause.

7

THE SECOND TRIUMVIRATE:
ONE-THIRD OF THE WORLD

It was probably early in September that Mark Antony and Lepidus, having received word of the Senate's action to revoke their status as public enemies and almost certainly already in regular communication with Octavian, decided to leave Gaul in control of lieutenants and march with strong forces into Italy. They apparently desired to make a show of collective strength that would aid them in their negotiations with Octavian.[1] Most sources credit Lepidus with acting as intermediary in bringing Antony and Octavian together.[2] Dio Cassius thought that Octavian concluded a pact with Antony first and then through him with Lepidus, but Octavian was more of a direct threat to Antony's position of leadership and they had fought each other at Mutina so it appears that Dio is in error here.[3]

The meeting of the three leaders took place in Cisalpine Gaul, near one of two towns located close to each other along the Via Aemilia, Bononia (Bologna) and Mutina (Modena). This region was a kind of home territory to Lepidus because his model ancestor had built the road and served as patron to the families of many of the area's inhabitants. It had apparently been a recruiting-ground for Carbo and for Lepidus' father and Cicero had only recently questioned the loyalty to the Republic of its towns Bononia, Regium Lepidi, and Parma.[4]

Although Appian mentions Mutina as the site for the negotiations of Octavian, Lepidus, and Antony, this is unlikely because of the recent conflict there between Octavian and Antony. To attempt to work out a peace agreement in the town where Antony had suffered two great defeats would seem to be a gratuitous insult to Antony. Dio Cassius, Plutarch, Suetonius, and Florus all name Bononia as the site and this seems a far more likely choice because it lacked any association with the enmities of the past. Both sites, however, fit the general description of being near a river with small islands in it. It was on such an island in late October or early November of 43 BC that the meeting was held.

According to Appian, each of the three leaders brought along five legions and an escort of three hundred men to accompany him to the bridges over the river.[5] The suspicion of a possible plot had to be carefully guarded against. Lepidus, playing his role of intermediary, went ahead and searched the island, finally waving his cloak as a signal to the other two that it was safe to proceed. The leaders also searched one another to make sure that no one had concealed a dagger. The three men held talks in plain sight in the middle of the island for two or three days, with Octavian as consul seated in the center.[6] Long hours were presumably spent in discussing how they should control the state, by what method they could best exact revenge on Caesar's murderers, and what the personal role of each of them would be in the united effort. All three had to be willing to compromise to some extent because each man knew that he had to secure the assistance of the other two.

The major decision reached at the conference was to form a triumvirate, a board of three men legally approved, in this particular case for five years and for the express purpose of bringing order to a state torn by civil strife. The appointment of such a trio was in keeping with Roman political tradition because similar boards of three had been used to establish colonies or distribute land, but the extent of its powers made it revolutionary. The closest precedent for it was Sulla's unlimited dictatorship to revise the constitution. The First Triumvirate had not been formalized and given such official status.

The three men were to receive consular power and, although they carefully avoided the title of dictator, they granted themselves dictatorial powers. They were at once to designate the city magistrates for the next five years, a move similar to that made by Caesar before his intended departure to fight the Parthians. They could also rule by decree, making laws with or without consulting the Senate or Assembly. The triumvirs also divided the western provinces among themselves: Lepidus was to keep Narbonese Gaul and to gain the rest of Spain in addition to his current province of Hither Spain; Antony would receive Cisalpine Gaul and the rest of Gaul north of Provence, called Gallia Comata; and Octavian would govern Africa, Numidia, Sardinia, Sicily, and other islands in that region. No claim was made to the eastern provinces then under the control of Brutus and Cassius, perhaps because the triumvirs did not wish to appear too ambitious.[7]

The initial division of the western provinces indicates the relative power of the three men in 43 BC. Antony seems to have taken the choicest portions because Cisalpine Gaul was the most important province strategically and Gallia Comata held tremendous potential for exploitation and enrichment, as Caesar had only recently demonstrated. Both areas were good for recruiting soldiers. Lepidus also received provinces of similar potential in Narbonese Gaul and both Spains. Those who see Lepidus as a nonentity or as Antony's lackey are hard-pressed to explain why he was allowed to take such a substantial portion of the provincial pie. Octavian got important provinces in Sicily, Sardinia, and Africa, but, as Eleanor Huzar has pointed out, Sextus Pompey controlled most of Sicily and Sardinia, and Africa was under the command of T. Sextius, a general loyal to Antony.[8] Africa, of course, would be turned over voluntarily, but Sextus Pompey was still a major obstacle yet to be overcome in the other two provinces. Octavian's share was practically humiliating. It is shocking to see him the weakest of the three partners at this point, but he knew that he just had to bide his time and before too long he would turn the tables on both his colleagues. Octavian was probably shrewd enough to see that by yielding seven of his legions Lepidus was effectively eliminating himself as an equal partner and that a victory over Brutus and Cassius would create a duovirate. The provinces could then be reshuffled accordingly.

The triumvirs also decided that Octavian would resign from the consulship for the last two months of the year in order to reward the praetor Ventidius with the office for the help he had brought to Antony. This move was probably necessary to preserve the external appearance of equality among the triumvirs after their return to Rome. The triumvirs also agreed that Antony and Octavian would carry on the war against Brutus and Cassius, while Lepidus would be consul in 42, resume his old role of running the government in Rome, and control his provinces through lieutenants. Lepidus would keep three of the ten legions he possessed by this time to guard Rome and Italy and turn over three legions to Octavian and four to Antony so that his two colleagues could each lead twenty legions into war in the east.[9]

The triumvirs put all of their agreements in writing and took oaths to uphold them. A public announcement of the decisions was made to the troops by Octavian as consul to produce a feeling of unity among them. The one part of the triumvirs' arrangements not relayed to their soldiers was the decision to carry out proscriptions against their enemies before departing for the war against Brutus and Cassius.[10] The trio must have considered this necessary to secure the home front before departure, as well as to build up the treasury needed to reward so many soldiers.

The unity attained by the triumvirs at Bononia would decide the course of Roman history for several years to come. However, just as happened to the partners of the First Triumvirate, human nature would eventually cause two of the participants, who were temporarily willing to accept a division of power among three, each to attempt to grab it all for himself.

The omens that generally portended important events in Roman history were not absent at the founding of the Second Triumvirate. In regard to Lepidus' future, a snake coiling around a centurion's sword and a wolf entering his tent and knocking over a table while he dined conclusively foretold future power followed by trouble.[11] The howling of a pack of dogs outside Lepidus' official residence as pontifex maximus augured ill for the Republic and an attack on the largest dog by the others naturally indicated disgrace for Lepidus.[12] Lepidus had in fact already reached the peak of his power. By becoming pontifex maximus and triumvir he had gained a level of recognition that would preserve his name and save a very small niche for him in the history of western civilization. However, in agreeing to yield seven of his legions and allow Octavian and Antony the glory of defeating Brutus and Cassius, he had consigned himself to a minor role in the future. The job of governing Rome and Italy was the natural one for him, given his past experience, and Antony had the military background to lead the triumviral armies, while Caesar's name would also be of tremendous help with the soldiers. The presence of the pontifex maximus in Rome might also help stabilize a tense situation. Lepidus may not have had any choice of role, but the initial distribution of provinces casts at least some doubt on that. Lepidus' mistake was his failure to see that, under the new rules that the violent disruptions of the first century BC had forged, and that he and his colleagues had helped create, trust in one's word was no longer the treasured Roman virtue that one could count on.

The proscriptions of the Second Triumvirate have marred the reputations of all three triumvirs to some extent, although imperial historians tried to excuse Octavian's involvement by placing most of the blame on his two colleagues. Proscription of political enemies was modeled on Sulla's policy and the triumvirs considered it essential because in their eyes Caesar's clemency had led directly to his assassination. In addition to protecting themselves and making political action easier to accomplish in an atmosphere of fear, the confiscations of property that accompanied proscriptions might help produce revenue quickly and this was needed to fulfill promises made to secure the allegiance of so many soldiers.

Many of the names placed on proscription lists were agreed upon at the conference near Bononia. Lepidus and Antony had both known the ignominy of being public enemies and they must have seen the proscriptions at first as an act of vengeance against their tormentors. Antony must have demanded Cicero's death as retribution for past harm that the orator had done him in both word and act. Cicero therefore joined a small list, reported to contain either twelve or seventeen names, that the triumvirs sent ahead to Rome with executioners and orders to murder those most dangerous individuals immediately, without warning. The initial blows of this very limited proscription caused panic in Rome, for no one could be sure of safety. The elderly consul Pedius, who died shortly thereafter, calmed the populace by publishing the abbreviated list and explaining his mistaken view that those included, who were responsible for civil war, were the only ones to be condemned.[13]

When the triumvirs reached Rome, they entered the city separately on three successive days. Octavian went first, presumably because he was still consul, followed by Antony and then Lepidus. A praetorian cohort and one legion accompanied each leader. On November 27, in the presence of armed soldiers, an Assembly meeting was held at which the tribune P. Titius proposed a law to set up a board of three men, specifically Antony, Octavian, and Lepidus, to serve for five years with consular power for the purpose of setting the state in order. This *Lex Titia* was passed immediately, without the customary period of time allowed for deliberation and debate. Sacrifices were also voted in honor of the three men for their successes, presumably in coming to the relief of the state.[14]

The passage of the *Lex Titia*, which gave the triumvirs a legal base that the members of the unofficial First Triumvirate never had, was followed that night by the proclamation of a proscription list with 130 names included. To this were soon added 150 more names and from time to time others would also appear, particularly to justify the murders of people killed by mistake or to gain additional property.[15] The figure of 150 proscribed on the first long list, cited by Appian, may well have included only senators. Livy, Florus, and Orosius all give figures between 130 and 140 for the total number of senators proscribed. The 150 on the next list may have been equestrians. This figure may have increased during the following months. Dio says that two white tablets of names were displayed, one for senators and one for the rest of the people.[16] This comment adds support to Appian's two separate lists and to the number of senators proscribed.

The inclusion of Lepidus' brother, Paullus, and Antony's uncle, L. Caesar, on the proscription lists has received condemnation by many sources as one of the most brutal acts of the triumvirs. These two men, according to Appian, had been the first to vote to denounce Lepidus and Antony as public enemies.[17] However, both men survived the proscriptions, Paullus through escape and L. Caesar by the intervention of his sister, Antony's mother.[18] Plutarch preserves another tradition which says that Lepidus sacrificed his brother to the demands of Octavian and Antony.[19] Aside from this, the fact that Lepidus was still corresponding with Paullus in April of 44 BC, Cicero's favorable mention of Paullus' public monument (the Basilica Aemilia) in his appeal to Lepidus in the thirteenth *Philippic*, and Dio's statement that Lepidus allowed his brother to escape to Miletus all point to a continuing positive relationship between the brothers that rose above politics.[20] Lepidus' 'surrender' of his brother's name to the proscription list is mitigated substantially by the fact that relatives of Antony, Plancus, and Pollio, and an alleged former tutor of Octavian were also included. The naming of relatives of the Caesarian leaders must have been a symbolic gesture to demonstrate the toughness and will of the new regime and make it clear that anyone who opposed the triumvirs would suffer a similar fate. Lepidus may also have felt compelled to proscribe his brother as an active leader of the opposition, while at the same time providing for his escape from Italy, where Paullus could no longer be safe whether proscribed or not.

Appian preserves a text of the official announcement of the proscription which seems to be an accurate representation because its content agrees with information supplied by other sources. In the document the triumvirs justified their action, explaining that Caesar's clemency towards his defeated foes had led to his death and that the war to avenge that murder could not begin abroad until all enemies at home could be rooted out. Everyone was warned that those who attempted to conceal or help the proscribed in any way would themselves be placed on the list. The searching of homes had to be permitted. People were encouraged to kill the proscribed and turn in their heads for a reward. A free man would be paid 25,000 denarii and a slave 10,000 in addition to his freedom and his master's right of citizenship. This kind of bounty system inevitably caused mistrust throughout the populace and led to informing and murder at the expense of innocent victims. To protect the informers and killers, no names of those receiving rewards were to be registered. This would save them from later prosecution, which had occurred after the proscriptions of Sulla. The triumvirs also claimed in the proclamation that they would single out only the worst offenders for prosecution and that they would not slay as many people as Sulla had done earlier.[21]

Appian and Dio Cassius have described very effectively the horror of the proscriptions late in 43 BC and during the early months of 42 in a series of individual experiences of the proscribed.[22] Although many undoubtedly died, it seems that a great number of those placed on the lists escaped, several of whom had been named only to justify confiscating their property when they fled into exile.[23] Appian estimates the total number of senators sentenced to death or confiscation of property at 300, along with about 2,000 equestrians.[24] François Hinard's research makes a good case for revising downward the number of men actually proscribed and for emphasizing the political motivation of the proscriptions, to avenge Caesar's death and use terror to remove the 'senatorial' party as an opposing force, rather than the economic one of raising money to pay the soldiers.[25]

The triumvirs did have to levy additional taxes to increase their financial resources for the war effort, especially since the wealthy east was paying its revenues to Brutus and Cassius.[26] Although the contents of the houses of the proscribed seem to have been easy to sell, the triumvirs ran into difficulty in the sale of the lands. Few buyers attended the auctions of the property either because they were ashamed to take advantage of the punishment of the proscribed, because they feared it would bring them bad luck, or, most probably, because they feared to increase their own property and draw attention to their wealth, lest they too join the lists. Those who took the risk, usually soldiers, were thus able to buy at very low prices. Appian says that despite these sales the triumvirs were still about 200,000,000 denarii short of the total that they needed.[27]

Other revenue-raising measures included placing a tax on the property of 1,400 of the richest women of the state and providing for fines for false evaluation and rewards for informers. The women rebelled at this unfair and discriminatory measure and asked the triumvirs to revoke their decision. Hortensia, speaking for the group, said that the women should not be taxed because they had no part in deciding affairs of state. She stated that the women would voluntarily contribute to defense against external attack, but not in a civil war. The triumvirs responded by reducing the number of women to be taxed from 1,400 to 400 and by ordering all men having more than 100,000 denarii to lend the state a fiftieth part of their property at interest and to contribute a year's income to the treasury.[28]

Several other attempts to raise money also helped make the triumvirs particularly unpopular. According to Dio, the promises to give the widows of the proscribed their dowries and to grant their male children a tenth of the property and the female children a twentieth were probably honored only in a few cases. The triumvirs also placed heavy taxes both on all houses of the proscribed and on the income from their land.[29]

When Lepidus and Plancus assumed the consulship in 42 BC, the triumvirs set up tablets proclaiming property confiscations of additional citizens who were not formally proscribed. The excessive taxation that the triumvirs levied in general on land and slaves seems to have strained the resources of all citizens except the soldiers, whose loyalty they were trying to purchase. Dio says that instead of a man yielding one-tenth of his property in taxes, in reality he had barely one-tenth left after all these exactions.[30] Plutarch even accuses the triumvirs of confiscating the money deposited with the vestal virgins, and Lepidus as pontifex maximus may even have accomplished this 'legally'.[31] In addition to all the taxes, specific contributions, such as furnishing slaves for the navy and repairing roads, could increase the burden. The citizens could assess the value of their own property, but greedy informers raised the threat of accusations of false valuation and swift punishment.[32] The whole situation made life an endless nightmare for the general population.

The proscription horror-story that most directly affects our image of Lepidus is preserved in a funerary inscription known as the *Laudatio Turiae*. In the course of a long account of Turia's defense of her husband's interests both during the period of Caesar's domination of Rome and later in the proscriptions, the husband relates how Octavian, then absent from Rome, had issued an edict that promised him restoration of citizenship. Turia then took this edict to Rome and appeared before Lepidus, who was in charge there, to officially complete the process. Lepidus rejected Turia's petition and, despite her humiliating prostration before him, had her dragged away. This story does make Lepidus appear cruel and inhumane, but, although the *Laudatio Turiae* is a touching and romantic account of the intense love that bonded two people for over forty years, it is far from objective. A diehard Pompeian/Republican who had been proscribed in the midst of a civil war composed this beautiful testament. The bereaved husband had reason to hold a grudge against Lepidus and be thankful to Octavian, who by the time of the composition of the piece was the respected and powerful emperor Augustus. Lepidus may have been cruel in this case, but if so he was most probably provoked by Octavian's interference in his area of responsibility and treatment of his colleague as a mere lieutenant expected to ratify Octavian's wishes (just as Octavian would act later in the Sicilian campaign against Sextus Pompey).[33]

Octavian's participation in the proscriptions can not be condoned by the excuses that he was too young or not a powerful member of the triumvirate. Antony probably deserves the largest share of guilt, mainly because he had the most enemies, but Octavian and Lepidus actively participated in the proscriptions, both to stabilize the regime and enrich the treasury, and this is not to their credit.[34] No one can defend the cruelties and general reign of terror associated with the proscriptions of the Second Triumvirate; however, such actions have unfortunately been only too characteristic of societies fragmented by civil war.

On the last day of the year 43 BC Lepidus received his second triumph, which recognized his achievements as proconsul in Spain, specifically his success in negotiating a settlement with Sextus Pompey. Plancus had also triumphed three days earlier for his conduct as governor of Gallia Comata.[35] It was unusual to celebrate two triumphs within such a short period, but it was necessary to avoid any conflict with the two men's joint assumption of the consulship for 42 on January 1. Velleius Paterculus preserves the story that the soldiers in the triumphal processions of Lepidus and Plancus mocked their leaders by chanting that the two men had triumphed over their brothers, who had been proscribed in both cases, rather than over a defeated foe.[36]

According to Appian, the edict proclaiming Lepidus' triumph ordered all men and women to celebrate the day with sacrifices and feasting, under pain of proscription if they failed to participate.[37] Lepidus' procession to the Capitoline therefore must have attracted great crowds of people, but their cheers must have had a hollow sound because Lepidus knew that the populace had been forced to honor him, though his deeds had merited no military triumph.

The consulship of Lepidus and Plancus in 42 was a direct result of the events of the previous summer and fall. Although Caesar had designated Plancus for the office in advance, he could hardly have served without joining the Caesarian cause. Lepidus as triumvir needed the additional honor and power of being consul so that he could better control affairs in Rome and in Italy while Antony and Octavian carried on the war against Brutus and Cassius.

When the proscriptions had achieved the triumvirs' purposes of both ridding Italy of their enemies and helping raise money for their eastern campaign, Lepidus addressed the Senate as consul to justify the horrors of the preceding months and to hold out hope of a policy of leniency in the future, although Octavian reportedly reserved the right to reopen the proscriptions if necessary.[38] To carry out their agreement to provide property for their soldiers in certain Italian cities, the triumvirs appointed commissioners in 42 to divide up lands and establish colonies. In accordance with this plan, Plancus as consul apparently began to distribute land to soldiers at Beneventum.[39]

The four moneyers of 42 BC issued an interesting series of gold coins in commemoration of the Second Triumvirate. The portraits of each triumvir are boldly displayed, following the recent precedent of Julius Caesar, accompanied by the individual names and the title 'III VIR R.P.C.' (*triumvir reipublicae constituendae*). Three of the moneyers struck groups of three coins and one of them struck two separate groups of three. The triumvirs share common reverse-types showing Mars, two clasped hands representing *concordia*, and a cornucopia symbolizing abundance. Lepidus' two individual types are of particular interest. One of them shows a female deity standing, holding a sceptre in one hand and a cornucopia in the other, Theodore V. Buttrey, Jr. has identified this figure as Felicitas and associated it with Lepidus' temple to that goddess.[40] The other one depicts a veiled female holding a *simpulum* and a sceptre. She is generally called the vestal virgin Aemilia, but the sceptre eliminates the mortal vestal who had saved the sacred fire with her veil and indicates instead that she is the Aemilia whom Plutarch says was the daughter of Aeneas and mother of

Romulus by Mars.[41] The figure could also represent the goddess Vesta herself and symbolize her close connection with the pontifex maximus. Although the moneyers of 42 minted coin-types equally for all three triumvirs, coins issued after this date reflect the reduced role of Lepidus by focusing on propaganda for Antony or Octavian and ignoring Lepidus.[42]

The triumvirs also passed legislation in 42 granting divine honors to Julius Caesar and providing for the construction of a temple on the spot in the forum where his body had been cremated. In addition, they had everyone take an oath swearing that Caesar's acts were all to be considered binding. In Caesar's memory they also began to construct the Curia Iulia (a new meeting-hall for the Senate) and Lepidus apparently supervised the completion of the Saepta Iulia (the permanent voting place begun earlier in the Campus Martius in accordance with Caesar's plans).[43] In deifying and honoring Caesar in these ways, the triumvirs added a religious sanction to their war of vengeance and institutionalized Caesarian government to a greater degree by associating the Senate building with Caesar's name. At the same time, of course, they were continuing Caesar's plans for beautifying Rome and also providing jobs related to construction work.

Dio Cassius says that the triumvirs passed a law authorizing the building of a temple for the Egyptian gods Serapis and Isis.[44] No evidence for its actual erection survives, but the fact that the temple of Isis in the Campus Martius was known to be situated close to the Saepta Iulia lends some support to construction by the triumvirs because Roman temples were frequently built in clusters as new areas opened up and Lepidus was in the process of completing the Saepta Iulia at precisely this time. A new temple to Isis and Serapis might help atone for the bad omens associated with decisions to tear down their sanctuaries in 53, 50, and 48 BC and Lepidus probably felt a personal need to be involved in restoring good relations with Isis both as pontifex maximus and because his brother Paullus had led the attack on Isis' temple as consul in 50.[45]

The early months of 42 witnessed preparations for the departure of Mark Antony and Octavian and their legions to meet the forces of Brutus and Cassius in Macedonia. As the triumvirs had agreed at Bononia, Lepidus, with his three remaining legions, stayed behind to administer Rome and the rest of Italy when his colleagues departed for their campaign in the east. His legions were considered sufficient defense against any internal rebellion or an attack from Sextus Pompey, who was based in Sicily.[46]

Very little is known about events in Rome during most of the year 42 because our sources shift their attention from the proscriptions to the impending war in the east. An inscription found in the Syrian coastal town of Rhosos, near Antioch, refers to a *Lex Munatia et Aemilia*, certainly passed in 42 in the name of the two consuls, which conferred citizenship and immunity from taxation upon a certain Seleucus and his family in recognition of his services.[47] Similar grants were probably made at the same time to others who had assisted the Caesarian cause. Aside from this kind of legislation and direction of ongoing building activity, we know very little about developments in Rome in the latter part of the year. We can assume that Lepidus maintained stability in Rome and Italy and performed his duties effectively because the sources would probably have reported failure here. Although most of the citizens were in difficult economic straits, Lepidus presumably governed as he had in the past, smoothing over internal difficulties and maintaining a strong defense against the threat of an external attack.

Octavian and Antony probably left Rome as early as April of 42 BC. They marched south, Octavian making a side trip towards Sicily to send an expedition by sea against Sextus Pompey. The battle was indecisive and Octavian decided that he would put off the struggle with Sextus until later because it would take too much time and energy from the war with Brutus and Cassius. He rejoined Antony and their forces embarked from Brundisium to cross the Adriatic to Macedonia.

The triumviral army marched from the coast into the interior and camped opposite Brutus and Cassius near the town of Philippi, close to the Thracian border. The Republican leaders did not join battle immediately because they hoped that delay might compel the forces of Antony and Octavian, who were short of supplies, to withdraw rather than face starvation. When the battle finally began, Antony succeeded in defeating Cassius, who soon afterwards committed suicide, but Brutus inflicted heavy losses on Octavian and captured his camp. The triumvirs also lost many soldiers from a force coming to assist them which had suffered a setback in a naval battle in the Adriatic on the same day. The mixture of victory and defeat had brought no final result and Brutus stalled for a while, hoping again that famine would remove the opposition. Late in October his own soldiers forced Brutus to fight and in the second battle near Philippi

Antony and Octavian won a great victory that resulted in Brutus' retreat and eventual suicide. The defeated army obtained pardon and was divided between the two victorious leaders.[48]

At Philippi the Republican cause was virtually wiped out. Many of the losers would return to fight once more under Sextus Pompey, but, with the eastern provinces now rejoined to the western ones, the issue had been decided and Caesarian monarchy had replaced Republican government for the duration of Rome's existence as a world power. The only question remaining to be answered concerned which leader or leaders would control the Caesarian government.

The battle of Philippi also ironically marked the end of Lepidus' effective power within the triumvirate and over the state. He was still consul, of course, and would administer Rome until Octavian returned, but the victory in Macedonia gave Mark Antony and Octavian the power and the glory with which they could ignore Lepidus' wishes. If they had lost to Brutus and Cassius, Antony and Octavian would have still needed Lepidus. However, because they had divested him of seven of his ten legions and because of the further increased military strength they presented after Philippi, Antony and Octavian could effectively reduce the triumvirate to a duovirate. No matter what guarantees they had given Lepidus about division of spoils and captured enemy soldiers, nothing compelled them to respect these agreements. With the intermediary removed, however, a struggle for one-man rule would inevitably ensue.

As a sign of the altered balance of power after Philippi, Antony and Octavian decided upon a new division of the provinces. They converted Cisalpine Gaul from a province to an independent section of Italy and, in compensation for this loss, Antony added Lepidus' former province of Narbonese Gaul to his own Gallia Comata. Antony also picked up the province of Africa, although Octavian retained Numidia. In addition, Octavian gained Spain from Lepidus and held title to Sicily and Sardinia, still under the control of Sextus Pompey. Lepidus received nothing in the new distribution, although Africa and Numidia could be offered to him if it became necessary or useful.[49] Appian says that Lepidus had been accused of betraying the triumvirs' cause to Sextus Pompey and that if this charge were to prove groundless he would receive one or both of the African provinces.[50] Although it is possible that Lepidus negotiated with Sextus in the absence of his colleagues, perhaps anticipating a loss of power upon their return, it seems more likely that the accusation was contrived merely as an excuse to justify confiscation of Lepidus' provinces.

In order to make good on all the promises they had made to their soldiers, Octavian went to Italy to distribute land and set up colonies, while Antony toured the eastern provinces to raise money and stabilize areas that had only recently supported Brutus and Cassius. Antony probably also entertained thoughts of controlling the region for his own personal advantage later.[51]

When Octavian returned to Rome in 41, after recuperating from a severe illness, he found discontentment and growing opposition to the triumvirate. The senatorial class in Rome still resented the triumvirs' arbitrary use of power and especially disliked the impotent role allowed to the Senate and the purging of many of its leaders in the proscriptions. Octavian had written ahead to calm the fears preceding his return to Rome and most probably also to forestall any defection on the part of Lepidus, who was still administering the city at that time.[52]

The triumvirs' plan to confiscate Italian lands for redistribution to the soldiers had also aroused much opposition from the middle-class farmers who feared being dispossessed. The tremendous amount of land needed and the replacement of hard-working farmers with men brutalized by the long years of civil war had to have a very destructive effect on the Roman economy, especially when the food supply was already diminished by the pirating of Sextus Pompey. The power exercised by the soldiers over their generals would also haunt Rome many more times throughout its duration as an empire.

Stirring up further discontent in 41 were Antony's wife, Fulvia, and his brother, L. Antonius, who was consul. Most probably because he wanted to strengthen his brother's position by weakening Octavian's, Lucius proclaimed to the senatorial class his opposition to the excesses of the triumvirate and also stood up for the cause of the dispossessed farmers, while simultaneously making other promises to placate the soldiers.[53] It was probably due to the activities of Fulvia and Lucius, and not because Lepidus had proved himself innocent of his alleged dealings with Sextus Pompey, that Octavian, deciding that he needed Lepidus' support, promised his colleague the province of Africa as compensation for the loss of his other provinces. It was to Octavian's advantage to keep Lepidus on his side rather than to allow his discontented colleague to be enticed into either joining Lucius and the senatorial opposition or negotiating a separate deal with Sextus

Pompey. Africa was thus a small price to pay for retaining Lepidus' assistance.[54]

Despite an agreement between Octavian and Lucius reached at Teanum, the struggle known as the Perusine War broke out between the two men during the latter half of 41. Octavian left Rome to command his troops in this war. He entrusted the city to Lepidus once again and gave him two legions for its defense. However, when Lucius suddenly marched on Rome, Lepidus was unable to put up sufficient resistance. The triumvir apparently sent out a cavalry force and followed it with foot-soldiers, but Lucius still succeeded in entering the city. Lucius won primarily because he had superiority in numbers, but also because, according to Dio, he had sent ahead soldiers to Rome who entered as individuals and attacked the defenders from the inside when the siege began.[55] Appian says that Lucius infiltrated the city by night and that during the battle the next day he gained admission through the betrayal of a certain Nonius and his troops guarding one of the gates. Lepidus, who apparently escaped to Octavian's camp, was not helped by the anti-triumviral mood then prevalent in Rome and in Italy.[56] The Roman populace, especially members of the senatorial class, probably welcomed Lucius to the city as their champion.

Upon hearing that Octavian was marching towards Rome, Lucius withdrew his forces and marched north, camping near the city of Perusia (Perugia) in Umbria. Octavian probably established Lepidus in control of Rome again, perhaps leaving him with additional troops with which he could protect Rome this time. Octavian then departed to pursue Lucius and besieged his opponent's forces within Perusia, slowly weakening them through hunger during the winter months late in 41 and early in 40 BC. Lucius eventually surrendered and received a pardon, but Octavian burned the city as punishment for its defection.[57]

Soon after the end of the Perusine War, probably late in the spring or early in the summer of 40, Octavian sent Lepidus to govern Africa, giving him the six of Mark Antony's legions whose loyalty was most suspect.[58] This act almost certainly pleased Lepidus and bound him closer to Octavian, while also removing him from the scene as a potential opponent. It also disposed of much of Antony's military strength in Italy, thus strengthening Octavian's cause if a war should erupt with his other colleague. In addition, Lepidus would be well situated to come to Octavian's aid, not so much against Antony, although his forces could have been called in for a war in Egypt, but especially to catch Sextus Pompey in a pincers movement, as indeed later proved to be the case.

When Lepidus left Rome in 40 BC he could not have known that he would not return again with either honor or power. He must, however, have realized that his strength had been slipping ever since he had allowed his two colleagues to take seven of his ten legions with them to fight Brutus and Cassius. He may have hoped to recoup his losses through his governorship of Africa and an eventual show of strength against Sextus Pompey and, perhaps also, against one or both of his colleagues.

Octavian apparently gave Lepidus both African provinces to govern, even though Antony had been in charge of the eastern one, which surrounded Carthage and was called Africa, since the redistribution and Antony's legate, T. Sextius, controlled both militarily. When Lepidus arrived in the summer of 40 to assume command, Sextius submitted himself to Lepidus' authority without hostility either because he believed that Antony had approved of Lepidus' appointment or because he did not have enough soldiers to resist.[59] At some point between Lepidus' arrival and Antony's call for troops to aid in fighting the Parthians late in 39 Lepidus took over control of four of Sextius' legions, perhaps with the approval of Sextius, but to the apparent surprise of Antony.[60] Later on in 40 both Octavian and Antony confirmed Lepidus' governorship of the two Africas in their pact of Brundisium, which temporarily halted the growing hostility between them and again redistributed the provinces so that Antony would govern the eastern ones and Octavian the western. Both men agreed that either one could raise troops in Italy and that Octavian would fight Sextus Pompey, while Antony fought the Parthians.[61]

Very little is known about Lepidus' administration of Africa between 40 and 36 BC. A very interesting inscription has been found in the coastal town of Thabraca (Tabarka), which lies a little over 100 miles west of Carthage. It records a decree of the decurions of Thabraca that honored Lepidus as the patron of their city. The dedication reads: M. LEPIDO. IMP. TERT. PONT. MAX. IIIVIR R. P. C. BIS. COS. ITER. PATRONO. EX. D. D.[62] Two important pieces of information are revealed in this inscription. First of all, this is the only evidence attesting to a third time that Lepidus was hailed as *imperator*. He had received the honor first for settling the dispute in Spain between Cassius and Marcellus in 47 and second for negotiating peace with Sextus

Pompey in Spain in 44. If the inscription is correct, and there is no reason to assume that it is not, there must have been some incident during his administration of Africa for which Lepidus received the title of *imperator* for the third time. Because the dedication also refers to Lepidus' second tenure as triumvir, which became official in 37, the date of the inscription can be placed between 37 and the middle of 36, when Lepidus left Africa for good. The third title of *imperator* was probably received for some scuffle with the forces of Sextus Pompey or for putting down some internal rebellion in Africa. Lepidus may have wanted the honor again to keep his record active and worthy of comparison with those of his two colleagues. He could have accepted the title from his own troops without receiving or requesting official confirmation in Rome.

The second fact newly revealed in the inscription is that the decurions of Thabraca selected Lepidus as the patron of their city. This honor probably resulted from some preferential treatment given Thabraca by Lepidus, in some area such as provincial taxes, port dues, building activity, or rights of citizens. The inscription appears to be a positive statement from the city of Thabraca indicating its favorable attitude toward Lepidus' provincial administration and, barring further evidence to the contrary, should be considered to Lepidus' credit. The fact that the inscription still stands today indicates that it was more than mere window-dressing because it was not destroyed (as Juvenal, for example, tells us Sejanus' statue was, as soon as that leader had fallen from power).[63]

Dio Cassius indicates that Lepidus had destroyed a part of the city of Carthage and thus abrogated rights that colonists had presumably received in the time of Julius Caesar.[64] Tertullian also alludes to some violence on the part of Lepidus.[65] Scholars have suggested that Lepidus as pontifex maximus saw to the destruction of that part of Carthage which had encroached on the area of the Punic city, which the Romans in 146 BC had destroyed and decreed unsuitable for any future habitation or construction.[66] Those who had settled on this unholy ground would quite naturally have been upset to see their homes levelled and to have to move elsewhere, especially when they most probably had no knowledge of these potential problems when they had first settled there. It was, of course, Lepidus' job as chief priest to preserve Rome's proper relationship with the gods by enforcing this religious ban on reconstruction on the site of Rome's greatest enemy, although Caesar, also a pontifex maximus, had apparently ignored it when he began the new colony there. The argument that Lepidus was enforcing a religious prohibition seems logical and it is hard to explain otherwise why Lepidus would focus on a particular part of the city for destruction. It could have been a pretext for moving a certain part of the population, but, in any case, the action is not likely to have made Lepidus popular in Carthage.

Carthage is also a likely site for Lepidus' mint and he seems to have coined money while in Africa, presumably to pay his soldiers.[67] T.R.S. Broughton speculated, on the basis of an inscription recording the career of the freedman Phileros, that Carthage may have honored Lepidus with the position of *duovir quinquennalis* in connection with the letting of the vectigalia and that Lepidus delegated his functions to Phileros. The inscription also records the construction of a temple of Tellus in Carthage in this same period.[68] In addition, epigraphic evidence indicates that the cult of the Cereres, two grain goddesses, was established there in 38 BC and Lepidus was most probably responsible for this, but there is no evidence to show whether or not the cult was introduced as a response to a famine or some other agricultural crisis. Duncan Fishwick and Brent D. Shaw have concluded that Lepidus was the one responsible for combining the two sections of Africa into one province with its administrative capital at Carthage. Their argument, which is quite convincing, relates Sextus Pompey's threat to Rome's grain supply to the need for a single African command, sees the revival of the cult of the Cereres as confirmation that Carthage was the administrative center of a large unified province, and ties in the rent-collection efforts of Phileros as well.[69]

Lepidus probably spent part of his time in Africa settling colonists who had been dispossessed from their property in Italy in order to meet the demands of the soldiers for land. François Bertrandy has discovered from his study of the inscriptional evidence at Thibilis in eastern Numidia and comparison with that from various other sites in Numidia and Africa Nova that there was a significant number of individuals taking the name 'Aemilius' or even 'Marcus Aemilius'. He concludes that Lepidus continued the work started by Caesar and granted Roman citizenship and extended municipal rights in the hope of creating an African clientele to support him in future dealings with his triumviral colleagues. The inscription from Thabraca could indicate that he bestowed municipal rights there as well.[70] A considerable amount of Lepidus' time and effort in Africa therefore could have involved settling natives, displaced Italians, and veterans in colonies dispersed around his provinces who would spread romanization and also serve as a personal base of future political and military support.

Lepidus must also have devoted time to building up his forces for the virtually inevitable clash with Sextus Pompey. He apparently constructed a large fleet, and perhaps at least part of this was stationed at Thabraca, for he used many ships to transport his troops to Sicily in 36 BC. Little else can be said about Lepidus' administration of Africa. None the less, the evidence reviewed indicates that Lepidus played a more active and important role in the colonization and romanization of north Africa than scholars in the past had given him credit for accomplishing.

Lepidus seems to have maintained little contact with his two colleagues during his stay in Africa. In 39 the Senate ratified all of the acts of the triumvirs and Octavian introduced additional unpopular taxes in Rome which, when combined with the famine caused by the piracy of Sextus Pompey, aroused further public outrage at the triumviral government.[71] When Sextus Pompey met with Antony and Octavian to negotiate a settlement of their differences, he came, according to Appian, with the expectation that he would replace Lepidus as the third triumvir.[72] Although he did not achieve this status, Sextus won significant concessions from the triumvirs and a peace agreement temporarily relieved some of the discontent in Rome.[73]

In 38 BC hostilities with Sextus Pompey resumed and Octavian lost numerous ships and men through battles and storms. Octavian sent for help from both Antony and Lepidus, but the planned meeting at Brundisium did not take place and it appeared as if his two colleagues were willing to let their colleague fight the war alone, perhaps even hoping for his defeat or at least for a reduction in his bargaining power with them.[74]

During 37 preparations were made to rebuild the fleet in anticipation of more battles with Sextus. Early in the year Antony and Octavian met at Tarentum, the latter agreeing to exchange soldiers for the ships of the former. They also decided to extend the extraordinary powers granted to the triumvirs for another five years. Their duties had technically expired at the end of 38, but no one dared bring up this fact and ratification of the extension was not sought from the Assembly.

Prior to the meeting at Tarentum, Octavian had been very cold towards Antony. He had charged, among other things, that Antony had sent his freedman Callias to persuade Lepidus to make a secret alliance with Antony. Octavia, who served as mediator between her brother and her husband, had replied that Callias had been sent to complete arrangements for the marriage, which had been arranged several years before, between Lepidus' son and Antony's daughter. Antony had even offered to send Callias to be questioned by Octavian on the matter, but Octavian had declined and instead agreed to the negotiations at Tarentum.[75]

Octavian was correct to question the mission of Callias because of the hesitance of both Lepidus and Antony to come to his aid against Sextus Pompey. The excuse that Callias was merely making arrangements for the marriage is questionable because of the length of time that had passed since the engagement and because there is no evidence that the marriage ever took place. If either child was still quite young, however, this could account for a long engagement period. It is more likely that Callias was negotiating an alliance to take advantage of the weakening position of Octavian. Antony may have been contemplating a showdown with Octavian and desired to know where Lepidus would stand. Lepidus must have blamed Octavian primarily for his diminished condition because Octavian had been the main beneficiary, but more recently Octavian had installed him in a position of command again in Africa. Although the triumvirate was renewed in 37, Octavian must still have felt uneasy about a future alliance of his two colleagues against him and this was probably the main reason for his deposition of Lepidus in 36. Antony and Lepidus perhaps intended to act jointly if Octavian were to suffer another defeat at the hands of Sextus Pompey, but before Antony was able to return again from his war with the Parthians, the threat of Sextus was removed and Lepidus had been stripped of his powers.

In 36 BC, before launching his campaign against Sextus, Octavian procured from Lepidus, probably with some difficulty, a promise to assist him. They planned a coordinated attack on the three coasts of Sicily for July 1. Octavian was to sail from Puteoli, near Naples, and land on the north coast. T. Statilius Taurus would depart from Tarentum in the heel of Italy and attack the east coast. Lepidus would sail from north Africa, perhaps from Thabraca, and land on the south-western coast. With attack coming from three directions, it would be harder for Sextus' fleet to maneuver and it would also force him to spread his defenses out to cover all three coasts simultaneously. Sextus Pompey positioned L. Plinius Rufus at Lilybaeum, on the western tip of the island, to oppose Lepidus with one legion and a group of light-armed troops. Sextus also protected the islands of Cossyra and Lipara, the former against Lepidus and the latter against Octavian, to prevent their use as naval bases to facilitate attacks on Sicily. The main body of Sextus' navy was stationed at Messana, located just across from the toe of Italy.[76]

Lepidus, Taurus, and Octavian all set sail at daybreak on July 1. Lepidus' fleet included 1,600 carrier vessels, 70 warships, twelve legions, 500 Numidian cavalry, and a large amount of military equipment, according to Appian.[77] Velleius adds that the twelve legions were only half their usual strength of 6,000 men each.[78] On July 3 a storm blew up from the south and capsized many of Lepidus' carrier ships. Lepidus lost several boats on the journey to Sicily as a result of this storm and because of an attack from Demochares, one of Sextus' lieutenants. Nevertheless, Lepidus landed his troops in Sicily, besieged Plinius in Lilybaeum, and gained control of several towns in the area, some through the use of force. Lepidus must have remembered the story of his ancestor who as praetor in 218 had defended Lilybaeum in the Second Punic War, with a feeling of *déjà vu*.[79]

Meanwhile, both Taurus and Octavian also encountered turbulent weather. Taurus returned quickly to Tarentum, but Octavian lost many men and ships before he was able to bring the rest of his fleet back for extensive repairs. Sextus sent Menodorus with a small force to harass Octavian's ships while they were being overhauled. Menodorus was angry at Sextus because he had not received the command against Lepidus and, after causing additional damage, he joined Octavian's side.[80] When Octavian was ready to sail again, he sent Messala with two legions to assist Lepidus' forces and cross over to Tauromenium, on Sicily's east coast.

In the meantime, four additional legions had sailed from Africa on merchant ships to join the rest of Lepidus' army. On their way, they were met by ships under the command of Papias, one of Sextus' lieutenants. Lepidus' men thought that these boats constituted a friendly convoy that Lepidus had sent out to escort them, so Papias was able to take them by surprise and destroy several vessels. When Lepidus' convoy did arrive to greet their comrades, those remaining on the merchant ships sailed off in fear of another attack. Two legions were lost at sea, including many soldiers that Tisienus Gallus' forces killed as they struggled to land. The remaining two legions eventually joined Lepidus much later, arriving separately after having returned to Africa to regroup.[81]

Sextus Pompey sent Tisienus Gallus to assist Plinius in defending Lilybaeum against Lepidus' attacks. While this struggle was going on, Agrippa scored a hard-fought victory over Sextus' naval forces off Mylae on the northern coast of the island. As soon as this battle ended Sextus sailed quickly around to the east-coast city of Tauromenium to take Octavian by surprise. He was successful in defeating Octavian both by land and by sea near Tauromenium and in inflicting heavy losses, but Sextus' troops did not follow up their victory.[82] At this time, Sextus decided to recall Tisienus Gallus, whose battles with Lepidus had been indecisive. Lepidus may also have received word from Octavian asking him to bring his forces east.

Both Lepidus and Gallus withdrew their troops from Lilybaeum and made their separate ways to the camps of Octavian and Sextus at Artemisium, near Mylae on the northern coast. Octavian tried in vain to intercept Gallus before he could join Sextus and, after witnessing an eruption of Mount Etna, Octavian ravaged the territory of Palaestena. Here he met up with the forces of Lepidus, who were out foraging, and the two triumvirs then set up camp near Messana.[83] According to Dio, the two men had difficulty working together because Lepidus demanded equal authority in everything and Octavian treated his colleague as he would any lieutenant. This treatment must have been very galling to Lepidus, who was about twice Octavian's age, held the high honor of being pontifex maximus, and had suffered demotion in the past at Octavian's hands. Sheer frustration helps explain why Lepidus later seized the only chance he saw to regain a real share of power. Dio says that Lepidus communicated in secret with Sextus, but this may have been just a fear in Octavian's mind. In any case, Octavian decided to move swiftly against Sextus, perhaps to prevent any defection on the part of Lepidus.[84]

In the naval battle that followed off Naulochus, to the east of Mylae, Agrippa engineered a decisive victory, losing only three ships to Sextus' twenty-eight. Sextus escaped from the scene with seventeen ships, sending word to Plinius in Lilybaeum to bring his legions to Messana. After his infantry and cavalry near Naulochus surrendered to Octavian, Sextus decided to flee to the east in the hope of concluding an agreement with Mark Antony.[85] Soon after Sextus' departure, Plinius arrived in Messana and Agrippa and Lepidus besieged him in that city. Plinius quickly sued for peace terms and Lepidus granted them, despite Agrippa's objection to making peace before Octavian's expected arrival the next morning. Lepidus gained the favor of Plinius' soldiers by letting them join in the plunder of Messana along with his own troops. This act probably gained Lepidus the support of Plinius' legions, but it alienated the loyalty of his regular soldiers who would naturally have resented sharing the booty with the just-defeated enemy.[86]

Dio Cassius says that Octavian interfered with Lepidus' burning and sacking of various parts of Messana and that Lepidus withdrew his forces from the city and occupied a strategic hill nearby.[87] Whether this actually happened or not, Lepidus did make his move to reassert his power in the state. He added the eight legions of Plinius to his fourteen, giving him the large number of twenty-two legions, although it must be remembered that most of these were probably at less than half-strength. Those sources that credit Lepidus with only twenty legions apparently failed to count the two surviving from the four legions that had come from Africa to reinforce him and were attacked on their way. Lepidus also had a large cavalry force under his command.[88]

Lepidus claimed that he should receive control of Sicily because he had been the first to land on the island and because he had personally gained the allegiance of many of the cities. He also sent word to his garrisons in these areas not to admit the representatives of Octavian. Octavian, of course, was not about to yield Sicily because of its strategic location and connection to the important Roman grain supply, nor would he consider making Lepidus an equal partner and potential rival again. Octavian therefore sent envoys to Lepidus to reproach him for his actions and explain that Lepidus had been requested to help Octavian as an ally and that he had no right to claim Sicily for himself. Lepidus complained of the treatment he had received from Octavian since Philippi and demanded full restitution of his power as a triumvir. He then offered to trade Africa and Sicily for his former provinces of Spain and Narbonese Gaul. The two men naturally failed to reach any agreement when they met together.[89]

Although most of the sources consider Lepidus' actions as outrageous because he dared to challenge the authority of Octavian, who was either the beloved emperor Augustus or a divine memory by the time these accounts were written, Lepidus' position does have some merit. First, Octavian had formed an agreement with him voluntarily at Bononia and then proceeded to betray him without apparent cause once Lepidus in good faith had yielded the bulk of his legions for the war effort against Brutus and Cassius. Second, the arrangements at

Bononia had been legally ratified by the *Lex Titia*. Third, Lepidus had performed loyally in the past and had been an important factor in the conquest of Sicily from Sextus Pompey. Unfortunately for Lepidus, however – and he and Octavian both must bear some blame for this fact – decisions in the Roman world were no longer made with any reference to fairness or the inviolability of one's word, but according to the will of the stronger.

Both Octavian and Lepidus surrounded themselves with guards and prepared for the inevitable contest of strength. Octavian anchored his ships offshore to protect them from burning.[90] Several different accounts of the way in which Octavian won over Lepidus' army are given. Velleius' romantic version has Octavian walk into Lepidus' camp unarmed and, although attacked on Lepidus's orders, carry off a legionary standard, thus inciting a mass desertion of Lepidus' army.[91] This story makes Octavian sound like Horatius Cocles or some other *exemplum* of Roman courage, but it is hard to believe that any commander could have been so foolhardy and impossible that someone as cautious and calculating as Octavian would have risked almost certain death.[92]

Lepidus' soldiers certainly did not want to fight again so soon, particularly against their comrades. It is important to note that of Lepidus' twenty-two legions six had been Antony's that Octavian gave to him because their loyalty was most suspect, four had been Antony's taken over from Sextius in Africa, and eight had been Sextus' troops that Plinius had surrendered. The majority of Lepidus' troops, therefore, had owed their loyalty to others and none of his soldiers had experienced much actual fighting under his command or, what was more important to them, received the booty and rewards that followed victory. The inclusion of the recent enemy troops in Lepidus' army was divisive and their participation in the pillage of Messana made the regulars jealous and discontented. Since Octavian was at that time a more powerful leader who possessed the magical name of Caesar, many were convinced that their fortune lay with him.

Appian reports that Octavian sent men to mix with Lepidus' troops to convince them that their personal interests would be served if they joined Octavian. Appian says that then Octavian came to Lepidus' camp with a large body of cavalry and, entering with a few supporters, succeeded in persuading some of Sextus' former soldiers to grab their standards and join him. They apparently feared that he would not ratify the peace terms that Lepidus had granted to them. When Lepidus became aware of what Octavian was doing he drove him out of the camp after a brief scuffle. Appian says that Lepidus' army slowly went over to the other side in small groups during the night and the next day. Lepidus armed some of his men to guard others and prevent them from defecting, but even the guards seized their standards and left. When Lepidus sent troops out from his camp, they too joined Octavian. The cavalry, according to Appian, was the last group to desert Lepidus, but even its leaders sent messengers to Octavian to get orders whether or not to kill their former general. Octavian told them not to kill Lepidus.[93]

Dio Cassius agrees with Appian for the most part in his account of how Lepidus lost his army. He adds the information that Lepidus sent messengers to Octavian to list his grievances and seek negotiation, but Octavian refused them admission. Dio then reports the first attempt of Octavian with a few followers to win over Lepidus' soldiers and his expulsion from the camp with the loss of some lives. Dio says that Octavian returned with his entire army and besieged the camp of Lepidus. This pressure explains the mass defections of the soldiers, which, according to Dio, were carried out in small groups out of respect for Lepidus to avoid a common desertion.[94] Orosius agrees that, after an initial attempt with a small force was repelled, Octavian drew up his whole army to cause Lepidus' soldiers to change their allegiance.[95] The date of the surrender of Lepidus' army to Octavian was September 3.[96]

The similarity between the descriptions of Octavian's takeover of Lepidus' troops in 36 BC and those of Antony's joining forces with Lepidus after Mutina in 43 casts some doubt on the accuracy of both stories. They appear to be far more believable for 36, if one can put aside the tendency of the imperial historians to glorify Octavian's actions and ignore, diminish, or even make a mockery of the deeds of those individuals with whom he had once shared equal power. Although these same sources quite naturally do not say anything about the use of bribery in wooing away Lepidus' soldiers, this is not unlikely because Cicero attests to Octavian's spending liberally in November of 44 to seduce soldiers from their loyalty to Antony.[97]

Although Lepidus' story that his troops had compelled him to join forces with Antony in 43 after Mutina may have been chiefly a fabrication intended to defend Lepidus against charges of treason, this propaganda tale may have had a real influence on many of his soldiers in 36 when the opportunity to join Octavian developed. The humiliation of losing his legions to Octavian has given rise to making sport of Lepidus' military competence, but it is important to note that desertions of commanders by soldiers were not exactly uncommon in civil wars, where the lure of bonuses and the desire to be on the winning side when the spoils were divided proved to be powerful motivating factors to switching sides, especially when both spoke the same language and shared the same traditions. Roman soldiers were a volatile lot, especially in the uncertainty of civil wars. Even Julius Caesar had difficulty with them at times and Octavian faced mutiny among his victorious legions almost immediately after capturing Lepidus.[98]

With Octavian successfully in control of the field, Lepidus apparently appeared before Octavian in civilian clothing and either threw himself at his feet or was prevented from doing so by his conqueror. Octavian sent Lepidus back to Rome as a private citizen and stripped him of his remaining triumviral authority. Lepidus may technically have resigned in exchange for an easier punishment. Lepidus was granted his life and his property and he did not lose his post of pontifex maximus, but he had to return to private life in perpetual exile, probably under guard, in Circeii, a coastal resort town, about midway between Rome and Naples, where his family held property.[99]

The reason for deposing Lepidus seems to have been Octavian's fear that Lepidus and Antony would unite against him. He did not want to reward Lepidus for his help against Sextus Pompey because this would weaken his own power. Octavian would probably have taken action against his colleague regardless of what Lepidus did because twenty-two legions was a considerable force and allowing Lepidus to retain them would only make them more dangerous as time passed and they became more loyal to their commander. With Sextus Pompey gone from the west, Lepidus had completed his utility and he had to be removed now lest he prove a hindrance to Octavian's future plans.

Octavian told Antony that he had deposed their colleague because he had abused his office, a charge that would have been very difficult to back up. All Lepidus had done, after all, was to help Octavian win the war with Sextus and then to demand as compensation restoration of the powers and authority of which he had been arbitrarily stripped. Antony was too busy to care about Lepidus' fate, but he later objected to Octavian's treatment of their colleague, particularly, of course, to the transferral of Lepidus' army, territory, and revenues to Octavian.[100] By removing Lepidus from power Octavian had eliminated the threat of his two colleagues combining against him, but he had also narrowed the competition for power down to a two-man race. With only two leaders struggling for control, and no third force seeming to side with one or the other or keeping some power for himself, Octavian and Antony would soon find themselves reaching for one-man rule.

8

EXILE AND DEATH: ON THE OUTSIDE LOOKING IN

During the thirteen years from his praetorship in 49 to his deposition in 36 BC, Lepidus had been one of the most important figures in Roman political life. If he had been an Aemilius Lepidus born in an earlier generation he might have spent many more years serving in the Senate and performing his functions as pontifex maximus. However, Lepidus both enjoyed unusual power and authority and suffered humiliating punishment as a result of the fact that his career was caught in Rome's transition from Republic to Empire. His days of power and prestige were now over and after 36 he was doomed to spend the final twenty-three years of his life in political impotence and virtual obscurity. Lepidus' brief taste of power became a subject for historians and moralists, and the inevitable clash between his two former colleagues was now the main focus of discussion.

Octavian was particularly shrewd in all the decisions that he made concerning Lepidus' fate. He could, of course, have executed his former colleague on a trumped-up charge of treason, but this would have been an unnecessary act of cruelty and allowing him to live earned Octavian great credit for clemency. The amazing thing is that Octavian permitted Lepidus to continue as pontifex maximus, especially when he considered this office rightfully his by inheritance from Caesar. If Octavian had killed Lepidus and then assumed this office a stigma would have attached itself permanently to this honored position and there was also the danger of incurring the wrath of the gods. Octavian could also have stripped Lepidus of the office, as his supporters apparently urged him to do, but he wisely saw that he could gain little additional power thereby, while he would be disregarding the long-standing Roman tradition that a pontifex maximus, or any pontifex, was elected for life.[1]

Octavian had learned well from his adoptive father's experience that rejection of traditional Roman customs caused great opposition among the people. Although some would have cheered him if he had usurped Lepidus' priestly office, he would have caused further damage to that respect for the Roman constitution that had given Rome political continuity and success for so many centuries. It was the challenge to such authority raised by the Gracchi, Marius, Sulla, Pompey, Caesar, Crassus, Antony, Lepidus, and Octavian himself that had plagued Rome with civil wars for the previous century. Octavian knew that, once he had removed Antony from the scene, he would need to re-establish respect for Rome's traditions to constitute a stable government over such a large area. It is unusual to find such insight and understanding in a political figure still so young, but his delicate treatment of Roman customs would help him and his 'reorganized Republic' succeed and Octavian apparently foresaw this.

When Octavian returned to Rome from Sicily he selected Lepidus' place of exile. Circeii offered seclusion from Rome and other large cities, but it was also close enough so that Octavian could keep close watch over Lepidus and bring him to Rome if he wanted to do so. If the place of exile were at a great distance, Octavian would be taking a risk that Lepidus might join Antony or some other enemy long before he would hear word of it. Octavian was obviously not going to allow Lepidus to continue his residence in the home of the pontifex maximus in Rome so he probably examined a list of Lepidus' property, which we know was not forfeited, and selected Circeii. Lepidus apparently already owned an estate there and his model ancestor of the second century had owned property in nearby Tarracina.[2] Octavian probably stationed a guard at Circeii to keep a close watch on Lepidus' activities and keep Rome informed.[3]

Although Lepidus was probably physically comfortable at Circeii, spending time as many other Roman nobles did, relaxing on a family estate in a lovely setting far removed from the urban disruptions at Rome, his spirit had been broken and the knowledge that he was not free to leave and travel at will back and forth to the center of power must have been intensely frustrating. As an Aemilius Lepidus, as an ex-consul and *imperator*, and as pontifex maximus, Lepidus had earned a place of respect in the Senate and in Roman society, yet he was not free to exercise it. It must have been particularly galling to receive word of Antony's Parthian failure and distractions with Cleopatra, while the star of Octavian, the man responsible for Lepidus' ill fortune, rose to ever greater heights. The defeat of

Antony at Actium in 31 BC established one-man rule once again at Rome, but this time Lepidus would not benefit from the situation.

In fact, the battle of Actium soon led, late in 31 or early in 30, to personal heartbreak and further humiliation for Lepidus from the conduct of his eldest son, M. Aemilius Lepidus [74]. This son was presumably the same one who had served as a hostage to bring Brutus and Cassius down from the Capitoline hill after Caesar's murder and who also had been engaged to a daughter of Mark Antony to conclude a marriage alliance that would bind Antony and Lepidus closer together. Young Marcus had the good looks that had characterized other members of his family and the impetuosity of his grandfather, the consul of 78. The young man, probably to gain revenge on Octavian for injuring his family name, formed a plot to assassinate the victorious triumvir upon his return to Rome from Egypt. Maecenas, who was administering Rome at the time, caught word of the plan, and swiftly, yet quietly, crushed the threat. He arrested young Lepidus, prosecuted him for high treason, and presumably executed him, although Appian says Maecenas sent him to Octavian at Actium, which, if true, only served to delay his eventual death.[4]

There must have been others involved in the plot, unless Lepidus tried to recruit conspirators who refused and turned him in to Maecenas. Otherwise it would have been close to impossible for Maecenas to have had advance knowledge of the plans of a lone assassin. It is a strange situation in any case because Octavian was still at Actium, but it is possible that young Lepidus hoped to assassinate Octavian and restore his exiled father to a position of authority. Perhaps Maecenas caught the young man stirring up rebellion in the city and sent him off to Octavian for punishment to prevent him from becoming a martyr to the discontented in Rome.

Velleius reports that young Lepidus' wife, Servilia, who was probably the daughter of the Caesarian consul of 48 and 41 BC, P. Servilius Isauricus, committed suicide by swallowing live coals.[5] She was most probably the same Servilia formerly engaged to Octavian, which may have provided the young man with another personal motive for the assassination. The couple could not have been married very long because as late as 37 young Lepidus was still engaged to Antony's daughter. The groom's mother, Iunia, may have helped arrange the marriage because her mother had been a Servilia. The Aemilii and Servilii had also been associated together several times in the past.[6]

Maecenas also implicated Lepidus' wife, Iunia, in the assassination plot for knowing of her son's intentions and not informing on him. This fact lends support to the view that mother and son hoped to gain revenge on Octavian and bring Lepidus back from exile. Iunia's reputation has suffered to some degree because of one of Cicero's gossipy letters to Atticus in 50 BC which told of the scoundrel P. Vedius whose baggage contained the images of five married women, including Iunia.[7] It is true that in his thirteenth *Philippic* Cicero referred to her as a 'most excellent wife' (*probatissima uxor*), but this statement has not carried as much weight because at that point the orator was still trying to court the support of Lepidus.[8]

Appian says that in order to spare Iunia the necessity of traveling to Actium for judgment, she had to pay bail to ensure that she would appear before Octavian when he returned to Rome. The fact that Iunia was indicted as an accomplice while her husband was declared innocent by the accusers indicates that she and young Marcus were probably residing in Rome, at least temporarily, while Lepidus remained in exile at Circeii. Iunia and Marcus may have traveled back and forth on a regular basis to visit friends and relatives and also to accumulate information about activities in Rome for Lepidus. Syme speculates that the young man may have been kept as a hostage in Rome during this critical period.[9] Appian plays on the reversal of fortunes exemplified by the situation where Lepidus, who as triumvir had been partially responsible for the proscriptions, pleaded before the court of Balbinus, who had been one of the proscribed. Lepidus apparently sought an audience several times, only to be removed, but when he finally received a hearing he explained that he had not proscribed Balbinus and asked that he be allowed to serve as bond for his wife's appearance or to join her on her journey. Balbinus then released Iunia from the requirement for bail.[10]

It is strange to find Lepidus this early in his exile being allowed to go to Rome to appear before Balbinus, although he must have received permission to do so. It is also very odd that Lepidus was unable to post bail if he indeed had held on to all of his property when he was exiled. Appian does make it clear that Lepidus was not involved in his son's plot against Octavian and this seems correct because he would probably have been executed if he were guilty of complicity. It is true, however, that to execute Lepidus would be to raise once again the possibility of charges that Octavian had killed to secure the chief priesthood.

Dio Cassius says that Octavian made Lepidus' life difficult by calling him to Rome and making fun of him in front of the Senate. He apparently even allowed Lepidus to vote at these meetings of the Senate, but purposely called on him last in the order of ex-consuls. This was certainly demeaning and abusive, but at the same time the *princeps* did at least acknowledge his former colleague's consular status. It is not clear how frequently Octavian brought Lepidus to Rome or over what period of time he did this, but Dio includes the information with his account of the adjustment of the Senate membership in 18 BC and it seems to suit this period.[11] By then Octavian had consolidated his position as the emperor Augustus and exercised all the power and authority held by Julius Caesar and more, but with such subtle action that the people loved him for it. It is probably festering anger over Lepidus' longevity and continued possession of the post of pontifex maximus that caused Augustus' mean-spirited and abusive treatment of the former triumvir. Dio says that when the future jurist Antistius Labeo proposed Lepidus' name for inclusion in the revised Senate Augustus threatened him with punishment. When, however Antistius responded that he had only named a man whom Augustus permitted to be pontifex maximus, the emperor calmed down.[12]

Although there is no evidence that Lepidus performed his religious functions as pontifex maximus during the period of his exile, the sources would probably not have recorded such activity. If Augustus actually summoned Lepidus to Rome, apparently against his will, on a regular basis and allowed him to vote in the Senate, even while he mocked him, it is also possible that Lepidus was permitted to attend such events as temple dedications, patrician weddings, public games, and inaugurations into consular office, where the chief priest would normally be involved, or even to participate in the cooptation of new pontiffs.[13] Lepidus' long term of exile may have been brightened to some small extent when he received word of his nephew's suffect consulship in 34 and censorship in 22 and of Q. Aemilius Lepidus' consulship in 21 and service as *quindecimvir sacris faciundis* during the spectacular Secular Games in 17, but these men succeeded through their ties to Augustus.[14] Lepidus' brother Lucius apparently never left Miletus, where he had gone after the battles of Philippi.[15] There is no evidence on how long Junia and her second son, Quintus, lived.[16]

Lepidus' long period of suffering public humiliation finally came to an end with his death late in 13 or early in 12 BC. Octavian could never have foreseen in 36 that he would have to wait almost twenty-three years to receive the treasured position of pontifex maximus, but his amazing patience was rewarded when he received the honor on March 6, 12 BC before the largest crowd assembled in Rome up to that time.[17] Few people probably mourned Lepidus' passing. He was a forgotten relic of the past, forced to live out his days watching the constantly growing glory attached to the man who had so rudely dropped him from his pinnacle of power.

Lepidus the triumvir is the most famous member of his noble family, although not the most distinguished. His two consulships and the honor of being pontifex maximus were, it is true, rewards for his service to Caesar and for carrying on the Caesarian cause after the dictator's death. Although his position as triumvir gave him for a short time tremendous power and enduring name-recognition, it was not an honorable office. Lepidus helped establish stability in the chaotic situation following Caesar's assassination and over the next few years. His name provided some legitimacy for the actions of Caesar and Octavian and, even though he was deposed and slandered after being used by the latter, he contributed indirectly to the transition from Republic to Empire. Sir Ronald Syme has concluded:

> In political operations the Triumvir reflects a past age, exploiting birth and family connections. Hence tardy and obsolete, so some in stern condemnation opine. Yet those claims proved not obsolete in the new order taking shape. Lepidus showed the future path for the high aristocracy: to eschew violence, to acquiesce before superior power, to respond to alliance with the dynasty.[18]

Several sources accuse Lepidus of laziness and they may be correct in this assertion.[19] In fact, Cicero's anecdote about a M. Lepidus lying in the grass while all the others exercised probably refers to the future triumvir rather than to his ancestor, Porcina, the consul of 137 BC: Lepidus commented 'I wish that hard work were what I am doing.'[20] However, Lepidus' coin portraits do not reflect the face of a particularly heavy man.[21] Even if a lazy disposition is conceded, Lepidus was not slow to act on the Ides of March and he performed very effectively in his numerous positions as provincial governor and administrator of Rome.

The claim that Lepidus was a terrible general who could not control his troops depends entirely on the confused story of his alliance with Antony after Mutina and on Octavian's seduction of his soldiers in Sicily. In both cases he was dealing with Caesar's veterans who wanted to join fellow veterans and a Caesarian commander. Lepidus had few tests of his military ability, but in his limited combat experiences he was generally successful. He never had the opportunity to work with a body of soldiers long enough to satisfy their desires for booty and gain their personal loyalty.

Some sources accuse Lepidus of being indecisive, but this resulted from his effort to keep his options open while awaiting the conclusion of other events, something that characterized so many men of the time. If one sets absolute standards of proper conduct, of course, failure to do the 'right thing' immediately will be interpreted as fickleness or lack of resolve.

Lepidus was a capable administrator and would likely have made an effective consul if he had lived much earlier in the Republic. Julius Caesar had trusted him with several important tasks and he performed well. However, with Caesar's death the power vacuum thrust him into a struggle in which the stakes were too high and the competition too vigorous for him to have a chance of emerging as the victor. His only hope lay in working with his adversaries, but, although he might side with one or the other, his opponents were bent on attaining sole domination, and he inevitably had to fall.

Lepidus perhaps lacked some of the moral qualities that many of his ancestors had displayed, but he was living in times characterized by immorality and he was more capable than many at getting the job done. Lepidus' role in the proscriptions and his other failings can not be excused, but neither should they totally dominate the interpretation of the man's place in Roman history. The writers who composed their works in the centuries immediately following his death have without cause blackened his memory in history. In their efforts to heap glory upon the emperor Augustus they have distorted the portraits of those around him. The invective of Cicero has been taken as fact and permanently damaged Lepidus' reputation much as it also did to that of Mark Antony. In any case, the picture that one might get of Lepidus as an indecisive and blundering fool is one that is not supported by a careful examination of all available sources.

9

NACHLEBEN: LEPIDUS IN HISTORY AND FICTION

Cicero's stinging words of invective, occasioned by Lepidus' resuscitation of Mark Antony's flagging cause in 43 BC, have determined more than any other source the prevailing course of Lepidus' *Nachleben*. It is not, however a result only of the great influence that the orator's views would have on future generations, but also of the fact that to attack the pretensions of the emperor Augustus' former triumviral colleagues also suited the purposes of Rome's imperial historians. The positive points about Lepidus' career would chiefly survive fragmented into isolated references, as pieces of flotsam in a sea of scorn, derision, and ridicule.

Cicero predicted correctly his impact on Antony's public reputation: 'I will brand him with the truest marks of infamy, and will hand him down to the everlasting memory of man.'[1] This statement rings just as true for the lasting impact of the orator's condemnation of Lepidus. Although Cicero had included plenty of praise of Lepidus in the *Philippics* in an effort to isolate Antony from the support of the Caesarian provincial governors, these statements have been overwhelmed by Cicero's view that Lepidus was a traitor who had placed personal gain above his obligations to the Republic.[2]

To Cicero's charge of betrayal of the Republic, Decimus Brutus, in a letter to the orator, added the label of indecision to Lepidus, calling him a weathercock (*homo ventosissimus*).[3] Velleius Paterculus went a step further by attacking the man's competence, claiming that all Roman commanders were better than Lepidus and calling him 'the most unreliable man' (*vir omnium vanissimus*) and 'the most wicked man' (*homo pravissimus*).[4] The other imperial historians were not nearly as blatant in attacking Lepidus. They chose instead through their selection of material to belittle his status in the triumvirate or his position of pontifex maximus and to shift blame for the

101

proscriptions away from Octavian to the shoulders of Lepidus and Antony. None bothers to explain Lepidus' career or how and why he became a triumvir and pontifex maximus. There was, of course, nothing to be gained by resurrecting the virtues of the losers in the struggle. As Eleanor Huzar pointed out in her discussion of the problems involved in dealing with the sources on Antony for this period; 'Authors contemporary . . . should provide the most reliable evidence; but, though best informed, these writers had the least political and personal detachment in this age of murderous civil wars.'[5]

One of the most important influences on the interpretation of the triumviral period in the works of the imperial historians was, quite naturally, the view of the emperor Augustus himself. Augustus' autobiography, extant only in fragments, must have justified his treatment of his former partners. The later *Res Gestae* carefully avoids mentioning either of Octavian's triumviral partners by name, but does take pains to make it clear that Lepidus had seized the office of pontifex maximus in a time of civil turmoil and that the emperor had declined assuming the sacred position while his former colleague was still living.[6]

One of the historians writing during the reign of Augustus, Nicolaus of Damascus, wrote a biography of Octavian's early life, but he makes only a few references to Lepidus. He repeats Cicero's statement about Lepidus' dissatisfaction with the crowning incident at the Lupercalia and emphasizes Lepidus' strong advocacy of revenge for Caesar's murder.[7] The work ends before addressing the major questions of the triumviral period.

Without the text of Livy for this period it is difficult to speculate about his attitude toward Lepidus, but a few indications of his views can be gleaned from summaries of his books or fragments cited by others. Livy believed that Lepidus had stolen the position of pontifex maximus. Although he credited Lepidus with bringing Octavian and Antony together to form the triumvirate, he also included Lucius Antony's driving Lepidus from Rome in the Perusine War and interpreted the key events of 36 BC as results of Lepidus making war on Octavian, thus leading to the desertion of his army, his deposition as triumvir, and the humiliation of having to beg for his life.[8]

Velleius Paterculus, as mentioned above, is the only imperial writer who makes a personal attack on Lepidus' character, questioning his competence and military prowess. Velleius, a strong supporter of Augustus and Tiberius, follows the *Res Gestae*'s view that

Lepidus had usurped the position of pontifex maximus.[9] Velleius also blames Lepidus and Antony for the proscriptions, focuses on the proscription of relatives, and repeats Livy's chain of events with Lepidus' pride leading to the loss of his legions, humiliation, deposition, and banishment.[10]

Tacitus presents a more anti-imperial view of history and, although his *Annals* begins with the accession of Tiberius, includes a few interesting comments relevant to Lepidus. Tacitus discusses two opposing opinions of Augustus' career following the emperor's death in AD 14. One stated that Octavian had conceded much to both Antony and Lepidus in order to gain their support for avenging Caesar's assassination. These concessions could include such things as the proscriptions and even the office of pontifex maximus, but the exact meaning is not clear. Tacitus goes on to say that after Lepidus became old and lazy (*socordia senuerit*) and Antony's lusts had destroyed him, the only solution to Rome's problems was government by one man.[11] The reference to laziness, even if it only applied to Lepidus' old age in Tacitus' meaning, may have unintentionally contributed another negative label to Lepidus' character that sometimes surfaces in later references.[12]

The opposing opinion on Augustus, according to Tacitus, places Octavian's route to power in a much less favorable light. Tacitus says that Octavian had deceived Sextus Pompey with the semblance of peace and Lepidus by the appearance of friendship (*specie amicitiae*).[13] This comment is particularly important because it lends weight to the view that Octavian had betrayed Lepidus' trust after Philippi when Lepidus had in good faith yielded the bulk of his legions to the common cause. It would also support Lepidus' contention in 36 BC that he was adding captured legions and demanding Sicily merely as compensation for the armies and provinces from which Octavian had arbitrarily stripped him earlier.

Most of Plutarch's references to Lepidus come within the context of his lives of Caesar, Cicero, Brutus, and Antony. He mentions Lepidus' proscription of his brother, but points out that others believed that Octavian and Antony had demanded that Paullus be included.[14] Plutarch also says that Lepidus supported Antony's insistence on Cicero's proscription.[15] In his *Moralia* Plutarch interprets Octavian's rise to power as the result of his fortune and sees Lepidus' command (and defeat) as almost predetermined to enhance Octavian's success.[16]

Suetonius' biographies of Caesar and Augustus also contain a few references to Lepidus. In a statement very similar to that in the epitome of Livy, Suetonius says that it was Lepidus' pride in the size of his army that caused him to challenge Octavian and led to the loss of his legions, having to beg for his life, and his exile.[17] Suetonius differs from other imperial historians by saying that although Octavian resisted the proscriptions at first, once they had begun he carried them on with more fervor than did either of his colleagues.[18]

Florus defends Octavian by saying that Antony and Lepidus forced him to join the triumvirate and by blaming the two partners for the proscriptions. He also says that Lepidus' motivation in joining the triumvirate was his greed for wealth and totally omits his role in the war with Sextus Pompey.[19]

The two sources that provide the most information about the triumviral period and about Lepidus' role are Appian and Cassius Dio.[20] Appian, writing in the mid-second century AD refers to some of Lepidus' posts under Julius Caesar and begins to provide greater detail about him immediately following the assassination. Appian includes Lepidus' movement of troops to stabilize the situation, but basically sees Lepidus as an ally and supporter of the historian's main focus, Mark Antony.[21] Both men are pictured as in accord in their desire to avenge Caesar's murder.[22] Appian ignores Lepidus' role in arranging the truce with Sextus Pompey, however, in favor of giving Antony sole credit.[23] Appian interprets the merger of Lepidus' army with Antony's after Mutina as a natural outcome for two Caesarians who had been in accord all along.[24] He goes on to record the repeal of the hostility decrees against Antony and Lepidus and then describes the formation of the Second Triumvirate, the *Lex Titia* that legalized it, and the ensuing proscriptions.[25] Appian and Cassius Dio are the only historians to record the initial division of the western provinces among the triumvirs, a crucial point in proving Lepidus' importance prior to Philippi.[26]

Appian does ascribe characteristics of inaction and laziness to Lepidus, but these appear to stem primarily from his loss of his troops to Antony and Octavian.[27] Appian says that Lepidus proscribed his brother first and Antony his uncle second, but the historian also provides some justification by pointing out that these two men had been first to vote Lepidus and Antony public enemies and he also hints at Lepidus' involvement in Paullus' escape.[28] In addition, Appian provides the touching scene of 'reversal in fortune' with Lepidus appearing before Balbinus, who had been proscribed by the triumvirs, to secure bail for his wife in connection with the conspiracy of their son against Octavian.[29]

Cassius Dio cites Antony alone as being Caesar's agent back home in 49 BC, although he does credit Lepidus with holding the election as praetor to make Caesar dictator.[30] Dio makes sport of Lepidus' triumph without enemy contact, but he totally ignores Lepidus' role in pacifying Farther Spain, an act that involved a show of force and driving back the attack of Bogud's auxiliaries on Marcellus' camp.[31] It is true that this action was not of sufficient stature to merit a triumph in normal times, but Dio misses the significance of the service to Caesar's cause.

Dio gives Lepidus a more active and independent role than does Appian, emphasizing his occupation of the forum with troops and demand for revenge against the assassins. However, he carries this too far by picturing Lepidus as desirous of leading a revolution, perhaps because of confusion with the image of Lepidus' father, the consul of 78 BC.[32] Dio interprets Antony's offer of an alliance through marriage between his daughter and Lepidus' son and his maneuvering as consul to have Lepidus selected as pontifex maximus as results of Antony's fear that Lepidus may upset his plans.[33] Dio also describes Lepidus' dual role of remaining in technical allegiance to the Senate while also helping Antony, but interprets their merger as following an agreement between Antony and Octavian.[34]

In addition to including the initial triumviral division of the western provinces, Dio places primary blame for the proscriptions on Antony and Lepidus, who as experienced Caesarian politicians quite naturally had made many more enemies than had their younger colleague. Dio singles out Antony as particularly guilty here and comments that Lepidus had allowed his brother to escape to Miletus and was somewhat lenient toward others.[35] The historian indicates that Antony and Octavian pushed Lepidus aside after they returned triumphant from Philippi, includes some reference to Lepidus' activities in Africa, and describes Lepidus' involvement in the war against Sextus Pompey and his subsequent challenge to Octavian that led directly to his deposition.[36] Although Octavian is Dio's primary interest, Dio records, in contrast to earlier accounts, that Lepidus' soldiers at first resisted Octavian's overtures.[37] Dio is also our source for the petty insults to which Octavian regularly subjected Lepidus in later years.[38]

Eutropius' brief sketch of Roman history, written in the late fourth century, reports a few facts about Lepidus, including his mediation between Antony and Octavian to form the triumvirate and equally shared responsibility for the proscriptions.[39] Eutropius makes no attempt to slight or mock Lepidus.

The fifth century proved less kind to Lepidus' reputation, however. The long poem of Rutilius Namatianus associates the triumvir and other members of his family with evil deeds. Lepidus is singled out for reversing the course of freedom won at Mutina.[40] Orosius, in his Christian view of Rome's pagan past, adds nothing to the traditions regarding Lepidus, but moralizes against the proscription of brother by brother and against the overblown pride that led to Lepidus' defeat in Sicily.[41]

It is interesting to note a very different view coming roughly a century later in the Christian eastern empire. John the Lydian was not writing a history, it is true, but he does refer to Lepidus in one place as *magister equitum* under the dictator Julius Caesar and in another as partner with Antony and Octavian in command and there is nothing negative attached to either reference.[42]

After surveying the predominant characterization of Lepidus that most imperial historians included in their works, however, one can understand why such a negative impression of his character and role in historical events would surface whenever future generations chose to refer to the man. During the Middle Ages, with the exception of the work of chroniclers, epitomizers, and copiers of ancient manuscripts who only repeated what they had read about him, if they mentioned him at all, Lepidus received no attention from writers or historians.[43] Even Dante, who displays extensive knowledge of Roman history through the *exempla* he regularly cites from antiquity in his *Divine Comedy*, makes no reference to either Lepidus or Mark Antony. Moralizing about pride, greed, or reversals of fortune relative to these two triumvirs might have been expected here.

A little later in the fourteenth century Boccaccio (1313–75) did address Lepidus and Antony as moral *exempla* in his *De Casibus Virorum Illustrium*. Boccaccio said that Lepidus was *illustris* because of his service as *magister equitum* under Caesar and because of his mediation between Octavian and Antony and sharing of power with them in the triumvirate. However, Boccaccio criticized the exile of Lepidus' brother and expressed the view that pride and arrogance had led Lepidus to challenge Octavian, thus resulting in his humiliation and banishment.[44] Boccaccio's treatment of Lepidus was later repeated in a French version by Laurent de Premierfait

(d. 1418) and in English by John Lydgate (*c*.1370–1451) in *Fall of Princes*.[45]

The Renaissance architect and writer Leon Battista Alberti (1404–72) wrote a comedy early in his life using the name 'Lepidus' and many assumed it to be an authentic Roman work. Alberti also used Lepidus as a character, but his purpose was to play on the adjective *lepidus*, meaning 'witty' or 'charming,' and not to recall any of the Aemilii Lepidi. It is hard to believe, however, that in the fifteenth century some did not conclude that Alberti was referring to the Roman name Lepidus.[46]

Poggio Bracciolini (1380–1459) mentioned Lepidus in connection with Octavian and the triumviral proscriptions, but did not single him out for individual discussion.[47] Erasmus reproduced an obscure anecdote from Pliny's *Natural History* concerning Lepidus as triumvir complaining about his lodging accommodation because the singing of birds had kept him awake. The problem was solved by the painting of a very large snake that kept the birds quiet.[48]

In the mid-sixteenth century Lepidus appeared on a Renaissance medal. The obverse showed the heads of all three triumvirs, accompanied by the inscription CONCORDIA IMPERATORVM. The reverse portrayed the three men at tribunals, presiding over the horrors of the proscriptions, including Cicero's execution.[49] Roughly two centuries later, the Swiss medallists Jean Dassier and his son Jacques-Antoine Dassier included a far more positive triumviral medallion in their series of Roman history medals. The obverse displayed the three men's heads and listed their names. The reverse, titled *Partage de l'empire*, showed the three colleagues examining a map on a table at the time of their division of land in 43 BC.[50]

Hubert Goltz published in 1563 a work that integrated Roman history and numismatics and featured several plates illustrating Lepidus' coins, both authentic and Renaissance fantasies, along with those of Julius Caesar and Mark Antony. In addition, Goltz cites details on Lepidus' early positions and mentions Cicero's statement about Lepidus' visible displeasure at the Lupercalia 'crowning' and the initial triumviral division of the provinces. Goltz also records Lepidus' humiliation after taking Messana and demanding Sicily, but his only real criticism of Lepidus concerns the brutal proscription of his brother.[51]

The Italian comic poet Cesare Caporali (1531–1601) spoofed the triumvirs in his *Vita di Mecenate*. Caporali mocked all three for the proscriptions and made particular sport of Lepidus concerning the division of the empire:

> The triumvirs divided the great tarte of the world among them, without using a knife: but every man taking hold of his piece, and pulling, the line slanted upon Lepidus' share, who therefore snatched at his next neighbor's; but lost his teeth and burnt his mouth in the attempt.[52]

The triumviral proscriptions appear to have assumed greater relevance in the sixteenth century as conflict between Catholics and Protestants escalated and produced modern examples of man's inhumanity to his fellow man. The French translation of Appian's history was especially popular in this period. When a trio of French nobles, the Constable de Montmorency, Jacques d'Albon de Saint-André, and the Duc de Guise, joined forces in persecuting Protestants and received the name 'the triumvirate,' the parallels between ancient and modern became especially timely. A series of massacre paintings and engravings appeared, the most famous of which were the work of a painter at the Valois court, Antoine Caron (1521–99), showing the triumvirs watching or even joining in the wanton slaughter of unarmed citizens and evoking the atrocities of the past either to condemn or to urge caution concerning the current horrors.[53] The Renaissance medal mentioned above and a bas-relief of the triumvirs in Dijon may also relate to this renewed interest in the triumvirate in a period of religious turmoil.[54] In any case, this publicity associated with the atrocities of the proscriptions only served to underscore the negative connotations attached to Lepidus' name.

For the political theorists, Lepidus and his colleagues provided suitable negative *exempla*. Jean Bodin (*c*.1529–96), in Book II of *Les Six Livres de la République*, commented on the nature of a triumvirate and its reduction first to a duovirate and then to a monarchy. What is particularly interesting here is that in the original French edition Bodin says that the initial reduction occurred after Augustus despoiled Lepidus, seemingly echoing Tacitus' view, while in the Latin version he wrote ten years later (which was also followed in the English translation of 1606) Bodin says that Lepidus, unfit for government, submitted his authority to Augustus, an interpretation closer to that shared by the other imperial historians.[55] The essayist Michel de Montaigne (1533–92) referred to the triumvirs as the 'three thieves' (*trois voleurs*).[56] According to Innocent Gentillet (*c*.1535–95), the sedition sponsored by the triumvirate brought death and destruction to Rome and the provinces as well as a change in government from Republic to monarchy. Though some may have justified all this because it led to the good government of Augustus, Gentillet adds that that period was followed by the tyrannical rule of five or six of Augustus' immediate successors.[57] An English political analyst, using the name D.P. Gent, 'a well-wisher to peace and unitie,' said that Octavian had overthrown his two colleagues 'out of ambition to reign alone.' He also listed Lepidus with Antony, Caesar, Augustus, and several others in a group of Romans who had abused their trust as government leaders.[58] Roughly a century later, Denis Diderot (1713–84) said that the conspirators should have assassinated Antony and Lepidus as well as Caesar.[59]

Classical themes also proved to be of great interest to Renaissance dramatists and it was in this field where the negative characterization of Lepidus would receive exposure on a grand scale, particularly through the pen of William Shakespeare. The playwright faced the same problem that people still have in trying to understand why Lepidus held the vaunted position of triumvir. The sources provided no apparent explanation of this enigma so Shakespeare must have concluded that Lepidus was the prototypical political cipher who possessed power without meriting it and exercised it only through his attachments to others. Shakespeare then sketched in the character to match his perception and in the process further denigrated Lepidus' reputation. This skewed image of Lepidus also suited the playwright's purposes by providing a foil for Antony and Octavius to act upon and by adding comic relief.

In *Julius Caesar* Shakespeare ignored Lepidus' close relationship with the dictator, although Plutarch makes it very clear, probably because its inclusion would have detracted from the character development of Antony and Brutus.[60] Shakespeare follows Plutarch over Appian and Cassius Dio by placing Lepidus in the Senate at the time of the assassination, but still has given him no speaking role to this point.[61] The playwright omits reference to Lepidus' service as *magister equitum* under Caesar, his swift occupation of the city with troops following the murder, his assumption of the office of pontifex maximus, his administration of Spain, and his giving aid to Antony after Mutina. In fact, Lepidus' only lines in this play come at the drafting of the proscription list when Octavius asks that Lepidus' brother Lucius be included and Lepidus agrees to consent if Antony will sacrifice his nephew.[62]

Antony then sends Lepidus off on an errand to Caesar's house to fetch the will so the 'real' triumvirs can get down to business and he delivers this devastating evaluation of Lepidus:

> This is a slight unmeritable man, meet to be sent on errands. Is it fit the three-fold world divided, he should stand one of the three to share it? . . . though we lay these honors on this man, to ease ourselves of divers slanderous loads, he shall but bear them as the ass bears gold, to groan and sweat under the business, either led or driven, as we point the way; and having brought our treasure where we will, then take we down his load and turn him off, like to the empty ass, to shake his ears, and graze in commons.[63]

Although Octavius points out that Lepidus was 'a tried and valiant soldier,' Antony continues:

> So is my horse . . . Lepidus . . . must be taught and train'd and bid go forth; a barren-spirited fellow; one that feeds on objects, orts and imitations, which, out of use and staled by other men, begin his fashion: do not talk of him, but as a property.[64]

These words provide powerful drama, which, of course, is the playwright's primary goal, but they also misrepresent the historical situation in a major way. Shakespeare has rejected the long-standing close relationship between Antony and Lepidus, a connection which, after all, played a big part both in creating stability in Rome following the assassination and in resurrecting Antony following the defeat at Mutina. He has also made Antony, instead of Octavian, the triumvir who wanted to push Lepidus aside. The impression of Lepidus created here just does not make sense when one considers the initial division of provinces in the west, but Shakespeare did not find that information in Plutarch, though he could have seen it in Appian. It is quite likely that Octavian and even Antony felt after their victory at Philippi that they no longer needed Lepidus as a partner, but this was unthinkable in 43 BC.

In *Antony and Cleopatra* Shakespeare has given Lepidus a larger role, but his character is developed to suit Antony's description of him in the earlier play and to provide moments of comic relief. Commentators have called this Lepidus character such things as 'vain, sychophantic, unprincipled, boobyish,' 'such an unequivocal nonentity that he becomes positively comic,' 'professional and weak-minded apostle of peace,' 'a mere cipher,' 'born to obey not to rule,' and an 'unctious and humble-mannered hypochondriac.'[65]

Most of Lepidus' lines in this play are short and calculated to preserve peace between Antony and Octavian through fawning praise or words of solace intended to still the passions of the moment. In the most degrading scene (Act II, scene 7) even the servants speak of Lepidus' getting drunk and Sextus Pompey repeatedly toasts Lepidus' health, encouraging him to consume more and more, while Antony provides inane replies to Lepidus' questions about animal life in Egypt. For example, to Lepidus' question 'What manner o' thing is your crocodile?', Antony replies: 'It is shaped, sir, like itself; and it is as broad as it hath breadth. It is just so high as it is, and moves with its own organs. It lives by that which nourisheth it; and the elements once out of it, it transmigrates.'[66] Lepidus is finally carried off by an attendant and is later hung over with the 'green sickness.'

Shakespeare does mention Lepidus' participation in the war against Sextus Pompey, but he then has Octavian arrest his colleague for alleged secret correspondence with Sextus and justify the action by stating that Lepidus had 'grown too cruel.'[67] Enobarbus correctly predicts that with the third triumvir removed, his partners would 'grind [th' one] the other.'[68]

Lepidus' constant interest in keeping the peace between Antony and Octavian is essentially a caricature of his earlier mediation between them to form the triumvirate. However, his extended meetings with his two colleagues and with Sextus Pompey never took place historically and, though there is some evidence testifying to Antony's heavy drinking, none of the sources mentions this concerning Lepidus. Shakespeare has molded his Lepidus character to suit the playwright's needs, but he has also damaged further the reputation of the historical Lepidus in the process.[69]

Some of the other Renaissance dramatists mention such things as Lepidus hosting Julius Caesar and others the night before the assassination, his occupation of the city with troops after the murder, his desire for revenge, or his aid to Antony after Mutina, but these are only isolated references and in several plays he is omitted entirely.[70] Kaspar B. Brülow (1585–1627), a poet and teacher, wrote several plays in the academic theater tradition in Strassburg, including one on Julius Caesar. These were composed in Latin and translated into German as textbooks.[71] In his play on Caesar, Brülow includes

Lepidus as a minor character who is a close friend to the dictator and warns him against potential danger. After the assassination, Lepidus joins with Antony and Calpurnia to console each other and plan revenge. Lepidus is also involved in the proscription scene with his triumviral colleagues.[72] Brülow does not use the Lepidus character in a negative way.

Georges de Scudéry (1601–67) gives Lepidus a substantial role in *La Mort de César*. Antony and Lepidus discuss the dangers of Caesar's policy of clemency and warn the dictator, to no avail, about Brutus and other opponents. There is no negative twist to Lepidus' character in this play. Antony calls his colleague *sage et prudent Lépide* and he is not being facetious.[73] Although Antony has a larger role, they both are true friends to Caesar and Lepidus' part is quite positive. In contrast to de Scudéry, the French dramatist Pierre Corneille (1606–84) treats Lepidus as a nonentity. In his *Mort de Pompée* Corneille includes Lepidus as a character in eight scenes, but gives him no speaking role. Lepidus even joins Caesar and Antony in Egypt, but whereas Caesar consults Antony at times, he only gives Lepidus orders.[74] In his play *Cinna or the Mercy of Augustus* Corneille has Cinna deplore the horrors of the triumvirate and refers to Antony and Lepidus as enemies of Octavian.[75]

Near the end of the seventeenth century, another French writer, Samuel De Broé, assembled a history of both triumvirates that was soon published in English translation as well as in French. The work details Lepidus' activities during the period of the second triumvirate, including his triumph and his meeting with Balbinus at the time of young Lepidus' failed conspiracy against Octavian. The author fails to question Lepidus' desire to proscribe his own brother and yet his assessment of Lepidus' character is unusually positive. According to De Broé, 'Lepidus belonged to a famous family and was very rich and highly respected in Rome for his honesty and for the great positions that he had held.' The author goes on to say that 'Lepidus' integrity was highly valued, but that he never had the firmness so necessary to all encounters and over everything involving the people with whom he came in contact.'[76]

The first work that attempts to analyze Lepidus' career with some degree of objectivity is *Fragmens sur Lépide* which was published among the posthumous works of the Abbé de Saint-Réal (1644–92), but was more probably written by one of his associates, such as the Marquis de la Bastie.[77] Although the author makes some mistakes in details, it is refreshing finally to find someone who questions the motivation behind his sources instead of merely parroting what they say! He states that the historians' portrait of Lepidus conforms more to their passions and to the interests of the emperor Augustus than it does to the truth.[78] He credits Lepidus for his loyalty to Caesar, his restoration of Antony's fortunes after Mutina, and with the idea to form the Second Triumvirate and he analyzes Lepidus' options when confronted with the opportunity to unite with Antony. The portrait is by no means a whitewash because the author admits that Lepidus had little experience or ability for war and evaluates him as being of moderate merit and excessive vanity.[79] In addition, he criticizes Lepidus' weakness and humiliation at the hands of Octavian as lacking in dignity. However, the author also rejects Velleius' attack on Lepidus as commander because of his success against Sextus Pompey and because Julius Caesar would never have placed such confidence in a person of no ability.[80]

Unfortunately, the revisionist view of Lepidus attributed to the Abbé de Saint-Réal was soon rejected (in 1734) by the Baron de Montesquieu in his *Considérations sur les causes de la grandeur des Romains et de leur décadence*. Montesquieu's dismissal of the argument, however, was based solely on his rejection of the testimony of one of Antony's letters and not on a serious consideration of all points.[81] Montesquieu went on to discuss the occupation of the Forum by the troops of Lepidus 'qui cherchait le trouble' and he branded Lepidus as 'the most wicked citizen in the Republic – always the first to begin disturbances, constantly forming evil projects in which he was forced to associate with men cleverer than himself'.[82] In his *De l'ésprit des lois*, Montesquieu said that Rome was 'deluged with blood' (*inondée de sang*) when Lepidus received his triumph, at the end of the year 43.[83] Unfortunately, this hyperbole and the authority of its author would further damn Lepidus' reputation and bury the more rational evaluation written under the name of Saint-Réal.

In England, Laurence Echard (1671–1730) published in 1699 a fairly detailed history of the Republic and mentioned Lepidus' service as praetor in naming Caesar as dictator, his joint consulship with Caesar, Caesar's last dinner at Lepidus' house, and Lepidus' desire for revenge after the assassination. Echard apparently followed Appian's text closely and although he does not really moralize concerning Lepidus and he places an unusual amount of blame on Octavian for cruelty in the proscriptions, he does emphasize Lepidus' humiliation at the hands of the future emperor.[84]

John Sheffield (1648–1721), Duke of Buckingham, wrote two plays, *Julius Caesar* and *The Death of Marcus Brutus*, that both excluded Lepidus as a character, but in the latter drama Sheffield has Cassius inform Brutus that Antony and Octavius are marching toward them 'with a mighty force' and that 'The useless Lepidus is left at Rome.'[85] In his *Dialogue between Augustus Caesar and Cardinal Richelieu*, Sheffield's Augustus maintains that Antony had tricked him into proscribing Cicero and that Lepidus, the only witness, would not offend Antony by declaring the truth, thus justifying his later vengeance on Lepidus. Richelieu then asks if Antony and Lepidus might be 'the merriest ghosts in Elysium, for methinks they have no such great cause.' Augustus responds that Lepidus does not laugh, but 'cries still for the loss of his army, which left him for me, nobody knows why.'[86]

William Guthrie (1708–70) and John Gray (*c.*1723–1811) wrote a general world history that contained a fairly straightforward account of the triumviral period and that is devoid of moralizing or gratuitous insults concerning Lepidus. They include Lepidus' speech declaring an end to the proscriptions, the initial division of the provinces, and his victory at Messana, as well as the more common story of Octavian's takeover of his troops.[87] The chronological tables of John Blair (d. 1782) listed Lepidus' and Octavius' defeat of Sextus Pompey and said Lepidus was degraded from the triumvirate and banished to Circeii for 'arrogating too much.'[88]

Another eighteenth-century writer, the Abbé Vertot (1655–1735), composed an *Histoire des révolutions de la république romaine* that went through several editions both in French and in an English translation. Vertot described Lepidus as 'a man more regarded for the merit of his ancestors, than his own worth; of a narrow mind; ambitious without courage; enterprizing, and yet timorous at the same time.'[89] Vertot basically follows Plutarch's account of Antony's takeover of Lepidus' army and interpreted Lepidus' role in the triumvirate as that of an arbitrator needed only to resolve disputes between his two colleagues.[90]

One of the most popular Roman histories of the eighteenth century was the multi-volume work of Charles Rollin (1661–1741), *Histoire romaine depuis la fondation de Rome jusqu'à la bataille d'Actium*, which appeared almost simultaneously in French and English editions over the period from 1739 to 1750 and was later translated into German and Italian as well. The volumes dealing with Lepidus were actually the work of Jean Baptiste Louis Crévier (1693–1765). Crévier described Lepidus as

> a man of much ambition and little genius, without principle or resolution, but ill affected to the Republic, and who had no other view than to aggrandize himself; this man, but from the circumstances of the times, would never have made any extraordinary figure in life.[91]

Although his assessment is very negative and reflects the influence of direct quotes from Cicero and Decimus Brutus, as well as that of the Abbé Vertot, Crévier does credit Lepidus with allowing his brother to escape Italy and with contributing to the victory over Sextus Pompey and having some justification in his claim to Sicily. However, he also refers to Lepidus' 'want of capacity' and 'narrowness of genius' and says Lepidus was the 'jest of his colleagues' and better suited to the high priesthood than to the position of triumvir.[92]

A more compact version of Roman history that went through numerous editions is the *History of Rome* by Oliver Goldsmith (1728–74). Goldsmith ignores Lepidus before Caesar's assassination, says Lepidus and Antony were 'fond of commotions' and describes Lepidus as 'a man of some authority and great riches at Rome.'[93] Goldsmith calls the triumvirs 'three usurpers of their country's freedom,' lists only Spain as Lepidus' initial share of command, and says Lepidus yielded his brother to his colleagues' vengeance.[94] Goldsmith also gives Agrippa total credit for the victory over Sextus Pompey, states that Octavian secured the loyalty of Lepidus' soldiers through 'secret intrigues and largesses' and 'private bounties,' and concluded that Lepidus was banished, 'despised by his friends, and to all a melancholy object of blasted ambition.'[95]

A recent article by Frank M. Turner has demonstrated very clearly how historians' interpretations of individual leaders and events in the last years of the Republic have often reflected their own personal political views.[96] This seems to be especially characteristic of histories written in the eighteenth century, when the classical world truly informed the modern, and applies to France as well as to England. For example, Conyers Middleton (1683–1750), an Anglican clergyman associated with the court Whigs, believed that the collapse of the aristocratic order and suppression of liberty were the results of subversion by 'evil, unpatriotic persons.'[97] Middleton, then, would quite naturally take a dim view of Lepidus and in fact he regularly quotes letters of Cicero and others attesting to Lepidus' treachery. He said Lepidus was the 'dupe' of his two colleagues and 'a vain, weak, inconstant man, incapable of empire, yet aspiring to the possession of it, and abusing the most glorious opportunity of serving his country, to the ruin of both his country and himself.'[98] Middleton believed that had Lepidus heeded Laterensis' advice and helped eliminate Antony and given 'liberty to Rome, the merit of that service, added to the dignity of his family and fortunes, would necessarily have made him the first citizen of a free republic.'[99] This statement shows very clearly why Cicero and those who revere him detest Lepidus and the switch to Antony's side so intensely.

Turner cites Thomas Blackwell (1701–57), who wrote *Memoirs of the Court of Augustus*, as 'a strong Scottish supporter of the Hanoverians' who blamed the demise of liberty on the powers of the tribunes and on the loss of morality at the hands of luxury.[100] Blackwell launched a blistering attack on all three triumvirs and even on Julius Caesar, 'the most ambitious profligate that ever was born.'[101] Blackwell's heroes are Cicero and the other Republicans and he uses his detailed account to attack all the Caesarians and to moralize about the evils of wealth, private pleasure, luxury, immorality, and vice, all of which threatened the 'glorious liberty' of all Britons.[102] Although Blackwell regularly refers to Lepidus as worthless and insignificant, he also defends the fairness of Lepidus' demands for a restoration of his provinces in 36 BC and criticizes Octavian's abuse of Lepidus in retirement.[103]

Turner indicates that portions of Blackwell's work appear to be a direct response to the multi-volume work of Nathaniel Hooke (d. 1763) whom he calls 'a Roman Catholic friend of Alexander Pope with Jacobite connections.'[104] Hooke blamed the Senate, not the Gracchi and their followers, for the decline of liberty and saw the Roman citizen's choice not as one between slavery and freedom, but one between triumviral government and anarchy.[105] Although Hooke credits Lepidus with securing the peace with Sextus Pompey in 44 BC, much of his narrative is accompanied by Cicero's correspondence, which condemns Lepidus' treachery. Hooke, despite his Caesarian leanings, calls Lepidus feeble and a weak general, but he also concludes, as the Saint-Réal author did, that Lepidus' services under Caesar, as governor of Rome, consul, and *magister equitum* show that he was not judged by Caesar to be without capacity. In addition, Hooke credits Lepidus with spirited action after the assassination, after Mutina, and in forming the triumvirate, but faults him for demonstrating weakness as triumvir and suffering extreme humiliation.[106]

One of Hooke's chief critics was Adam Ferguson, a professor of moral philosophy at Edinburgh who dedicated his *History of the Progress and Termination of the Roman Republic* to King George III.[107] Ferguson, like so many writers of this period, believed that Lepidus' survival after his defeat by Octavian was a result of his being 'too inconsiderable, even to be an object of resentment to those he had injured.'[108] According to Ferguson, Lepidus became 'almost the only example of an ignominy and disgrace, which so many others had merited no less than himself.'[109] This interpretation, however, ignores Lepidus' relegation to exile in Circeii as well as the fact that killing Lepidus would have besmirched the sacred office of pontifex maximus and made its next occupant appear to have secured the honor through murder.

An anonymous British pamphlet from the mid-eighteenth century touches upon the Lepidus tradition in an unusual way. It is titled *The Fair Triumvirate at War* and it parodies relationships within the British cabinet by reporting a conversation involving three ladies, given the Roman names of Antonia, Octavia, and Lepida, who are 'the consorts of the three powerfullest subjects in the nation.'[110] It is odd to find the wives given feminine forms of their husbands' names, but this, of course, is a literary vehicle for relating ancient and modern triumvirates. During the conversation, Lepida complains about a scandalous pamphlet, *Miscellaneous Thoughts*, that makes 'a cypher and a fool' out of her husband. Although it skewered Antony and Octavian as well, Lepida was upset because her husband was portrayed as a man 'they could easily impose upon and work to their purpose,' someone to be used and then cast aside.[111] Although Lepidus is not the direct target here, the negative image, echoing that presented by Shakespeare, is still important.

John Adams (1750–1814), in his *History of Rome*, despite his praise for Julius Caesar, calls Lepidus 'a man of mean capacity but profligate disposition' who 'wonted but resolution and abilities to erect himself into the master of the Roman world.'[112] Instead of crediting Lepidus for securing peace with Sextus Pompey in 44 BC, Adams says Sextus 'listened to the insidious negociations of Lepidus.'[113] Although he refers to Lepidus' desertion and abandoning the cause of freedom, Adams places ultimate blame for the fall of the Republic on 'the treachery of Octavius.'[114] Adams also says that Messana's legions 'yielded to the promises rather than the arms of Lepidus,' that Lepidus' life 'was secured by the weakness of his character,' and that Lepidus 'was a rival whose abilities he [Octavius] despised too much to dread.'[115]

In French drama of the eighteenth century, Lepidus was a significant, though still negative, character in *Le Triumvirat, ou la mort de Cicéron*, a play written late in life by Prosper Jolyot de Crébillon (1674–1762). The choice of the double title reflects the playwright's devotion to Cicero and the triumvirate is viewed in light of the orator's proscription. In spite of this perspective, however, Crébillon is still somewhat sympathetic to Lepidus as a character, in contrast to Antony, the arch-enemy who has no role except through slanderous reference. In Lepidus' conversation with Cicero's daughter Tullia he appears troubled by the Senate's accusations against him. He does not really grasp why he is in such disrepute, but he still tries to distance himself from the crimes of his impious colleagues.[116] The orator at first rebukes Lepidus as a tyrant and then implores him to return to the fold and save the Senate and Roman people in their time of greatest need. Lepidus warns Cicero that Antony has marked him for death and offers to take him and his daughter along to Spain, where Lepidus hopes to save his honor, name, and virtue by exiling himself from the horrors of Rome. Cicero naturally refuses to consider the offer and says that Lepidus and his colleagues are all the same.[117] Even though Cicero obviously holds Lepidus in low repute and Lepidus lacks the nobility and courage to 'fight the good fight' in this play, Lepidus' desire to separate himself from the evils of his colleagues is more than just an excuse and his generous offer to help Cicero and Tullia is sincere. These are positive actions and that is significant in light of the treatment Lepidus usually receives.

Voltaire (1694–1778) wrote his play *Le Triumvirat* about a decade after Crébillon's appeared. Voltaire's view of Lepidus is similar to that reflected in Shakespeare's *Julius Caesar*. Lepidus plays no role in this play and Antony refers to him with scorn as someone who is no longer needed and now can safely be put aside to tend exclusively to religious matters.[118] In the play *La Mort de César* Voltaire has Brutus list Lepidus with others who are Caesar's minions.[119] In one of Voltaire's letters, he refers to Lepidus as 'chief priest, a fool, and a rogue' (*grand pontife, sot, et fripon*).[120]

Marie-Joseph de Chénier (1764–1811) also wrote a play, in the tradition of Corneille and Voltaire, called *Brutus et Cassius ou les derniers Romains*. Chénier has Brutus renounce his ties to his brother-in-law Lepidus, whom he calls a 'meek monster' (*monstre débonnaire*). Brutus also denounces Lepidus' desertion of the cause of liberty and his aspirations to the throne and says that Lepidus' odious colleagues intend to leave him to his religious duties.[121] The triumvirs, needless to say, do not have roles in this drama. Most of the French writers of this period, and many British as well, quite understandably viewed the struggle between Cicero's followers and the Caesarians in light of their own intense concern to secure freedom from tyranny. In addition, the emphasis that Voltaire, Crévier, and Chénier placed on Lepidus' religious position and his forced retirement from government to perform those ceremonial functions is particularly interesting in light of the hostility toward religious power in the state that many Frenchmen of the Revolutionary period shared.

The Roman historians of the nineteenth century were in general less judgmental, moralistic, and dogmatic in their evaluations of Lepidus and the triumvirate than were their eighteenth-century counterparts, who had been very emotionally involved in the struggles of their period and tended to view individuals and events in absolute terms of good and evil. As the establishment of the French Republic and individual freedom gave way to the Terror, historians began to see that first impressions could be deceiving. When nationalism and imperialism became powerful forces and pushed liberalism aside in the hearts of many Europeans, views of Roman history received some modification as well. This would not mean that Lepidus would undergo full-scale rehabilitation, of course, but merely that he would not be used so frequently as an immoral example and that statements about him would more often be neutral in tone.

Ennio Quirino Visconti (1751–1818) included Lepidus in his *Iconographie romaine*. Visconti was familiar with Saint-Réal's *Fragmens sur Lépide*, but says the effort to enhance the character of Lepidus was in vain.[122] In spite of this comment, however, Visconti gives positive details on Lepidus' services under Caesar.[123] He points out that Lepidus all by himself did not have the genius or energy to both avenge Caesar and replace him, thus explaining his support for Antony in 44.[124] Visconti mentions Lepidus' disapproval of the Lupercalia charade, his treaty with Sextus Pompey that earned him an equestrian statue, and the formation of the triumvirate.[125] He points out correctly that Lepidus had not demonstrated his personal valor or his ability to command sufficiently to be considered an equal by his colleagues, even though he surpassed them in consular dignity.[126] Visconti also shows how Lepidus' ambition reasserted itself in Sicily and led to his humiliation.[127] All in all, Visconti provides a fair overview of Lepidus' career.

Thomas Arnold (1795–1842), the renowned headmaster of Rugby, died before completing his major history of Rome, but several of his early essays were later collected into a book titled *History of the Later Roman Commonwealth*. According to Frank Turner, Arnold believed Roman history 'manifested the follies of fallen human nature' and its value was chiefly as a contrast to Christian times.[128] Although Arnold would naturally disapprove of Lepidus, his references are not generally abusive or condemnatory, as were many written by his predecessors in the previous century almost as a matter of custom.[129] Arnold clearly views Lepidus as a man deserving notice 'more from the elevated situation to which circumstances afterward raised him, than from any merit or abilities of his own.' He does credit Lepidus with 'quieting the disturbances' in Spain for Caesar, but instead of also citing Lepidus' arrangement of a peace treaty in 44 BC, Arnold says Lepidus negotiated because he was afraid to fight Sextus, citing as his source only Velleius' statement about Lepidus' poor generalship.[130] Arnold also accepts Dio's belief that Lepidus aimed to replace Caesar, says Lepidus had insisted on his brother's proscription, and refers to Lepidus' treason and treachery in switching sides.[131] Arnold's basic assessment of Lepidus' motivation is that he

> was likely to join that party which could most work upon his hopes of personal advantage; but his inclination would lead him to oppose the cause of the commonwealth, inasmuch as the forms of the old constitution would confine within moderate bounds his irregular ambition.[132]

Victorian period histories of the Republic tended to praise Caesar and, although this did not necessarily result in a reappraisal of his friend Lepidus as well, it probably did contribute to a muting of criticism of the triumvir and to some neutralization in the prevailing attitude toward him, at least in many writers. This was not true, however, of Charles Merivale (1808–93), an Anglican clergyman and dean of Ely, at least in his popular, multi-volume history of Rome that appealed to the Victorian middle class. Frank Turner says: 'Merivale's extraordinary hatred and contempt for the landed oligarchy of the later republic led him to justify virtually all of its enemies and the suffering and violence that had marked its collapse.'[133] Although Merivale calls Lepidus 'an hereditary opponent of the oligarchy' and lists many of his services to Caesar, the author accepts Dio's statement that the only trophies he had acquired for his triumph were presents extorted from provincials.[134] Merivale also does not place Lepidus among those who enjoyed Caesar's 'personal intimacy and confidence' despite his having been raised 'nominally to the first place among the dictator's adherents.'[135] In his discussion of the proscriptions, Merivale says: 'Lepidus, a man neither of feeling nor of foresight, was easily persuaded to crimes, of which he could estimate neither the advantage nor the odium.'[136] Merivale goes on to say that Lepidus in joining Antony had pretended 'to be coerced by his own soldiers' and, after Lepidus' humiliation by Octavian, he adds: 'Undoubtedly Lepidus had owed his great public distinctions more to his high rank and family influence than to any abilities he had displayed even in his earlier and more active years.'[137]

Only a few years after the appearance of the third volume of his history, however, Merivale edited *An Account of the Life and Letters of Cicero*, translated from an earlier (1835) work of Bernard Rudolf Abeken (1780–1866) and in this pro-Ciceronian book the strongest negative references to Lepidus are to his being 'wary' and to his 'treacherous acts.'[138] It is also interesting to note that in his book on *The Roman Triumvirates* written later in life little of Merivale's hostility toward Lepidus remains. Here he calls Lepidus 'the least ambitious and least strong of the confederates, but a man of high position, great wealth and wide connections.'[139] When relating Octavian's deposition of Lepidus, he does refer to the latter as 'so feeble a pretender', but he also describes him as 'as magnate illustrious from his birth and from the dignity which he held as chief pontiff.'[140]

Henry G. Liddell (1811–98) wrote a one-volume history of the Republic that went through several reprintings. Although he calls Lepidus 'a feeble and fickle man', his other references are neutral in tone and he suggests that if Antony had agreed to use force against the conspirators Lepidus would probably have become Rome's master.[141] James Anthony Froude (1818–94), in his biography of Caesar, refers to Lepidus as 'a person of fickle character', but does mention Caesar's 'last supper' at Lepidus' house.[142] Samuel Eliot (1821–98) avoids disparaging remarks in his references to Lepidus, but he makes it clear that Lepidus was 'no match' for challenging Octavian.[143] In a popular reference work, the *Dictionary of Greek and Roman Biography and Mythology*, William Smith (1813–93), after describing Lepidus' life in some detail and without derogatory comment, concludes by both attacking Lepidus' character and raising the possibility of a different interpretation:

> Lepidus was one of those men who have no decided character, and who are incapable of committing great crimes for the same reason that they are incapable of performing any noble acts. He possessed great wealth, and, like almost all his contemporaries, was little scrupulous about the means of acquiring it. Neither in war nor in peace did he exhibit any distinguished abilities; but that he was not so contemptible a character . . . seems pretty certain from the respect with which he was always treated by that great judge of men, Julius Caesar. It seems clear that Lepidus was fond of ease and repose, and it is not improbable that he possessed abilities capable of effecting much more than he ever did.[144]

According to Anthony Trollope (1815–82), writing in his *Life of Cicero*, Lepidus was 'a coward,' 'false from the beginning,' and 'a vain inconstant man, looking simply to his own advantage in the side which he might choose.'[145] George Long (1800–79) presents a very neutral account of Lepidus, but his work stops in 44 BC. Long goes into great detail on Lepidus' pacification of Spain for Caesar and doubts Dio's assertion that Lepidus was seeking supreme power following the dictator's assassination.[146] T.M. Taylor also writes a fair, non-judgmental record of Lepidus' career, but he does conclude that 'Lepidus, who was naturally a weak man and owed his position to the fortunate accident of having been Master of the Horse at the time of Caesar's death, was of little account.'[147] Another British writer, H.F. Pelham (1846–1907), said that Lepidus 'possessed neither ability nor resolution enough to win for himself the prize to which he aspired,' but, aside from his assumption that Lepidus was aiming at replacing Caesar, which is at least questionable, few would disagree with Pelham and his overall account is a fair one.[148]

The images left in more general and less scholarly texts have also contributed to and reinforced Lepidus' negative reputation. For example, *The Comic History of Rome* referred to Lepidus as one of Caesar's 'creatures.'[149] John Bonner (1828–99) in *A Child's History of Rome* says Lepidus was 'a stupid, coarse-minded soldier' who 'would agree to any thing, if Antony and Octavian would let him kill his own brother.'[150] Bonner also says Octavian saw that

Lepidus was 'too stupid to be mischievous' so he 'sent him to Rome to be high-priest – or pope.' Bonner concludes: 'And I dare say he [Lepidus] made as good a pope as a politician'.[151] An exception to the generally negative portrait of the triumvir that typifies these works can be found in Elizabeth M. Sewell's *The Child's First History of Rome*, where the author refers to Lepidus as 'one of Caesar's greatest friends' and ascribes his obscurity after Philippi to his being 'an old man' whom people began to forget after he went to his province of Africa.[152] In his text, William F. Allen says simply: 'the incompetent Lepidus was set aside by his more energetic colleagues.'[153] Arthur Gilman (1837–1909), in *The Story of Rome*, is very neutral in reporting Lepidus' activities, but in commenting on Lepidus' forced retirement, Gilman says: 'He [Lepidus] lived in the ease that he loved until 13 BC.'[154] Such comments can help perpetuate misinformation and skewed impressions.

Nineteenth-century French writers, though very conscious of the parallels between Julius Caesar and Octavian and Napoleon I and III and therefore positive toward Caesar, were not particularly warm to Lepidus. Pierre-Charles Levesque (1736–1812) detects an ambivalence in Lepidus, describing him as 'cowardly in spirit and courageous in heart' and subject to a weakness 'that mild manners usually accompany and which was not incapable of harm because it yielded to every impulse.'[155] Levesque credits Lepidus with mediating between Antony and Octavian because they both trusted him but not one another, and says Lepidus yielded his brother to the hatred of his two colleagues, yet allowed Paullus to escape.[156] Levesque mentions the initial division of the provinces, yet does not see any inconsistency between this and his view that Lepidus was subordinate to his two colleagues from the start. According to Levesque, Lepidus' soldiers despised his sluggish delaying.[157] Emile Egger (1813–85), speaking of Octavian's rivals, says Octavian reduced Lepidus 'to conceal through inaction the most complete nonentity.'[158] The educator and government minister Victor Duruy (1811–96), whose multi-volume *History of Rome and of the Roman People* appeared in several printings in both French and English, presents a very neutral view of Lepidus' activities and includes several illustrations of coins and purported busts of Lepidus. However, Duruy also quotes Montesquieu's 'worst citizen' statement about Lepidus.[159]

The popular French historian from the Romantic period, Jules Michelet (1798–1874), says Antony had proscribed his uncle and

Lepidus his brother 'to show that no mercy would be granted' and he points out that both men escaped, 'probably by the connivance of the triumvirs.'[160] Michelet includes no disparaging remarks about Lepidus though he is rather tough on Octavian, calling him the most cruel of the triumvirs, and also on Antony.[161] However, Lepidus is practically ignored throughout Michelet's version of the triumviral period and only receives mention a few times.[162] Pierre Deschamps (1821–1906), in his tribute to Cicero, contrasts the triumvirs with Julius Caesar, who had repudiated the 'crimes of ambition' they were practicing and who had 'accepted all means of achieving empire, except the cowardly and disgraceful ones.' According to Deschamps:

> Rome belonged to force, belonged to young Octavian, to Lepidus, to Marc Antony, to the three masters who, just now, after the manner of tigers on their prey, are dividing the world, each one giving to his neighbor, an exchange of the same sacrifices, the head of their dearest friends.[163]

In the nineteenth-century German tradition, Lepidus received mixed responses. Although Julius Caesar was generally accorded praise, this attitude usually did not transfer to the Caesarian leaders of the Second Triumvirate. Bartold Georg Niebuhr (1776–1831) believes Lepidus could have ended Antony's career after Mutina, but that he had no resolution to do so, was 'a contemptible person' (*eines verworfenen Menschen*), and was raised to the office of pontifex maximus 'without having any claim to it.'[164] Niebuhr suggests that Sicily, though at the time occupied by Sextus Pompey, was included with Africa as Lepidus' share in the redistribution of the provinces and therefore that Lepidus was justified in demanding Octavian evacuate Sicily. He also adds: 'Lepidus did not enjoy the esteem or love of any man, not even among his soldiers.'[165] Wilhelm Karl August Drumann (1786–1861), whose *Geschichte Roms* became a standard on the Roman families, after several pages of recounting Lepidus' career in a relatively neutral fashion, presents what amounts to a legal brief or indictment of negative statements and anecdotes about the triumvir. Drumann calls Lepidus rich, weak, sluggish, negligent, driven by vanity and avarice, treacherous, hypocritical, unprincipled, and fickle, among other things.[166] Drumann cites references for his statements, but there is no attempt to understand why people had denounced Lepidus or how Caesar could have appointed such an incompetent and wicked person repeatedly to serve in positions of critical responsibility. One wonders how the label of drunkard was omitted from Drumann's list, though that one, of course, had no backing in classical texts. It is unfortunate that such a slanted picture of Lepidus was circulated in one of the standard reference works of the time.

German scholars of the nineteenth century, however, also produced some more moderate assessments of Lepidus. Karl Wilhelm Nitzsch (1818–80) provides a very straightforward account of the triumviral period and, although he includes only a few comments about Lepidus individually, he does avoid making personal attacks on him.[167] Theodor Mommsen (1817–1903), the dean of Roman historians, refers to the triumvir only a few times in his works, but these comments are objective and non-judgmental. Benedictus Niese (1849–1910) also is relatively neutral in his version, though he does refer to the 'helpless' Lepidus merging with Antony after some vacillation.[168] Ludwig Lange (1825–85) likewise, though calling Lepidus 'lazy,' presents a fair account overall.[169] Carl Peter accuses Lepidus of joining Antony out of cowardice and calls him 'insignificant' when describing the formation of the triumvirate, but he avoids any extensive negative comment.[170]

Near the end of the century three scholars focused more closely on Lepidus and the triumviral period, rather than just including these studies within much broader Roman histories. Felix Brueggemann's dissertation in Latin, *De Marci Aemilii Lepidi vita et rebus gestis*, presents the events of Lepidus' life without extensive analysis or editorial comment. Brueggemann correctly emphasizes Caesar's trust in Lepidus, but he also refers to the triumvir's laziness and quotes Velleius' comment about all commanders being better that Lepidus.[171] Viktor Gardthausen, in his classic study *Augustus und seine Zeit*, assesses Lepidus very negatively, referring to his personal insignificance, weaknesses, and incompetence and labeling the triumvir as a *Null*. However, Gardthausen also says that Lepidus was 'the firmest of all the friends of Caesar' in speaking out publicly for revenge against the assassins and also that Lepidus was able to achieve a certain importance through combining with others.[172]

Paul von Rohden summarized Lepidus's career for Pauly–Wissova's *Realencyclopädie*. Von Rohden naturally cites dates and sources on various stages of the triumvir's life. He says that Lepidus owed his consulship chiefly to his insignificance, echoing Gardthausen, in combination with his nobility and wealth.[173] Von

Rohden also recounts Lepidus' services under Caesar and his occupation of the forum and speech against the conspirators following the dictator's assassination.[174] Von Rohden credits Lepidus with bringing together Antony and Octavian and points out that by the time of Lepidus' yielding seven of his ten legions to his colleagues for the common effort it was decided that Lepidus would play only a subordinate role.[175] On Lepidus' character, von Rohden cites the 'unanimous opinion of writers' that he was weak and sluggish and says Cicero knew nothing to praise about him in the *Philippics* other than his nobility, honors, distinguished priesthood, and private fortune.[176] Although the orator was clearly grasping for some way to secure Lepidus' support for the Senate when hopes were fading, these words of praise cannot be dismissed so lightly and used as evidence that Cicero could not find anything else about Lepidus to honor.

Starting in the late nineteenth century and continuing to the present, books focusing on the lives of individual Roman leaders have become a popular vehicle for both scholarly and mass-market authors who write about Roman history. One might expect biographies of Cicero to be especially hostile toward Lepidus, but, although this is generally true, this was not automatically the case because neither William Forsyth nor J.L. Strachan-Davidson describe Lepidus in derogatory terms in their early biographies of the orator.[177] Gaston Boissier makes reference to 'the incapable Lepidus' and another French historian, Gaston Delayen, claims, without citation, that Suetonius had pictured Lepidus 'as a brutal, irascible person' and that Lepidus was 'a constant prey to fear.'[178] Torsten Petersson, in his biography of Cicero, says Lepidus was 'intensely hostile to the assassins, and, being a man of weak character, he allowed himself to become the tool of Antony.'[179] G.C. Richards, another biographer of the orator, goes about as far as one can in condemning Lepidus: 'There is hardly a more contemptible figure to be found in all Roman history.'[180] R.E. Smith believes that Lepidus and Plancus together could have destroyed the forces of Antony. He says Lepidus was 'weak and colourless, pushed by events into the centre of the stage' and that he 'must be persuaded or cajoled into doing his duty to the state.'[181] More recent biographies of Cicero by D.R. Shackleton Bailey, Elizabeth Rawson, W.K. Lacey, and Thomas N. Mitchell have treated Lepidus in a far more objective, non-judgmental tone, however.[182]

Max Radin's life of Brutus portrays Lepidus as a troublemaker who arouses Caesar's veterans to demand vengeance. According to Radin, 'Lepidus, always a swaggerer and boaster, overweeningly puffed up by the fact that he, and he only, had an army [in March of 44 BC], was already putting on the airs of a full dictator.'[183] Radin also says that Lepidus was sulky at the reconciliation dinner with Brutus because nothing was going as he had planned.[184] Gérard Walter and M.L. Clarke, in their studies of Brutus, handle the triumvir without noticeable bias, though Clarke does state that 'Lepidus was not a man of much weight.'[185]

Biographers of Augustus tend to view Lepidus in a dim light, probably for the same reason that the imperial historians did. John B. Firth describes the triumvir's activities in relatively neutral terms, although he emphasizes such things as Lepidus' untrustworthiness, his 'unearned triumph,' and his proscription of his brother.[186] Firth also has this to say about Lepidus:

> This clumsy soldier and still clumsier intriguer, who had owed his partnership in the Triumvirate not to his own abilities but to the accident that he had had so many legions under his command, was practically helpless in the absence of his patron and protector, Antonius.[187]

Although he credits the triumvir with helping defeat Sextus Pompey in Sicily, Firth believes that Lepidus' renewed strength 'seems to have turned the brain of the Triumvir.'[188] E.S. Shuckburgh acknowledges that Lepidus' claims against Octavian in 36 BC were sound, but adds, correctly, that they needed to be backed by a fixed determination and the loyalty of his army. Shuckburgh also states that Lepidus' whole career had been 'weak and shifty' and concludes that 'he certainly presents the most pitiful figure of all the leading men of the day.'[189]

In René Francis' biography of Augustus, Lepidus, the 'negligible quantity' of the Second Triumvirate, is compared to Crassus and his relative lack of importance in the First. Francis also points out the irony that Lepidus in 36 BC was only allowed to keep the one office, that of pontifex maximus, 'that had induced him to join the other triumvirs.'[190] John Buchan is the most hostile of the Augustan biographers in his attitude toward Lepidus. Buchan says the triumvir was 'vain, unstable, self-indulgent, a lesser Antony.'[191] Buchan also states that Lepidus 'had never been more than a cipher, important only for the legions which he brought into the pool.'[192] He also refers to the triumvir as 'trivial' and describes him as the slave of Fulvia. Although acknowledging that there was some justice in Lepidus' complaints against Octavian, Buchan says he was 'the type of man who, having no fixity of purpose or dignity of character, invites cavalier treatment' and that he retired, 'enriched by the loot of his triumvirate.'[193] In contrast to Buchan, Dietmar Kienast's biography of Augustus takes a very neutral attitude toward the actions of Lepidus and avoids negative rhetoric.[194]

The biographers of Mark Antony, including Arthur Weigall, Jack Lindsay, Hermann Bengtson, Eleanor Huzar, François Chamoux, and Alan Roberts, as a group are relatively neutral toward Lepidus, even though one might have expected them to be fairly positive because of the close relationship between Antony and Lepidus and because the two men both suffered the same kind of 'hatchet job' at the hands of the imperial historians.[195] Although the Antony scholars are not revisionists toward Lepidus, they do, however, avoid the negative formulae so often used by others to describe the triumvir. Eleanor Huzar makes some excellent points regarding the difficulties of trusting the sources for the period and emphasizes the importance of Lepidus' role as 'a significant brake to the rivalry between Antony and Octavian.'[196]

In the more general histories of this century, Lepidus has received mixed, though generally negative, references. W.E. Heitland, in his excellent survey *The Roman Republic*, describes Lepidus' actions in a fairly straightforward manner, though he does refer to the chief pontiff as 'weak and shifty,' thus echoing Shuckburgh. Heitland also comments on the mint's ceasing to issue coins with the head of Lepidus as an indication of 'the nullity of the senior partner.'[197] Tenney Frank refers to Lepidus as a 'willing tool' of Caesar, but otherwise describes his actions in a fair manner, as do T. Rice Holmes and André Piganiol as well.[198]

H.G. Wells, in *The Outline of History*, says very little about the Second Triumvirate, but, in commenting on Lepidus' receiving 'that picked bone,' Carthaginian Africa, in the redistribution of provinces, he makes this astounding observation on the triumvir: 'He seems to have been a good man of good traditions, set upon the restoration of Carthage rather than upon wealth or personal vanities.'[199] It would be interesting to know what influenced Wells to reach that rare estimation of Lepidus. The author mentions the 'advice and editorial help' of classicists Ernest Barker and Gilbert Murray, among others, but no conclusions can be drawn on Wells's source without additional information. In contrast, the author of another general history, Henry Smith Williams, refers to Lepidus as 'a feeble and fickle man.'[200]

In the *Cambridge Ancient History*, volume X, M.P. Charlesworth and W.W. Tarn report Lepidus' actions without much editorial comment except Tarn's observation that 'the soldiers were weary of civil war and still less inclined to enter one for Lepidus, whose sluggishness they despised.'[201] Tarn also believes that the size of Lepidus' force leaving Africa for Sicily indicates 'that he had carefully planned his coup' against Octavian.[202] Charlesworth makes this insightful comment:

> It is easy to brand the vacillation of a Lepidus or Plancus or Pollio, but hard to descry what other course than joining Antony was feasible for them. All three were men of distinction who had served under Julius Caesar and owed their rank and provinces to him ... ; in addition it was highly doubtful whether their men would fight against their fellows in Antony's army, for one of the most remarkable features of these years is the 'war-weariness' of the troops and their constant efforts to secure conciliation.[203]

Frank Burr Marsh, in his Methuen series volume, says that what Lepidus really intended in the spring of 43 BC cannot be known and that his assurances to Cicero may not have been insincere because he did not have a strong hold over Caesar's veterans and may have finally decided that they simply would not fight their comrades under Antony.[204] Marsh does conclude, however, that 'Lepidus was not a man of much ability or energy.'[205]

Other twentieth-century scholars who comment on the triumvir include Ernst Hohl, who, in an article in *Klio*, refers to Lepidus as 'a notorious simpleton' (*ein notorischer Schwachkopf*).[206] Michael Grant labels Lepidus 'a mediocrity,' Erich Gruen describes him as 'absorbed in vanity and idleness,' and Paul MacKendrick mentions 'Augustus' obscure and cruel colleague Lepidus.'[207] Both Christian Meier and Alfred Heuss call the triumvir 'a weak character' (*ein schwacher Character*) and Meier also adds the adjective *unsicherer* (unstable). Ernst Kornemann describes Lepidus as 'a completely incompetent man' (*ein gänzlich unfähiger Mann*) and as the 'straw man' of the triumvirate. However, N.A. Maschkin, Helga Botermann, Joseph Vogt, and Peter Wallmann all managed to write accounts of Lepidus without including any such derogatory references.[208]

Sir Ronald Syme (1903–89), in his classic work *The Roman*

Revolution, is not kind to Lepidus. Although he concedes to Lepidus' 'primacy in rank and standing' of all the patricians, Syme also describes him as 'ambiguous,' 'a flimsy character,' a 'cipher,' and 'perfidious and despised.'[209] However, in this work Syme also provides an unusual defense of the actions of the Caesarian generals, including Lepidus, in 43 BC. Syme states:

> Where and with whom stood now the legitimate government and the authority of the Roman State, it was impossible to discover ... They [these men] acted as they did from a reasoned and balanced estimate of the situation ... Even ... Lepidus may yet in treachery be held true to the Roman People at a time when patriotism and high principle were invoked to justify the shedding of Roman blood.[210]

In the Todd Memorial Lecture of 1950 Syme says 'Lepidus was a flimsy character, rapidly discarded, and by his very insignificance at the same time removed from blame and unworthy of rehabilitation.'[211] In his study of Sallust, Sir Ronald refers to 'the pretentious and flimsy Lepidus (pedigree, not principle or capacity)' and to Lepidus and his father as 'both flimsy and calamitous.'[212] Syme also says: 'Lepidus deserted the cause of the Republic – and he used noble and fraudulent language to cover his treachery.'[213] In his work on Tacitus Syme repeats the 'flimsy and pretentious' description and indicates that Sallust had had the satisfaction of witnessing the calamitous fall of the triumvir. He also suggests that Tacitus used 'Sallustian language' in describing Lepidus' decline, citing particularly the use of the word *socordia*.[214]

However, in an article on Livy and Augustus Syme mentions Lepidus as one of the scapegoats available to the imperial historian seeking to deflect blame from Octavian. Syme says Lepidus was displayed 'as a decayed and pretentious relic.'[215] In *The Augustan Aristocracy* Syme also summarizes Lepidus' career without derogatory references and says: 'Such was the end of M. Lepidus, who equalled as *bis consul* and *pontifex maximus* the great ancestor – and surpassed him with two triumphs. When they wrote history, men of the time were put in mind of the calamitous parent.' Syme continues,

> Disliked and distrusted by partisans eager for action or heroism, and failing to win approbation from sober senators who rated civil war the greatest of evils, or were prepared to

recommend even '*inertissima consilia*' in a dangerous conjunc-
ture, Lepidus was duly arraigned for personal vanity, vain
ambition, and persistent torpor.[216]

In one of his last articles, Syme defends Lepidus against condemnation for the proscription of Paullus:

> Marcus Lepidus the Triumvir earns reprobation for pro-
> scribing his own brother. That is to misconceive the procedure
> of the Caesarian leaders. Needing money, not revenge, they
> published aristocratic names on the lists in order to advertise
> firm concord and a ruthless resolve.[217]

It appears that late in his career Sir Ronald had reassessed the
veracity of some of the damaging sources on Lepidus.

In the field of literature, the single work that has nurtured the
negative image of Lepidus in the popular mind more than anything
since Shakespeare's two plays is Alfred Duggan (1903–64)'s historical novel *Three's Company*, published in 1958. This book received very
favorable reviews and one of these commented that:

> one is struck by Mr. Duggan's originality and imaginative
> insight in choosing such a psychologically interesting but
> unheroic hero. His choice of an obscure puppet about whom
> little is known has enabled him to create his own version of
> Lepidus, the eternal conservative stuffed shirt without the
> moral strength to live by the traditional virtues he admires
> and pretends to possess.
>
> Marcus Lepidus, according to Mr. Duggan, was vain,
> pompous, proud and simple-minded. A bit of a prig and
> a terrible snob, he was shocked by rakes and rascals like
> Mark Antony and appalled by ruthless dictators like Octavius
> Caesar. Conventional, honorable about little things, Lepidus
> wanted so much to be a great man that he never hesitated to
> accept the expedient and opportunistic choice. Such conduct
> might have made an abler man all powerful.[218]

Duggan begins his novel, quite appropriately, with the funeral of
Sulla in 78 BC, a year in which the young Lepidus underwent the
traumatic shock of his father's sudden fall from power in disgrace.
After the prologue, the action commences with the year 49 BC and
even then Duggan has Lepidus vacillating over whether to join
Caesar or Pompey. The novelist paints Lepidus as a man of the

noblest blood who relies on his wife Junia for decisions and appears out of touch with the cruder and craftier characters who vie for power in revolutionary Rome. His excessive caution keeps Lepidus in a perpetual quandary and a regular state of inactivity and he wants always to compromise and avoid war at any cost. In one humiliating scene Lepidus mistakes Fulvia's body language as an invitation to love and she quickly slaps him to the ground and calls him a 'fat miserable slug.'[219] Duggan's Lepidus means well – he questions the need to execute the proscribed, but is not forceful enough to influence his two colleagues. Lepidus in this novel combines his words of swashbuckling bravado with a lack of understanding of the world around him that together remind the reader of a Don Quixote in a toga. Although Duggan's Lepidus is pitiful, innocent of evil thoughts, and treated sympathetically, the caricature of a bumbling, inept, cowardly, and submissive triumvir would further tarnish Lepidus' public image.

In the novels of W.G. Hardy, *The Scarlet Mantle* and *The Bloodied Toga*, Lepidus is depicted as a relatively strong character, though he is referred to as pudgy or fat in the latter work. Lepidus acts quickly both as *interrex* in 52 and as troop commander following Caesar's assassination. On the Rostra Lepidus demands vengeance on Caesar's murderers and receives thunderous cheers in response. He persuades Antony to include Cicero in the negotiations of March 44 BC and also, at the request of his mother-in-law Servilia, stations guards to protect the conspirators' houses from violent attack. Lepidus' maxim is 'Never make enemies' and after his merger with Antony he brings Octavian and Antony together at Bononia.[220] Hardy, commenting on the initial triumviral division of the provinces, says: 'Even the stupidest soldier knew that Octavianus had been given only a wormy apple compared to the juicy fruits on the plates of Lepidus and, in particular, of Antony.'[221] Lepidus also questions whether or not proscriptions are worth losing public support for and resists the inclusion of Cicero on the list and the creation of large rewards for informers and bounty hunters, although he finally yields to his colleagues on these issues.[222]

Thornton Wilder only makes a few brief references to Lepidus in *The Ides of March*. In one letter Calpurnia relates that during a meal Caesar and Cicero had 'baited one another with such sharpness that Lepidus did not know where to rest his eyes.'[223] Phyllis Bentley, in her novel *Freedom, Farewell!*, refers to Lepidus as 'an officer of Caesar's, son to the long-dead Lepidus of the conspiracy, and about as much use' and ascribes this view to the dictator.[224] On the formation of the Second Triumvirate, Bentley says 'Lepidus was really negligible, but useful as representing religion, and to make a third . . . in the alliance.'[225] She also has him perform secretarial duties for his two colleagues.[226] Dyke Williams, in *Twilight at Janiculum*, relates Lepidus' gradual merger with Antony from Octavian's perspective, but there are no negative slurs against Lepidus and he is not a major character.[227]

In Allan Massie's *Let the Emperor Speak*, however, Lepidus is once again the target for extreme abuse. Massie has Octavian relate the story and he treats Lepidus with scorn and derision from the beginning. Lepidus is described as handsome, true to his name, but Octavian refers to him as 'nothing but a bag of wind' and says that Cicero had called Lepidus 'the most sordid and base of fellows': 'He takes hold of your elbow and mutters dishonourable filth in your ear.'[228] Octavian describes Lepidus as a gladhander whose lack of ease kept him chattering and in perpetual motion: 'He couldn't stop talking and his hands fluttered from man to man, a press here, a squeeze there, a light deprecating touch on the next shoulder.'[229] Even when Lepidus raises an excellent point in the triumviral negotiations, Octavian wondered 'which of his advisers had put him up to it.'[230] When discussion turns to the proscriptions, Lepidus warms up and proposes Atticus' name, 'with a snake flick of his tongue. "No one will spill more gold than that fat banker."'[231] Lepidus is outvoted by his colleagues on Atticus and Octavian concludes that: 'a weak man's thirst for blood is fiercer than a strong man's. In drawing up this list Lepidus was repaying the world for his own sense that he was less than his name.'[232] Massie also features Lepidus' demands in Sicily, Octavian's gradual turning of the issue against him, and Lepidus' final humiliation, embracing Octavian's knees and licking dust from his feet in thanks that his life was to be spared.[233]

Lepidus' public image also received another jolt in 1953 when Joseph L. Mankiewicz's cinema production of Shakespeare's *Julius Caesar* played to large-screen audiences and later reached additional viewers on television and as an educational resource. In this version, the bulk of Antony's 'slight, unmeritable man' speech does its damage very effectively, although the last section, about the 'barren-spirited fellow,' is not included.[234] In the early 1980s, television screened all Shakespeare's plays and *Julius Caesar* and *Antony and Cleopatra* spread Shakespeare's view of Lepidus to large numbers, especially when one considers that these versions continue to be used for educational purposes. Although Lepidus' role is admittedly small in both plays, their portrait of him is very negative and thus still damaging.

The Second Triumvirate naturally continues to be associated with power politics and the proscriptions and there was even a reference to Lepidus and his colleagues in a *New York Times* column in 1988 that grouped three of the American Democratic presidential candidates into a triumvirate.[235] Lepidus was also a character in a new play, Sam Segal's *Cicero*, as recently as 1986.[236] The triumvir will probably continue to be a stock figure in literary or dramatic presentations of the Caesarian–Augustan period in the future, especially if the author or playwright chooses to abuse him for comic relief. Although it has appeared to be dwindling in recent years, the image of a bumbling, hapless Lepidus will reappear at times in scholarly works because there is not enough proof to destroy it permanently.

In spite of the avalanche of negative opinions of Lepidus presented above, there is still sufficient evidence to justify a more positive assessment. Cicero pursued a personal vendetta, the imperial historians who wrote about Lepidus had a specific agenda, and most of the negative comments in modern scholarship are direct reflections of attacks in the classical sources rather than the result of careful evaluation.

Over the last twenty years, however, scholarly reevaluation of Lepidus and his historical role has begun to portray the triumvir in a different light. In an article published in *Acta Classica* in 1971, Léonie Hayne demonstrated that Lepidus acted 'skillfully and consistently in support of Antony and (indirectly) of the Caesarian faction' in 44 and 43 BC and was not the 'weak, shifty creature' that most authors seemed to think he was.[237] Two additional articles soon followed: one examines the confusing sources surrounding Lepidus' marriage and establishes his devotion to his wife, something not characteristic of a '*homo ventosissimus.*'[238] The other questions criticisms of Lepidus for challenging Octavian in 36 and concludes that his gamble was not unjustified nor his defeat inevitable.[239]

In his article 'Untersuchungen zum mutinensischen Krieg,' Hermann Bengtson claims that Cicero and the Senate failed to take advantage of the opportunity to pursue peace with Antony and ignored Lepidus and treated him as a political cipher. He also questions whether or not the portrait of Lepidus as an extremely weak figure is accurate. Bengtson uses Lepidus' letters to the Senate very effectively and shows the difficulties of his situation. After admirably defending Lepidus' character in this period, however, Bengtson points out that Lepidus' actions during the proscriptions cannot be erased from staining his reputation.[240]

Recent work on Lepidus' administration of Africa allows us to reconstruct the triumvir's activities there to some degree and indications concerning his role are generally positive. The testimony of the Thabraca inscription has been especially helpful.[241] François Bertrandy suggests that Lepidus' romanization of Thibilis in Numidia was part of a larger program to develop an African *clientela* in support of his reassertion of his original status as triumvir.[242]

Alain Gowing has also furthered the rehabilitation of Lepidus, first in his dissertation, 'The Triumviral Period in Appian and Cassius Dio,' and then in a paper assessing the bias of the *Laudatio Turiae*. In the former, Gowing concludes his section on the triumvir with this statement:

> Though admittedly more a follower than a leader, Lepidus was neither incompetent nor inexperienced; he had, after all, enjoyed a position of particular prominence under Julius Caesar. But as partner to Octavian and Antony, it might be argued, Lepidus found himself out of his league and unequal to the situation. One may doubt that at any point Lepidus schemed to acquire supreme power for himself. His revolt in Sicily in September of 36 was no more and no less a futile attempt to regain a position from which he had been unfairly thrust. Lepidus had quickly outlived his usefulness, though there can be no question that initially his cooperation was essential. Both Appian and Dio realized, for different reasons, that he could not be ignored.[243]

In my dissertation (1973) on Lepidus' family and in subsequent articles I have tried to show that many, if not most, of our sources on Lepidus cannot be taken at face value because they are biased against him for very specific reasons. In spite of this bias, however, one can still see that a record of effective, competent performance characterized most of Lepidus' career, that Julius Caesar trusted Lepidus sufficiently to place him in positions again and again where poor leadership could threaten disaster, and that our sources have featured Lepidus' merger with Antony and ultimate humiliation before Octavian in a way that has produced an overwhelmingly negative view of Lepidus in subsequent years.[244]

Without additional source material, it will be impossible ever fully to remove the tarnish from Lepidus' reputation and that is not our goal. Devotees of Cicero will tend to view Lepidus as a traitor who intervened at a crucial time to stifle attempts to resuscitate the Republic. Others, of course, see the vision of a restored Republic as little more than an impossible dream that sounds beautiful but has no substance. It is also unfortunately characteristic of human nature to cheer when the mighty have fallen and jump in and kick them while they lie sprawling on the ground. It is particularly sweet when the toppled statesman happens to be a blueblood. I hope that in the future historians and authors will avoid this tendency and treat Lepidus in less strident terms. The tarnished triumvir was no saint, but neither was he a stupid oaf. He performed effectively in most positions and made choices that were consistent with the times and the government that he had seen work under Julius Caesar.

With hindsight we can say that Lepidus was clearly outclassed by his two colleagues, almost from the very start, but we must remember that Octavian did not appear as formidable a figure in 43 BC as he later became and that Antony had been soundly beaten at Mutina. Both men drew strength from Lepidus and, in the process, left him weakened and vulnerable. With his departure, however, the stage was set for a showdown between his revivified colleagues.

A thorough examination of Lepidus' career shows that Lepidus carried out his duties capably in several different positions as an agent of Caesar, on his own following Caesar's death, and as a triumvir. He displayed considerable administrative competence and the ability to compromise both when directing the city of Rome and as a provincial governor. It is likely that he would have made an excellent consul and pontifex maximus if he had lived much earlier in the Republic. Lepidus had very few tests of his military skills, but on the whole he was quite successful. He never had the opportunity to work with soldiers long enough to satisfy their greed and gain their personal loyalty. The attacks on his character are more substantial than those on his competence. Lepidus clearly did not display the unimpeachable moral values that were attributed to Roman nobles of the early Republic and that Cicero demanded of him, but in the chaos of the Civil Wars neither did most of his peers. The indecisiveness or sluggishness ascribed to Lepidus seems rather to have been the result of a calculated effort to keep his options open, while at the same time remaining consistent in his loyalty to the Caesarian cause. Did Cicero really believe that Lepidus could or even should support the efforts of men who had murdered his close friend and patron? Apparently he did, because in his own mind he could justify and even praise the murder, but Lepidus would have had to reject his whole career in order to take that giant step.

Caesar's death suddenly put Lepidus into an unfamiliar position where he had to act independently of his leader. Although he moved quickly and effectively, his natural inclination was to work closely with Caesar's other followers, especially with Antony and Octavian, and joining Cicero and the assassins would have meant betrayal for him. His mistake lay in trusting his colleagues to keep their promises to him rather than pursue their own personal advantage, and this miscalculation allowed him to be pushed aside and then dropped unceremoniously from his lofty perch. No attempt should be made to picture the triumvir as a shining example of the ideal Roman statesman, but neither should he be portrayed as a nonentity, a political dwarf inexplicably found associating with the giants of his time.[245] A careful examination of all available sources shows that a reassessment of Lepidus is justified, that he was both competent and consistent, and that he played a more important role in Roman history than most historians recognize.

NOTES

References to my dissertation, 'The Aemilii Lepidi' (Newark, Delaware, 1973, University Microfilms 74–8754), will be indicated by the abbreviation *AL*. References to *Corpus Inscriptionum Latinarum* (Berlin, 1869–1959) are indicated by the abbreviation *CIL*.

1 AN INTRODUCTION TO THE PROBLEM

1 Cic. *Ad Brut.* 3.1 (Loeb translation by M. Cary).
2 Ibid, 22.1 (Loeb translation by M. Cary); see also 23.2 and 24.9.
3 Cic. *Fam.* 11.9.1 (Loeb translation by W. Glynn Williams). On the expression *homo ventosissimus*, see A.-M. Guillemin, 'Un cliché de la poésie élégiaque et de la langue politique,' *Mélanges Paul Thomas* (Bruges, 1930), 394–406.
4 Vell. Pat. 2.63.1 and 2.80.1 (Loeb translation by Frederick W. Shipley).
5 William Shakespeare, *Julius Caesar*, Act IV, scene 1.
6 Ibid.
7 Baron de Montesquieu, *Considérations sur les causes de la grandeur des Romains et de leur décadence*, ed. Gonzague Truc (Paris, 1954), ch. 13, p. 67 (translation mine).
8 Alfred Duggan, *Three's Company* (New York, 1958), 182; see also the negative impressions of Lepidus in 25–8, 36–8, 53, 106, 119, 205, and 210.
9 W.E. Heitland, *The Roman Republic* (3 vols, Cambridge, 1909), vol. III, 404.
10 F.B. Marsh, *A History of the Roman World from 146 to 30 B.C.* (2nd edn, London, 1953), 294.
11 Ronald Syme, *The Roman Revolution* (Oxford, 1939), 166, 180.
12 Ernst Hohl, 'Das Angebot des Diadems an Cäsar,' *Klio* 47 (1941), 107.
13 Erich S. Gruen, *The Last Generation of the Roman Republic* (Berkeley, 1974), 103.
14 Dio 47.8.1.

2 THE AEMILII LEPIDI

1 Plut. *Aem.* 2.1–2, *Numa* 8.9–10, 21.1–2; Paulus in Festus 22L ('Aemiliam gentem . . .')

2 Plut. *Rom.* 2.3.

3 Paulus in Festus 22L; Sil. Ital. *Punica* 8.293–7.

4 Numbers in square brackets are those used in Pauly–Wissowa, *Realencyclopädie der classischen Altertumswissenschaft*, to distinguish between individual members of the Aemilian *gens*.

5 On the father's heroic death, see Livy 22.49.6–12. On the son, see Erhard Meissner, *Lucius Aemilius Paullus Macedonicus und seine Bedeutung für das römische Reich (229–160 v.Chr.)* (Bischberg/Oberfranken, 1974) and William L. Reiter, 'The Anatomy of a Conqueror: The Image and Reality of Lucius Aemilius Paullus' (Diss., SUNY/Binghamton, 1977).

6 Plut. *Fab. Max.* 16.4–8; Livy 22.49; Polyb. 3.116. On the tragic end of the family line, see Livy 45.41.11 and Polyb. 32.14.2.

7 Livy 37.29–31.

8 Val. Max. 1.1.7. See my entry ('Aemilia 150b') in Pauly–Wissowa, *Realencyclopädie der classischen Altertumswissenschaft*, Supplement XV (Munich, 1978), 4.

9 Livy 23.30.15; see also F. Münzer, *Römische Adelsparteien und Adelsfamilien* (Stuttgart, 1920), 168, n. 1 and *AL*, 13–24.

10 Livy 21.49–51; *AL*, 24–44.

11 Livy 21.45–7 and 21.52–57.4; *AL*, 64–9.

12 Cic. *Brut.* 95–6; *AL*, 103–16.

13 On this man's life, see *AL*, 52–64, 69–101. For a discussion of the coins, see *AL*, 324–30, and my article, 'The Coins Issued by Lepidus as *Triumvir Monetalis*,' *SAN* (Society for Ancient Numismatics Journal) 5 (1973–4), 51–2.

14 Val. Max. 3.1.1.

15 Val. Max. 6.6.1.; Justin. 30.3.3–5.

16 Livy 35.10.11–12.

17 Livy 36.2.6, 10–13.

18 *AL*, 71–8; my article, 'The Duplication of Temples of Juno Regina in Rome' in *Ancient Society* 13/14 (1982–3), 179–92; J.W. Rich, *Declaring War in the Roman Republic in the Period of Transmarine Expansion* (Coll. Latomus 149, Brussels, 1976).

19 Livy 39.55.6–8.

20 See my article 'The Censors of 179 B.C.,' *Ancient World* 2 (1979), 51–3.

21 Livy 40.52.1–7.

22 See *AL*, 86, and W.B. McDaniel, 'Basilica Aemilia,' *American Journal of Archaeology* 32 (1928), 155–78.

23 See below, ch.4, n.13, for a different interpretation of this coin type.

24 Livy 41.27.3–4; *CIL* I, p. 459.

25 Diod. 31.9; Plut. *Aem.* 37.

26 See E. Badian, *Foreign Clientelae* (Oxford, 1958), 162–3, 275–6.

27 Polyb. 28.1.1 and 32.5–6.

28 Livy *Per.* 48.

29 Münzer, *Römische Adelsparteien*, 307, dates Lepidus' birth around 95 BC, but this appears to be several years too early, given the dating of his political career.

3 LIKE FATHER, LIKE SON?

1 *AL*, 101–18.
2 Cic. *Brut.* 96; *AL*, 101–17; E. Gruen, *Roman Politics and the Criminal Courts, 149–78 B.C.* (Cambridge, 1968), 73, 127–9; and Münzer, *Römische Adelsparteien und Adelsfamilien* (Stuttgart, 1920), 243–5. The opposition within the Senate to Porcina's activities in Spain, the fines levied against him in 136 and especially in 125, and the trial of the vestal virgins in 115 all raise questions about potential involvement of political factionalism.
3 Pliny *NH* 7.122, 186; App. *BC* 1.32. Appuleia could easily have been the daughter of some distant relation of Saturninus or even of a relative who did not support his policies. The marriage need not be Lepidus' first, although Pliny testifies to his devotion to Appuleia. Pliny, of course, may not have been referring to the consul of 78 as the husband of Appuleia. See n. 5 below.
4 Cic. *Pro Rab. Perd.* 7.21.
5 R. Syme, 'Paullus the Censor,' *Athenaeum* 65 (1987), 7–26, esp. 24. Syme believed that the M. Lepidus who was married to Appuleia (Pliny *NH* 7.122, 186) was a son of the consul of AD 6.
6 *CIL* VI.37045; C. Cichorius, *Römische Studien* (Stuttgart, 1961), 147; N. Criniti, *L'Epigraphe di Asculum di Gn. Pompeo Strabone* (Milan, 1970), 16–18, 106–8.
7 Oros. 5.22; E. Badian, 'Waiting for Sulla,' *Journal of Roman Studies* 52 (1962), 47–61, esp. 53; Münzer, *Römische Adelsparteien*, 307–11.
8 On Lepidus' alleged benefit from the proscriptions, see Sall. *Hist.* 1.55.18 and Gruen, *Roman Politics*, 274–5.
9 Bartolomeo Borghesi, *Œuvres complètes* (10 vols, Paris, 1862–97), vol. IV, 73; Elimer Klebs, 'Aemilius 84' in Pauly–Wissowa, *Realencyclopädie* 1.1 (Stuttgart, 1893), 567 (no. 84).
10 Pliny *NH* 35.13 and 36.49, 109–10.
11 Sall. *Hist.* 1.55.18.
12 App. *BC* 1.94–5.
13 Badian, 'Waiting for Sulla,' 53; Broughton, *Magistrates* II, 71.
14 Ps.-Ascon. 187, 259 Stangl; Gruen, *Roman Politics*, 274–5; L. Hayne, 'M. Lepidus (cos. 78): A Reappraisal,' *Historia* 21 (1972), 662–3.
15 Cic. *Verr.* 2.8.
16 Ibid., 212.
17 Plut. *Sulla* 34.3–5, *Pomp.* 15.1–2.
18 Plut. *Caes.* 1.2 (also related in Suet. *Caes.* 1.3).
19 Robin Seager, *Pompey: A Political Biography* (Berkeley, 1979), 14. For the opposite view, see John Leach, *Pompey the Great* (London, 1978), 39–41.
20 Cic. *De Off.* 2.58; R. Syme, *Sallust* (Los Angeles, 1964), 183; *AL*, 131.

21 App. *BC* 1.105.

22 On these possible sources of conflict, see Sall. *Hist.* 1.54; Pliny *NH* 35.13; App. *BC* 1.105; Plut. *Sulla* 38.1, *Pomp.* 15.3, *Comp. of Pomp. and Ages.* 1.2; Livy *Per.* 90; *CIL* I.2.734–7; *AL*, 132–4.

23 See N. Criniti's 'M. Aimilius Q.f.M.n. Lepidus, *"ut ignis in stipula"*,' *Memorie – Istituto Lombardo Accademia di Scienze e Lettere* 30 (1969), 319–460, and 'Tre noterelle di storia Lepidana,' *Rendiconti – Istituto Lombardo Accademia di Scienze e Lettere* 103 (1969), 865–74; Hayne, 'M. Lepidus'; L. Labruna, *Il console 'sovversivo'* (Naples, 1975). To get a better perspective on the issues involved in recent scholarship on Lepidus, see in addition the reviews of Criniti's work by J. Andreau in *Latomus* 31 (1972), 576–80, and K. Raaflaub in *Gnomon* 46 (1974), 50–5, and the reviews of Labruna's work by Criniti in *Rivista di Filologia e di Istruzione Classica* 106 (1978), 348–51, by R. Bauman in *Labeo* 24 (1978), 60–74, and by J. Carter in *Journal of Roman Studies* 69 (1979), 186–7.

24 Hayne, 'M. Lepidus,' 663–4.

25 Gran. Licin. 36.10.

26 Gell. 2.24.12; Macrob. *Sat.* 3.17.13.

27 Florus 2.23.3.

28 Gran. Licin. 36.10; see T. Rice Holmes, *The Roman Republic and the Founder of the Empire* (3 vols, Oxford, 1923), vol. I, 365–6.

29 App. *BC* 1.107; see also Gran. Licin. 36.10.

30 See Cicero's doubts about the loyalty of this area in 43 BC (*Fam.* 12.5.2).

31 Plut. *Pomp.* 16.3–5; Oros. 5.22; Livy *Per.* 90.

32 See *AL*, 138–40; App. *BC* 1.107; Florus 2.11.6–7; Livy *Per.* 90.

33 Plut. *Pomp.* 16.4, 16.6, 31.7, *Sert.* 15.2; Sall. *Hist.* 1.82M; Jul. Exup. 6; Ascon. 19C; Florus 2.11.7; App. *BC* 1.107; Pliny *NH* 7.122, 186; Zon. 10.2; Holmes, *The Roman Republic*, 305–6; M. Deutsch, 'The Death of Lepidus, Leader of the Revolution of 78 B.C.,' *University of California Publications in Classical Philology* 5 (1918), 59–68. On the connection between Lepidus' followers and Sertorius, see Philip Spann, *Quintus Sertorius and the Legacy of Sulla* (Fayetteville, Arkansas, 1987), 75–7 and 82–8.

4 THE FIRST TRIUMVIRATE

1 Pliny *NH* 7.122, 186; Plut. *Pomp.* 16. See above, ch. 3, p.13 and n.5 and R. Syme, 'Paullus the Censor,' *Athenaeum* 65 (1987), 7–26, 24. Plutarch's statement that Lepidus died as a consequence of learning of his wife's infidelity is very weakly linked to Pliny's reference to a M. Lepidus divorcing his wife Appuleia.

2 See G. V. Sumner, 'Manius or Mamercus?,' *Journal of Roman Studies* 54 (1964), 41–8, on the possible confusion of their names. See also E. Parrish, 'Influence of Consular Senators at Senate Meetings, 69 through 60 B.C.' (Diss., University of Pennsylvania, 1969), 25–7, 67–8.

3 Suet. *Caes.* 12.

4 Cic. *Att.* 8.9.3.

5 See E. Gruen, 'The Consular Elections for 53 B.C.,' in J. Bibauw, ed.,

Hommages à Marcel Renard (2 vols, Brussels, 1969), vol. II, 311–21. E. Badian, in 'M. Lepidus and the Second Triumvirate,' *Arctus* 25 (1991), 5–16, makes a strong case for dropping the misleading term 'First Triumvirate' in references to what was in essence a *conspiratio*. See below, p. 68.

6 There were apparently marriage ties linking the Lepidi with C. Aurelius Cotta and with Q. Metellus Scipio and Lucius was related to C. Scribonius Curio. Marcus' marriage to Iunia gave him a connection to M. Iunius Brutus, C. Cassius Longinus, and P. Servilius Isauricus. See E. Gruen, *The Last Generation of the Roman Republic* (Berkeley, 1974), 103–4, esp. 104, n. 53; E. Courtney, 'The Prosecution of Scaurus in 54 B.C.,' *Philologus* 105 (1961), 150–6, esp. 154–5; and R. Syme, *The Roman Revolution* (Oxford, 1939), 69, 136.

7 Sall. *Cat.* 31.4–6.

8 Cic. *Fam.* 15.13.1–2.

9 L.R. Taylor, 'Caesar's Colleagues in the Pontifical College,' *American Journal of Philology* 63 (1942), 385–412, esp. 391–3.

10 See my article, 'The Coins Issued by Lepidus as *Triumvir Monetalis*,' in *SAN* 5 (1973–4), 51–2. For a different interpretation of the inscription on Lepidus' equestrian statue coin, see S.P. Thomas, 'A Coin of M. Aemilius Lepidus,' *Numismatic Chronicle* 15 (1915), 520.

11 M. Crawford's *Roman Republican Coinage* (2 vols, Cambridge, 1974), vol. I, 443–4, dates the coins to 61 BC; a recent article by C. Hersh and A. Walker, 'The Mesagne Hoard,' *Museum Notes* 29 (1984), 103–34, uses additional hoard evidence to place their issue in 58 BC.

12 On Egypt as an issue at Rome, see I. Shatzman, 'The Egyptian Question in Roman Politics (59–54 B.C.),' *Latomus* 30 (1971), 363–9.

13 See my article, 'A Reevaluation of Lepidus' "Basilica Aemilia" Denarius' in Ian Carradice, ed., *Proceedings of the 10th International Congress of Numismatics* (London, 1990), 147–52, where I suggest that the building is a Porticus Aemilia rather than the more famous Basilica Aemilia.

14 E. Gruen, 'Pompey, the Roman Aristocracy, and the Conference of Luca,' *Historia* 18 (1969), 71–108, esp. 87, and *The Last Generation*, 60, 157, 302, 303, 334, 466, and 478; L. Hayne, 'L. Paullus and his Attitude to Pompey,' *L'Antiquité Classique* 41 (1972), 148–55. For the opposite view, see my article 'The Career of L. Paullus, cos. 50' in *Latomus* 38 (1979), 637–46.

15 Cic. *Phil.* 13.13, *Att.* 15.29; Dio 45.10.6.

16 Cic. *Har. Resp.* 12.

17 Ascon. 29. P. Willems (*Le Sénat de la république romaine*, 2 vols, Louvain, 1883, 1885, vol. I, 519, and vol. II, 12–13) and E.S. Staveley ('The Conduct of Elections during an Interregnum,' *Historia* 3, 1954, 196–7 and 197, n. 3) are most probably correct in their interpretation of Asconius and Lepidus' curule aedileship must have occurred just prior to his service as *interrex*. See also J. Seidel, *Fasti Aedilicii* (Breslau, 1908), 70; T.R.S. Broughton, *The Magistrates of the Roman Republic* (3 vols, New York, 1951–2, Atlanta, 1986 Supplement) vol. II, 228; and B. Marshall, *A Historical Commentary on Asconius* (Columbia, Missouri, 1985), 169–70.

18 Cic. *Att.* 4.17; for a discussion of this rebuilding, see L. Richardson, Jr,

'Basilica Fulvia, Modo Aemilia,' in G. Kopcke and M.B. Moore, eds, *Studies in Classical Art and Archaeology* (Locust Valley, New York, 1979), 209–15, esp. 213–14.

19 Cic. *Milo* 13; Asconius 33, 36, 43C; Dio 40.48–9. James Ruebel, in 'The Trial of Milo in 52 BC,' *TAPA* 109 (1979), 231–49 (esp. 234–5), suggests that the *interrex* was actually Manius Lepidus (cos. 66), but Broughton (*MRR* 3, 7–8) doubts this because of the need to amend the texts of Asconius and Cicero.

20 Staveley, 'Conduct of Elections,' 197, n. 3.

21 Asconius 36C; Plut. *Pomp.* 54.5.

22 See the discussion in L. Hayne, 'M. Lepidus and his Wife,' *Latomus* 33 (1974), 76–9; Marshall, *Historical Commentary*, 192.

23 Plut. *Pomp.* 16.2–5; Oros. 5.22; Livy *Per.* 90. See above, p.114 n.6.

24 See Sumner, 'Manius or Mamercus?,' esp. 41, n. 19.

25 For a more detailed account of L. Paullus' career, see Hayne, 'L. Paullus and his Attitude to Pompey,' and my article, 'The Career of L. Paullus, cos. 50.'

26 Cic. *Vat.* 25.

27 App. *BC* 2.26; Dio 40.59.4; Cael. in Cic. *Fam.* 8.4.4.

28 For more complete account of Paullus' consulship, see *AL*, 168–73.

29 App. *BC* 2.26–7; Plut. *Caes.* 29.2–3, *Pomp.* 58.1; Suet. *Iul.* 29.1; on the question of the bribery of Curio, see W.K. Lacey, 'The Tribunate of Curio,' *Historia* 10 (1961), 318–29.

30 Caes. *BG* 8.50; Suet. *Iul.* 29.2.

31 Plut. *Ant.* 6.4; App. *BC* 2.41. Felix Brueggemann points out in his dissertation on Lepidus (*De Marci Aemilii Lepidi vita et rebus gestis*, Münster, 1887, 9) that Dio (41.18.2–3) omits Lepidus' governing of the city and emphasizes Antony's command in Caesar's absence. However, Lepidus' performance as *praetor urbanus* makes Plutarch's and Appian's testimony to a division of authority seem more logical. If Antony had governed the city, one would expect Plutarch to have stated that in his biography of Antony. Dio is either mistaken or, as elsewhere (43.1.1–3, 44.34.4–6), is intentionally slighting Lepidus. Brueggemann (p. 8) also correctly emphasizes the importance of the confidence that Caesar placed in Lepidus to assume the major task of governing the city: 'Caesar ... in Lepido tantam fiduciam collocavit, ut ei urbem gubernandam traderet.'

32 Cic. *Att.* 9.9.3 and 15.2; see F.E. Adcock's analysis of Caesar's actions in *Cambridge Ancient History*, vol. IX (Cambridge, 1932), 654–5. Cicero's angry attack (*Att.* 9.9.3) on the unnamed individual who claimed that consular elections could be held by a praetor ('iste omnium turpissimus ac sordidissimus') has been interpreted by some as referring to Lepidus. See, for example, E.O. Winstedt's Loeb translation ('That disgraceful mean blackguard M. Lepidus'). D.R. Shackleton Bailey (*Cicero's Letters to Atticus*, 7 vols, Cambridge, 1965–70, vol. IV, 1968, 374) points out that Lepidus was a '*nobilis* of *nobiles*' and not likely to be called 'sordidissimus' by Cicero (at least not before 43 BC). The person in question could have been any outspoken supporter of Caesar who had angered Cicero for similar reckless actions in the past. One additional action of Lepidus'

praetorship can be added if Focke Hinrichs is correct in changing the name of the Lex Mamilia Roscia Peducaea Alliena Fabia to the Lex Aemilia Roscia Peducaea Alliena Fabia. Hinrichs, in 'Das Legale Landversprechen im Bellum Civile,' *Historia* 18 (1969), 521–44, esp. 532–7, argues convincingly that this land bill was Caesarian legislation passed in 49 and that Lepidus was its chief sponsor.

33 Dio 41.36.1, 43.1.1; Caes. BC 2.21.5.

34 Caes. *BC* 3.1–2; see additional sources in Broughton, *Magistrates* II, 256–7.

35 Dio 43.1.1; App. *BC* 2.48. The statement of Francis Hobler (in *Records of Roman History*, 2 vols, Westminster, 1860, vol. I, 17) that Lepidus 'took a part in the battle of Pharsalia' is a mystery without apparent source unless Hobler misinterpreted Lucan's reference (*Phar.* 7.583) to Lepidi and other great families having fallen on the battlefield. This is difficult to believe because Hobler discusses Lepidus in connection with a coin issued by him later as triumvir. It must just be a mistake.

36 Dio's statement (43.1.1–3) that Lepidus sent back from Spain only the money that he had plundered from the allies must be seen in its context as a mockery of Lepidus' receipt of a triumph without having conquered or even encountered an enemy. There is not enough evidence to conclude that Lepidus was 'guilty of extortion,' as Israel Shatzman states in *Senatorial Wealth and Roman Politics* (Coll. Latomus 142, Brussels, 1975), 289. When one considers the revolt stirred up by Cassius' exactions, Lepidus' return to the same province later without any indication of opposition, and the absence of any references to Lepidus being guilty of extortion, especially in Cicero, it seems that Dio means that Lepidus had only sent back to Rome the normal money 'plundered' from the provincials and not the spoils of war that would truly enrich the Roman treasury and earn him a triumph.

37 Hirt. in Caes. *Bell. Alex.* 48–62; Dio 42.15–16. Dio emphasizes the willingness of Marcellus to lead his revolt in either Pompey's or Caesar's direction, depending on circumstances. He does not even mention Lepidus' involvement in his account of the incident and plays down Lepidus' role when he records the triumph (43.1). See the summary of the incident in W.E. Heitland, *The Roman Republic* (3 vols, Cambridge, 1909), vol. III, 320–1.

38 Hirt. in Caes. *Bell. Alex.* 59.

39 Ibid., 63–4; Dio 42.16.2. See M.P. Galve Izquierdo, *Lépido en España – Testimonios* (Zaragoza, 1974), 16–19, on Lepidus' involvement in the dispute.

40 The naming of a colony after Lepidus reminds one again of his model ancestor, the colonies he had founded, and the establishment of Regium Lepidi, located naturally on the Via Aemilia. M.P. Galve Izquierdo summarizes a lot of the scholarship on the founding of Colonia Victrix Julia Lepida in *Lépido en España*, 30, 35, 43–5. The work of Miguel Beltran-Lloris, Antonio Mostalac Carrillo, and José Antonio Lasheras Corruchaga, *Colonia Victrix Iulia Lepida-Celsa* (Zaragoza, 1984) is also helpful. See also the comments of E. Hubner, 'Celsa' in Pauly–Wissowa, *Realencyclopädie* 3.2, (Stuttgart, 1899), 1880–1; C.H.V Sutherland, *The*

Romans in Spain (London, 1939), 128; and G. Hill, *Notes on the Ancient Coinage of Hispania Citerior* (New York, 1931), 78–9.

5 FRIEND OF CAESAR

1 Plut. *Ant.* 9–10; Dio 42.27–33; App. *BC* 2.92–4; see also the account of these events in Eleanor G. Huzar, *Mark Antony: A Biography* (Minneapolis, 1978), 65–9.

2 See Ettore Pais, *Fasti Triumphales Populi Romani* (Rome, 1920), 269. Aside from Lepidus and Caesar himself, during the period of the dictator's dominance only Q. Fabius Maximus and Q. Pedius received triumphs (in 45 BC for their service as Caesar's legates in Spain). See Dio 43.42.1–2 and Pais, *Fasti*, 283–4. An *ovatio* might seem to have been a more appropriate reward for Lepidus' service than would a triumph. However, there were very probably some casualties involved in fending off the attack on Marcellus' camp (see the criteria for an *ovatio* in Aulus Gellius 5.6.21 and Paulus 213L). The option was perhaps never even raised because Caesar had the power to grant whatever rewards he chose.

3 Dio 43.1.1–3, 33.1.

4 Dio 43.28.2, 48.1–4. These sources refer to the situation as it was a little later in time, but Caesar seems to have developed a regular pattern for entrusting Roman affairs in his absence to the team of Lepidus, the city prefects, and other agents and Dio supports this view.

5 Dio 43.2.1.

6 Dio 43.14.3–7, 19.1–4. See Pais, *Fasti*, 270–82.

7 Livy *Per.* 48 (Loeb translation by A.C. Schlesinger). See above, ch.2, p.9.

8 Cic. *Phil.* 5.38, 13.17.

9 Suet. *Caes.* 40; Dio 43.26; see W.E. Heitland, *The Roman Republic* (3 vols, Cambridge 1909), vol. III, 345–7.

10 Suet. *Caes.* 41; Dio 43.25; see Heitland, *Roman Republic* III, 339–45.

11 Cic. *Fam.* 13.26. See also the comments of D.R. Shackleton Bailey, *Cicero: Epistulae ad Familiares*, (7 vols, Cambridge, 1965–70), vol. II, 1977, 447–8.

12 Eutrop. 6.23.

13 *Inscriptiones Italiae* (ed.) A. Degrassi, 13.1 (Rome, 1947), 56–7. The Fasti Capitolini list Caesar's second dictatorship in 47 BC and his third with 45 BC. Since we know from Dio 43.14.3 that Caesar's third dictatorship began in 46, there is no reason to question Dio's statement (43.33.1) about Lepidus' office of *magister equitum* just because of its omission from the Fasti Capitolini for 46. W. Drumann, *Geschichte Roms*, vol. I (Berlin, 1899), 10, n. 1, dates the position to July of 46, when Caesar returned from Africa. See also F. Brueggemann, *De Marci Aemilii Lepidii vita et rebus gestis* (Diss., Münster, 1887), 14–16 and T.R.S. Broughton, *The Magistrates of the Roman Republic* (3 vols, New York, 1951–2, Atlanta, 1986 Supplement), vol. II, 295.

14 Dio 43.33.1.

15 Ibid.

16 Dio 43.28.2, 48.1.

17 Dio 43.33.1. See also Heitland, *Roman Republic* III, 350, n.1.
18 Caes. *Bell. Hisp.*; Dio 43.35–40. See Heitland's account in *Roman Republic* III, 350–2.
19 Cic. *Att.* 4.17.
20 Dio 53.23.2.
21 See L.R. Taylor, *Roman Voting Assemblies* (Ann Arbor, 1966), 47–55.
22 Dio 44.5.2–3. On the relationship between Caesar and Felicitas, see the comments of Stefan Weinstock, *Divus Julius* (Oxford, 1971), 117–18, 127.
23 Cic. *Att.* 13.42.
24 Dio 44.5.2–3.
25 Cic. *Att.* 13.47a.
26 Ibid., 46.
27 Cicero's references regarding Lepidus' wealth are in *Philippics* 13.8, 17, and 49. See the list of senatorial estates in the appendix to Maria Jaczynowska's article on 'The Economic Differenciation of the Roman Nobility at the End of the Republic,' *Historia* 11 (1962), 486–99. I. Shatzman, in *Senatorial Wealth and Roman Politics* (Coll. Latomus 142, Brussels, 1975), 289, n. 8, suggests that Lepidus may have also had an estate near Tibur, but the emended text in Cicero (*Att.* 8.14.3) still seems to refer to an estate of Manius Lepidus (cos. 66), not to one in Marcus' direct family: see D.R. Shackleton Bailey's comments in *Cicero's Letters to Atticus*, vol. IV (Cambridge, 1968), 353–4. The estate at Circeii, the site of Lepidus' exile later (Suet. *Aug.* 16.4), could very well have been handed down through the family line from his model ancestor (cos. 187, 175), who owned property nearby at Tarracina (Livy 40.51.2).
28 Cic. *Att.* 13.47a; see additional comments on Balbus and Oppius in *Fam.* 6.8.1, Tac. *Ann.* 12.60.4, and Brueggemann, *De Marci Aemilii Lepidii vita*, 17–18.
29 Dio 43.44.6–45.4.
30 On Caesar's honors and inclination towards monarchy and divinity, see the account of Weinstock, *Divus Julius*, esp. 270–341.
31 Broughton, *Magistrates*, II, 319.
32 App. *BC* 2.107; Dio 43.51.8.
33 For a survey of the sources and their interpretations, see the excellent article by Helga Gesche, 'Hat Caesar den Octavian zum Magister equitum designiert?,' *Historia* 22 (1971), 468–78.
34 Dio 43.49.1, 51.7.
35 Dio 43.51.8.
36 App. *BC* 2.107, 3.9.
37 Degrassi, *Inscriptiones Italiae* 13.1, 58–9, no. XLI.
38 Pliny *NH* 7.147.
39 Vell. Pat. 2.59.4; Suet. *Aug.* 8.2, 10.1.
40 For an excellent discussion of these events, see Weinstock, *Divus Julius*, 318–31.
41 I am assuming here that Cicero's statement (*Phil.* 5.38, 13.17) about Lepidus' expression of disapproval of the diadem episode at the Lupercalia a few weeks later has at least some truth to it.
42 See the accounts in Plut. *Ant.* 12, *Caes.* 61; App. *BC* 2.109; Dio 44.11,

45.30; Nic. Dam. 21; Cic. *Phil.* 2.84–7, 3.12, 13.17 and 31; Vell. Pat. 2.56.4; and Livy *Per.* 116.

43 See Livy 2.22.6, 3.57.7, 7.38.2, 28.39.15, 44.14.3–4. These passages refer to foreign envoys dedicating the *coronae* to express thanks or renew the ties of *amicitia*, but in 437 BC the dictator Mam. Aemilius Mamercinus dedicated one there 'ex publica pecunia populi iussu' (Livy 4.20.4).

44 See the summary of various interpretations in K. Welwei, 'Das Angebot des Diadems an Caesar und das Luperkalienproblem,' *Historia* 16 (1967), 44–69. See also Weinstock, *Divus Julius*, 331–41 and M. Gelzer, *Caesar: Politician and Statesman* (translated by Peter Needham, Cambridge, Mass., 1968), 321–2.

45 Cic. *Phil.* 13.41.

46 Ibid., 5.38, 13.17. See also the reference in Nic. Dam. 21.72 and the comments of Dietrich Felber on Lepidus' displeasure with the offer of the diadem in F. Altheim and D. Felber, *Untersuchungen zur Römischen Geschichte*, vol. I (Frankfurt, 1961), 282–3.

47 On the Venus Genetrix episode, see Suet. *Caes.* 78 and Nic. Dam. 22. See Cic. *Phil.* 2.87 and Gelzer, *Caesar: Politician and Statesman*, 320, n. 3, concerning the assumption of the title *dictator perpetuus*.

48 See above, ch.4, p.24. F. Münzer, *Römische Adelsparteien und Adelsfamilien* (Stuttgart, 1920), 157–9 and 168, n. 1, sees a relationship between the Aemilii and Iunii in general, as well as one between the Aemilii Lepidi and Iunii Bruti in particular. For some examples of these ties, see *AL*, 9, 22–4, 62, 108–9, 112, 139, 146, and 194.

49 See my article 'The Meetings of the Roman Senate on the Capitoline,' *L'Antiquité Classique* 55 (1986), 333–40.

50 Suet. *Caes.* 79; Dio 44.15.3–4; Plut. *Caes.* 60.1, 64.2.

51 Dio 44.19.1; Nic. Dam. 27.105; see Huzar, *Mark Antony*, 79.

52 Dio 44.11.1–2; App. *BC* 2.114; Plut. *Ant.* 13.2, *Brut.* 18.2–3; Cic. *Phil.* 2.34; Nic. Dam. 25. Brutus would very probably also have objected to Lepidus' proposed murder on personal grounds, given Brutus' later efforts to intervene with Cicero on the behalf of his brother-in-law and his nephews: see below, ch. 6, n. 90.

53 Suet. *Caes.* 87; Plut. *Caes.* 63.4; App. *BC* 2.115.

6 PONTIFEX MAXIMUS – AND *HOSTIS PUBLICUS*

1 Plut. *Caes.* 67.2.

2 Dio 44.19.2.

3 App. *BC* 2.118.

4 Ibid. See Dio 42.32 and App. *BC* 2.92 for a recent precedent for Lepidus' action (Antony as *magister equitum* in 47 sanctioned by the Senate to use troops in the city to maintain order). Although there may have been additional military units in the vicinity of Rome that were intended to go with Caesar on the Parthian expedition, it seems likely that Lepidus' legion stationed on the Tiber island would have remained behind, at the disposal of the *magister equitum*, to keep the city peaceful. See J. Malitz, 'Caesars Partherkrieg,' *Historia* 33 (1984), 21–59, esp. 44 and n. 117.

5 Dio 44.22.2. See the comments of Léonie Hayne, 'Lepidus' Role after the Ides of March', *Acta Classica* 14 (1971), 109–17.
6 Cic. *Att.* 14.10. Cicero was, of course, irritated that Antony had seized the initiative by summoning the Senate to the temple of Tellus on the 17th. The precise timing of the assassination may have been determined by more than Caesar's impending departure for Parthia and the rumored announcement of a Sibylline oracle supporting Caesar's kingship (Suet. *Caes.* 80.4). The Ides of March had been the traditional beginning of the consular year until 153 BC and an act of tyrannicide on that particular day was especially symbolic of the eagerly anticipated return to the government of the pre-Gracchan Republic. On the significance of Senate meetings *in Capitolio*, see my article, 'The Meetings of the Roman Senate on the Capitoline,' *L'Antiquité Classique* 55 (1986), 333–40.
7 App. *BC* 2.119; Suet. *Caes.* 82.4.
8 Dio 44.22.2; Zon. 10.12.
9 Nic. Dam. 27; App. *BC* 2.123–4; Dio 44.34.4–7.
10 App. *BC* 2.126; Dio 44.22.3; Zon. 10.12; on Cinna, see T.R.S. Broughton, *The Magistrates of the Roman Republic* (3 vols, New York, 1951–2, Atlanta, 1986 Supplement), vol. II, 320–1.
11 App. *BC* 2.127–32.
12 Ibid., 132–5; Dio 44.22.3–34.2; Vell. Pat. 2.58.4.
13 App. *BC* 2.142; Dio 44.34.7; Plut. *Ant.* 14.1, *Brut.* 19.2; Livy *Per.* 116; Zon. 10.12.
14 App. *BC* 2.143–8.
15 Dio 44.53.6; Cic. *Fam.* 12.2.2; App. *BC* 5.93; P. von Rohden, 'Aemilius 73' in Pauly–Wissowa, *Realencyclopädie* 1a (Stuttgart, 1893), 560–1.
16 Dio 44.5.3.
17 Dio 44.53.6–7; see L.R. Taylor, 'The Election of the Pontifex Maximus in the Late Republic', *Classical Philology* 37 (1942), 421–4. See also Léonie Hayne's account ('Lepidus' Role', 114–15). Her statement that 'Antony *as a pontifex* [italics mine] could have secured the office for himself' is probably the result either of confusion between Antony and his brother, C. Antonius, who was a pontifex or of simply following Dio. See also Richard D. Draper, 'The Role of the Pontifex Maximus and its Influence in Roman Religion and Politics' (Diss., Brigham Young University, 1988), 344–7, and Paul Jal, 'La propagande religieuse à Rome au cours des guerres civiles de la fin de la république,' *L'Antiquité Classique* 30 (1961), 395–414, esp. 403–4.
18 Cic. *Fam.* 16.23.2; see L.R. Taylor, 'Caesar's Colleagues in the Pontifical College,' *American Journal of Philology* 63 (1942), 385–412, esp. 411–12.
19 Livy *Per.* 117; *Res Gestae* 10; Vell. Pat. 2.63.1; App. *BC* 2.132.
20 Cic. *Att.* 14.7.1.
21 Ibid., 8.1.
22 Ibid., 5.1; see Hayne, 'Lepidus' Role,' 116.
23 Dio 44.53.7.
24 The reading of Cic. *Att.* 16.5.4 to indicate that Cicero mentioned in July Lepidus' selection of an inauguration day (see Taylor, 'Election,' 424 and n. 15, and Hayne, 'Lepidus' Role', 114, n. 33) is questionable.

See D.R. Shackleton Bailey, *Cicero's Letters to Atticus* (Cambridge, 1967) vol. VI, 284. The *Lepidianis feriis* mentioned by Cicero on November 5 (Cic. *Att.* 16.11.8) make more sense as the public celebration of Lepidus' *supplicatio* for his negotiation of peace with Sextus Pompey. It is true that the reference comes in a letter of November 5, while the *supplicatio* vote in the Senate was not taken until 28 November, but the agreement had taken place around the end of June and Balbus may simply have indicated to Cicero at the beginning of November that the celebration was planned for the end of the month. It is also possible, of course, that the *feriae* recognized Lepidus' chief priesthood (see Taylor, 'Election,' 424, n. 15, citing Cic. *Phil.* 3.23), but if so Lepidus does not appear to have been around to enjoy the festivities and the official induction probably still took place earlier in the year. F. Münzer, *Römische Adelsparteien und Adelsfamilien* (Stuttgart, 1920), 361, selected the latter part of May for Lepidus' inauguration, but does not indicate why he preferred this date.

25 Cic. *Att.* 15.29.
26 Dio 45.9.4.
27 App. *BC* 3.4, 4.94.
28 Dio 45.10.6.
29 Cic. *Att.* 15.29, 16.1.4.
30 Cic. *Phil.* 3.20–4.
31 Cic. *Att.* 16.11.
32 Cic. *Phil.* 5.38–41, 13.8.; Dio 46.51.4.
33 Cic. *Fam.* 10.34a and 35 (prescripts); App. *BC* 4.31; Broughton, *Magistrates* II 326; *CIL* 1, p. 461, 1.1, p. 50; Degrassi, *I.I.*, vol. XIII, 567.
34 See ch. 4, n. 40 above.
35 See *AL*, 348–50. On Antibes, see Jean Arazi, *Histoire de la ville d'Antibes* (Paris, 1880), esp. 71–2.
36 App. *BC* 3.27–48; Dio 45, 5–15; see W.E. Heitland, *The Roman Republic* (3 vols, Cambridge, 1909), vol. III, 385–93.
37 App. *BC* 3.49.
38 Cic. *Phil.* 5.12; App. *BC* 3.50–63; Dio 46.29.4–6.
39 Cic. *Phil.* 3.23.
40 Ibid., 5.38–40.
41 Ibid., 40–1.
42 Cic. *Fam.* 10.27.
43 Ibid., 31.
44 Cic. *Phil.* 13.7–17, 43, 49–50; on the left-overs: *Fam.* 10.28 and 12.4. Hermann Bengtson, in 'Untersuchungen zum mutinensischen Krieg,' *Kleine Schriften zur alten Geschichte* (Munich, 1974), 479–531, esp. 521–2, says that the Senate missed an irretrievable opportunity to draw back from reopening the Civil War when on March 30 it failed to respond positively to Lepidus' letter advocating a peaceful solution with Mark Antony and instead, on the advice of Cicero, pressed forward with the campaign around Mutina.
45 Cic. *Ad Brut.* 3.1 (Loeb translation by M. Cary). See above, ch.1, p.1.
46 App. *BC* 3.65–70; Dio 46.37–8; Cic. *Fam.* 10.30.1 and 10.34.2.
47 App. *BC* 3.71–2.

48 Ibid., 74; Dio 46.39.3; Cic. *Phil.* 14.29, 37.
49 App. *BC* 3.74;. Dio 46.39–41.
50 Cic. *Fam.* 10.34.2; Dio 46.51.1.
51 Dio 46.50.3–6. Plancus generally receives full credit for founding Lyons. Lepidus was close enough geographically to have assisted him initially, as the Senate had ordered, but he probably did not have enough time to be involved and, in any case, Plancus completed the operation. On Plancus, see Emile Jullien, *Le Fondateur de Lyon: Histoire de L. Munatius Plancus* (Paris, 1892); Amable Audin, *César et Plancus à Lyon* (Lyons, 1951); and the forthcoming monograph by Thomas Watson. Hermann Bengtson, in 'Die letzten Monate der römischen Senatsherrschaft,' *Kleine Schriften* (Munich, 1974), 532–48, esp. 542–3, emphasizes the weakness of the Senate in deciding to send Lepidus to found a colony after he had already joined Antony. Paul Stein, *Die Senatssitzungen der Ciceronischen Zeit (68–43)* (Diss., Münster, 1930), 93, also lists the events in that order, but Dio's narrative (46.50.3–6) ties the Senate's decision in after Silanus' help to Antony at Forum Gallorum and before his account of the merger between Antony and Lepidus. See the summary of arguments in Julien Guey, 'A propos de la fondation de Lyon,' *Bulletin de la Societé Nationale des Antiquaires de France* (1959), 129–73.
52 Cic. *Fam.* 11.20.1. 'Tollendum' could be interpreted as either 'elevated' or 'destroyed' and the latter meaning was not lost on Octavian. See D.R. Shackleton Bailey's commentary in *Cicero: Epistulae ad Familiares*, vol. II (Cambridge, 1977), 541, and the interpretations in Vell. Pat. 2.62.6 and Suet. *Aug.* 12.1. See also Paul MacKendrick, *The Philosophical Books of Cicero* (New York, 1989), 249.
53 Cic. *Fam.* 10.9, 11, and 14.
54 Ibid., 11.9.
55 Ibid., 11.11, see also 10.
56 Ibid., 10.15.
57 Ibid., 17–18 and 21.
58 Ibid., 34.
59 Ibid., 20, 11.14 and 23.
60 Ibid., 10.33.
61 Ibid., 11.13a.3.
62 Ibid., 10.16.1.
63 On Ventidius, see Eleanor G. Huzar, *Mark Antony: A Biography* (Minneapolis, 1978), 109, 111; James E. Seaver, 'Publius Vendidius, Neglected Roman Military Hero', *Classical Journal* 47 (1952), 275–280, 300; and Hans Gundel, 'Ventidius 5 in Pauly–Wissowa, *Realencyclopädie* 8A.I (Stuttgart, 1955), 795–816.
64 App. *BC* 3.83.
65 Cic. *Fam.* 10.17.1.
66 Vell. Pat. 2.63.1; Plut. *Ant.* 18.1; App. BC. 3.83.
67 Dio 46.51.1.
68 App. BC 3.83–4.
69 Dio 46.51.3–4; Vell. Pat. 2.63.2. On Laterensis, see Friedrich Münzer, ('Iuventius 16') in Pauly–Wissowa, *Realencyclopädie* 10.2 (Stuttgart, 1919), 1365–7.

70 Vell. Pat. 2.63.1.
71 Plut. *Ant.* 18.1–3.
72 Cic. *Fam.* 10.35. Bengtson, 'Untersuchungen,' 526–31, emphasizes Lepidus' use of the words 'misericordia' and 'pax' in his letter of May 30 to the Senate explaining his merger with Antony and says that Lepidus represented the primary concern of the majority of citizens and soldiers alike for peace, while Cicero responded with his condemnation of Lepidus out of an inflexible desire for revenge. For a discussion of the preference of many of the veteran soldiers for peace, see Helga Botermann's section on the 'pietas-Motiv' in *Die Soldaten und die römische Politik in der Zeit von Caesars Tod bis zur Begründung des zweiten Triumvirats* (Munich, 1968), 275–9. David. F. Epstein, in *Personal Enmity in Roman Politics, 218–43 B.C.* (New York, 1987), 69, points out that Lepidus implies in his letter that senatorial objections to his alliance with Antony could only result from *inimicitiae*. See also Gabriela Pianko, 'Korespondenci Cycerona: Marek Emiliusz Lepidus,' *Meander* 26 (1971), 32–42.
73 Eutrop. 7.2; Livy *Per.* 119.
74 Dio 46.51.2.
75 App. *BC* 3.84; Cic. *Fam.* 10.15.2; see Botermann, *Die Soldaten*, 197, 200; P.A. Brunt, *Italian Manpower* (Oxford, 1971), 478–9; and W.C. Schmitthenner, 'The Armies of the Triumviral Period' (Diss., Oxford, 1958), 37.
76 Dio 46.51.4; Vell. Pat. 2.64.4; App. *BC* 3.96; Cic. *Fam.* 12.10.1; Broughton, *Magistrates* II, 341.
77 Cic. *Fam.* 10.23.
78 Cic. *Ad Brut.* 3.1, 18.2; 22.1–2, 24.4, and 24.9–10. See above, ch.1, p.1. On Cicero's language and Roman political invective in general, see P. Jal, '"Hostis (publicus)" dans la littérature latine de la fin de la république,' *Revue des Etudes Anciennes* 65 (1963), 53–79; J. Roger Dunkle, 'The Greek Tyrant and Roman Political Invective of the Late Republic,' *Transactions of the American Philological Association* 98 (1967), 151–71; and André Oltramare, *Les Origines de la diatribe romaine* (Lausanne, 1926). See also P. Jal, *La Guerre Civile à Rome, Etude littéraire et morale* (Paris, 1963), esp. 349–50 on Cicero's language. This book is worth consulting in general on the period of the civil wars.
79 Cic. *Off.* 1.55–6 and 66, 3.13, 17–18, 26, and 38. For additional discussion of Cicero's views on individual obligations to the state, see Harry G. Edinger's introduction to his edition of Cicero, *De Officiis/On Duties* (New York, 1974), pp. ix–xxix; Hubert A. Holden's introduction and commentary on *Cicero: De Officiis* (Cambridge, 1899); MacKendrick, *Philosophical Books*, esp. 232–57; James M. May, *Trials of Character* (Chapel Hill, 1988), esp. 154–61; Torsten Petersson, *Cicero: A Biography* (New York, 1919), esp. 575–80; R. Syme, *The Roman Revolution* (Oxford, 1939), esp. 144–6; Neal Wood, *Cicero's Social and Political Thought* (Berkeley, 1988), esp. 74–8; P. Fedeli, 'Il "de officiis" di Cicerone' in *ANRW* I.4 (1973), 357–427; E. Gabba, 'Per un' interpretazione politica del *De Officiis* di Cicerone', *Lincei – Rendiconti Morali* 34 (1979), 117–41; W.K. Lacey, 'Boni atque Improbi', *Greece and Rome* 17 (1970),

3–16; T.N. Mitchell, 'Cicero on the Moral Crisis of the Late Republic', *Hermathena* 136 (1984), 21–41.

80 Cic. *Off.* 1.57, 64–5, 68, and 84, 3.21, 26, 37, 82, and 115. See also Cicero's warning to Plancus in *Fam.* 10.6.

81 Cic. *Off.* 3.83.

82 Ibid., 60.

83 Ibid., 36–7.

84 Cic. *Fam.* 12.8–9, *ad Brut.* 18.2. On the actions of Plancus and Lepidus in 43, see the different interpretations of C. Bardt, 'Plancus und Lepidus im mutinensischen Kriege', *Hermes* 44 (1909), 574–93, esp. the map on p. 579 and 591–2; W. Sternkopf, 'Plancus, Lepidus und Laterensis im Mai 43', *Hermes* 45 (1910), 250–300; and Bengtson, 'Untersuchungen.' See also Ludwig Holzapfel, 'Zur Geschichte des mutinensischen Krieges,' *Jahrbuch für Classische Philologie* 149 (1894), 400–5.

85 App. *BC* 3.80–1.

86 Dio 46.41.5 and 51.2; Livy *Per.* 119.

87 Dio 46.42; App. *BC* 3.82.

88 App. *BC* 3.80–94; Dio 46.43–6.

89 Cic. *Fam.* 12.10, *ad Brut*, 23.2, 24.4, 9–10, and 12.

90 Cic. *ad Brut.* 21.1, 22.1–2, 24.2, 24.9–10, and 24.12–13. On the question of *hostis publicus* declarations, see Jal, 'Hostis (publicus)', 53–79; Jurgen Baron Ungern-Sternberg von Purkel, *Untersuchungen zum spätrepublikanischen Notstandsrecht* (Munich, 1970).

91 Cic. *ad Brut.* 23.2, *Fam.* 10.24.6, 12.8.1, and 9.2.

92 Vell. Pat. 2.65.1.

93 App. *BC* 3.94–5; Dio 46.47–9.

94 App. *BC* 3.96; Dio 46.50.1 and 52.

95 App. *BC* 3.97–8; Dio 46.53.

7 THE SECOND TRIUMVIRATE: ONE-THIRD OF THE WORLD

1 Dio 46.54.

2 Eutrop. 7.2; App. *BC* 4.2; Livy *Per.* 119; Oros. 6.18.

3 Dio 46.51.2 and 52.1–2.

4 Cic. *Fam.* 12.5.2. See E. Badian, *Foreign Clientelae* (Oxford, 1958), 275–8.

5 App. *BC* 4.2.

6 Ibid; Dio 46.55.1–2; Plut. *Ant.* 19.1, *Cic.* 46.2–4; Florus 2.6.1–3; Suet. *Aug.* 96.1. See Viktor Gardthausen, *Augustus und seine Zeit* (6 vols, Leipzig, 1891) vol. 1.1, 129.

7 Dio 46.55–6.1; App. *BC* 4.2–3. See F. Millar, 'Triumvirate and Principate,' *Journal of Roman Studies* 63 (1973), 50–67.

8 E. Eleanor G. Huzar, *Mark Antony: A Biography* (Minneapolis, 1978), 116–17.

9 Dio 46.55–6.1; App. *BC* 4.2–3.

10 App. *BC* 4.3.

11 Dio 47.1.

12 Dio 45.17.5–7; Obseq. 68.

13 App. *BC* 4.6.

14 Ibid., 7.

15 Ibid., 7. On the proscriptions in general, see François Hinard, *Les Proscriptions de la Rome républicaine* (Rome, 1985); Ronald Syme, *Roman Revolution* (Oxford, 1939), 187–201; Hermann Bengtson, *Zu den Proskriptionen der Triumvirn* (Munich, 1972); and Alain Gowing, 'The Triumviral Period in Appian and Cassius Dio' (Diss., Bryn Mawr, 1988), 334 ff.

16 Livy *Per.* 120; Florus 2.6.3; Oros. 6.18; Dio 47.3.2–4.

17 App. *BC* 4.12.

18 Ibid., and 37; Dio 47.6.3; see also Plut. *Cic.* 46.4; Vell. Pat. 2.67.3–4; Livy *Per.* 120; Florus 2.6.4; Oros. 6.18.

19 Plut. *Ant.* 19.2–3. See Kenneth Scott, 'The Political Propaganda of 44–30 B.C.' *Memoirs of the American Academy in Rome* 11 (1933), 7–49, esp. 19, n. 5.

20 Cic. *Att.* 14.8.1, *Phil.* 13.8; Dio 47.8.1. On the other hand, Cic. *ad Brut.* 2.2 lends support to the view that Lepidus was hostile to Paullus. See Hinard, *Proscriptions*, 419–21.

21 App. *BC* 4.7–11; Dio 47.6.4–6. Appian's decree lists the triumvirs' names in the order of Lepidus, Antony, and Octavian. R.E.A. Palmer, in 'Octavian's First Attempt to Restore the Constitution (36 B.C.),' *Athenaeum* 56 (1978), 315–28, esp. 315–16, suggests that this order reflects the priority of their consulships and their ages. This decree could have been issued in 42 and Lepidus' first position could also have reflected his incumbency in the consulship. On this decree, see also Ernesto Trilla Millás, 'Aspectos menos conocidos del triunvirato,' *Cuadernos de Filología Clásica* 14 (1978), 329–88, esp. 348–53; Luciano Canfora, 'Proscrizioni e dissesto sociale nella repubblica Romana,' *Klio* 62 (1980), 425–37, esp. 430–4; and the legalistic analysis of Sibylle Bolla, *Aus römichem und bürgerlichem Erbrecht* (Vienna, 1950), 25–34.

22 App. *BC* 4.12–30; Dio 47.9–13.

23 App. *BC* 4.36–51.

24 Ibid., 5.

25 See Hinard, *Proscriptions*, esp. 259–318. Hinard provides on pp. 415–552 a detailed catalogue of known individuals who were proscribed; see also the older list in Heinrich Kloevekorn, *De Proscriptionibus a. a. Chr. n. 43 a M. Antonio, M. Aemilio Lepido, C. Julio Caesare Octaviano Triumviris Factis* (Diss., Königsberg, 1891), 31 ff.

26 App. *BC* 4.5.

27 Ibid., 31; Dio 47.14.5 and 17.3–5.

28 App. *BC* 4.32–4.

29 Dio 47.14.1–2.

30 Ibid., 16.5 and 16–17 in general.

31 Plut. *Ant.* 21.3.

32 Dio 47.16.5–17.1; see also T. Frank, *An Economic Survey of Ancient Rome* (6 vols, Baltimore, 1933), vol. I, 340; W.E. Heitland, *The Roman Republic* (3 vols, Cambridge, 1909), vol. III, 418.

33 Alain M. Gowing argues in 'Lepidus' Role in the Proscriptions of 43/42 BC' (a paper he presented at the annual meeting of the American

Philological Association in 1990), 8–9, that the story of Lepidus' abusive treatment of Turia 'is orchestrated and exaggerated to emphasize Octavian's own *clementia* by contrasting it with the vile behavior of Lepidus' and that it was a 'form of public humiliation' for Lepidus. Gowing goes on to describe the account as 'precisely the type of slander so characteristic of a historiographical tradition that sought to exculpate Octavian and incriminate his partners.' See Erik Wistrand, *The So-called Lavdatio Turiae* (Göteborg, 1976), esp. 47–9. The text and English translation are included; the relevant portion of the text is on pp. 25–7 (2.11–21). See also Marcel Durry, *Eloge funèbre d'une matrone romaine* (Paris, 1950); Arthur E. Gordon, 'Who's Who in the *Laudatio Turiae*', *Epigraphica* 39 (1977), 7–12; Wilhelm Kierdorf, *Laudatio Funebris* (Meisenheim am Glan, 1980); Nicholas Horsfall, 'Some Problems in the "Laudatio Turiae",' *Bulletin of the Institute of Classical Studies* 30 (1983), 85–98; W. Warde Fowler, *Social Life at Rome in the Age of Cicero* (London, 1908), 158–67; and R.S. Conway, 'New Light on Old Authors,' *Discovery* (1921), 261–5. An abbreviated translation of the text is also available as selection 183 in N. Lewis and M. Reinhold, *Roman Civilization Sourcebook I: The Republic* (New York, 1951), 484–7.

34 Vell. Pat. 2.66.1; Plut. *Cic.* 46.2–4, *Brut.* 27.5; Eutrop. 7.2; Suet. *Aug.* 27. Florus (2.16.6.2) says that Lepidus' greed for riches motivated his involvement in the proscriptions, but he is trying here to separate Lepidus and Antony from Octavian's 'nobler' reasons for participating. Hermann Bengtson, 'Untersuchungen zum mutinenischen Krieg,' *Kleine schriften zur alten Geschichte* (Munich, 1974), 530, who defends Lepidus's character at various other crucial points, is critical of his conduct during the proscriptions and correctly sees this activity as a serious blot on the triumvir's reputation. I would only add that a large part of this image comes from the proscription of Lepidus' brother, which seems to have been essentially a 'media event' and did not result in death.

35 *CIL* I, p. 461. I.l, p. 50; A. Degrassi, *I.I.* 13.1, 567.

36 Vell. Pat. 2.67.3–4. Such vulgar chants were apparently a customary feature of the general's triumph and should not be read as a sign that the soldiers lacked respect for Lepidus and Plancus. On Caesar's Gallic triumph, see Suet. *Div. Iul.* 49.4 and 51. See A.J. Woodman's comments in *Velleius Paterculus: the Caesarian and Augustan Narrative* (Cambridge, 1983), 155, and J.E. Stambaugh, *The Ancient Roman City* (Baltimore, 1988), 239.

37 App. *BC* 4.31.

38 Suet. *Aug.* 27.2. See Scott, 'Political Propaganda,' 20 n. 1; Hinard, *Proscriptions*, 310.

39 Dio 47.14.4; *CIL* X.6087; T.R.S. Broughton, *The Magistrates of the Roman Republic* (3 vols, New York, 1951–2, Atlanta, 1986 Supplement), vol. II, 357.

40 Theodore V. Buttrey, Jr. *The Triumviral Portrait Gold of the Quattuorviri Monetales of 42 B.C.* (ANS Numismatic Notes and Monographs no. 137, New York, 1956), 8–10 and n. 41. Michael Crawford in *Roman Republican Coinage* (Cambridge, 1974), 503 and 510 suggests a closely

related goddess, Fortuna, but Buttrey's inscriptional evidence makes his argument stronger.

41 Plut. *Rom.* 2.3.

42 For a more detailed analysis of Lepidus' triumviral cointypes, see *AL*, 336–53. See also Buttrey, *Triumviral Portrait Gold*, and Crawford, *Roman Republican Coinage* (above), Peter Wallman, *Münzpropaganda in den Anfangen des zweiten Triumvirats* (Bochum, 1977), esp. 23–5; and Leslaw Morawiecki, *Political Propaganda in the Coinage of the Late Roman Republic* (Warsaw, 1983). The two triumvirs also issued edicts recorded in inscriptions that omitted Lepidus' name; see Joyce Reynolds, *Aphrodisias and Rome* (London, 1982), 40 and 49.

43 Dio 47.18–19 and 53.23.2; Broughton, *Magistrates* II, 358. See above, ch. 4, pp. 34–5 (on Saepta Iulia). Robert E.A. Palmer tries to link up Vitruvius and Mamurra through Lepidus and the construction of the Saepta Iulia in 'On the Track of the Ignoble,' *Athenaeum* 61 (1983), 343–61, esp. 347–51.

44 Dio 47.15.4. See Juv. 6.528–9; Mart. 2.14.7; Platner–Ashby, *Topographical Dictionary* (London, 1929) 283–4; E. Nash, *Pictorial Dictionary of Ancient Rome*, vol. II (New York, 1968), 510–11; Peter Tschudin, *Isis in Rom* (Aarau, 1962), esp. 16–17; R.E. Witt, *Isis in the Graeco-Roman World* (Ithaca, 1971), 223.

45 Dio 40.47 and 42.26.2. On Paullus' role in the destruction of Isis' temple in 50 BC, see Val. Max. 1.4 and Witt, *Isis* 223.

46 Plut. *Ant.* 21.4; Eutrop. 7.3; Flor. 2.7.5; App. *BC* 4.3; Dio 46.56.1 and 47.20.1.

47 Salvatore Riccobono, *Fontes Iuris Romani Anteiustiniani*, (3 vols, Florence, 1941–3) vol. I, 308–15 (item 55); Broughton *Magistrates* II, 357.

48 App. *BC* 4.85–138; Dio 47.36–49; Broughton, *Magistrates* II, 358.

49 Dio 48.1–2 and 22.2.

50 App. *BC* 5.3; Broughton, *Magistrates* II, 358.

51 Dio 48.2.

52 Ibid., 3.

53 App. *BC* 5.12–19; Dio 48.4–8; Huzar, *Mark Antony*, 131–3; E. Gabba, 'The Perusine War and Triumviral Italy,' *Harvard Studies in Classical Philology* 75 (1971), 139–60, esp. 146–51; Heitland *Republic* III, 426–9. On Lucius Antony's aims, see J.-M. Roddaz, 'Lucius Antonius,' *Historia* 37 (1988), 317–46, esp. 344–6.

54 App. *BC* 5.12.

55 Dio 48.13.3–4; App. *BC* 5.20–1; Livy *Per.* 125; Huzar, *Mark Antony*, 133; Broughton, *Magistrates* II, 371.

56 App. *BC* 5.29–30.

57 Dio 48. 13.5–14; App. *BC* 5.32–49.

58 App. *BC* 5.53; Dio 48.20.4.

59 Dio 48.22–23.

60 App. *BC* 5.75. Palmer, 'Track of the Ignoble,' 349, suggests that Lepidus continued the rewards to the followers of P. Sittius that Caesar and T. Sextius had initiated.

61 App. *BC* 5.65; Dio 48.28–9; Plut. *Ant.* 30.3–4; Broughton, *Magistrates* II, 380.

62 J. Guey and A. Pernette, 'Lépide à Thàbraca', *Karthago* 9 (1958), 79–89; the inscription is pictured on 89 (plate I). See also J. Guey, 'Dédicace à Lépide', *Bulletin de la Société Nationale des Antiquaires de France* (1957) [1959], 186–7 and pl. XV, 1. On Lepidus' third recognition as *imperator*, see Leonhard Schumacher, 'Die imperatorischen Akklamationen der Triumvirn und die Auspicia des Augustus,' *Historia* 34 (1985), 191–222, esp. 202. E. Badian suggests that, despite the evidence of the Thabraca inscription and the Capitoline *fasti*, Lepidus may have losts his status as a triumvir in the renewal of powers at Tarentum in 37 BC ('M. Lepidus and the Second Triumvirate,' *Arctos* 25 (1991), 5–16).

63 Juv. *Sat.* 10.54–72. See Guey and Pernette, 'Lépide', 79–89, and Leo Teutsch, *Das Städtewesen in Nordafrika* (Berlin, 1962), 42–3, 128–9, and 162–3. Teutsch in ns. 226–7 cites evidence suggesting that the inscription may have been moved to Thabraca from other sites, but if true this would not weaken the importance of the inscription as a testimonial to Lepidus. It would, however, diminish support for the argument that Thabraca was one of Lepidus' main bases in Africa. Marcello Gaggiotti, in 'L'importazione del marmo numidico a Roma in epoca tardo-repubblicana', *L'Africa Romana: Atti del IV convegno di studio Sassari, 12–14 dicembre 1986* (Sassari, 1987), 201–13, connects the Aemilii Lepidi with support of the Numidian marble trade from the early second century on and sees the Thabraca inscription as an expression of thanks to their current patron from the citizens of the port city from which Numidian marble was shipped to Italy.

64 Dio 52.43.1.

65 Tertullian, *De Pallio* 1.1; Auguste Audollent, *Carthage romaine* (Paris, 1901), 44–7, esp. 46.

66 Yvan Debbasch, 'Colonia Julia Carthago; la vie et les institutions municipales de la Carthage Romaine', *Revue Historique de Droit Français et Etranger* 31 (1953), 30–53, esp. 38–9; Audollent, *Carthage* 44–5.

67 On Lepidus' coins attributed to his governorship of Africa, see *AL*, 339–41 and 352–3; Michael Grant, *From Imperium to Auctoritas* (Cambridge, 1946), 50–1. Rodolfo Martini, in 'Un probabile ritratto di M. Aemilius Lepidus su monete del secondo triumvirato emesse a Carthago,' *Rivista Italiana di Numismatica e Scienze Affini* 84 (1982), 141–76, has suggested that a coin that Grant, *From Imperium* (149–50), attributes to Karalis in Sardinia is actually a piece that Lepidus issued in Carthage, with portraits of Lepidus and Octavian backed by a representation of the temple of Venus.

68 *CIL* X.6104; T.R.S. Broughton, *The Romanization of Africa Proconsularis* (Baltimore, 1929), 61–2 and n. 92.

69 *CIL* VIII.26255; Stéphane Gsell, *Histoire Ancienne de l'Afrique du Nord*, vol. 8 (Paris, 1928), 194–6. See Duncan Fishwick and Brent D. Shaw, 'The Formation of Africa Proconsularis,' *Hermes* 105 (1977), 369–80; it is not clear why the authors, citing Gsell, seem to think that Lepidus' activities in Carthage took place before he became pontifex maximus (p. 372). See also Timothy Barnes, *Tertullian* (Oxford, 1971), 86. For a detailed discussion of the cult, see Duncan Fishwick and Brent D. Shaw, 'The Era of the Cereres,' *Historia* 27 (1978), 343–54.

70 François Bertrandy, 'Thibilis (Announa), de Juba Ier au triumvir M. Aemilius Lepidus,' *Karthago* 19 (1977–78) [1980], 87–106, esp. 100–6. P. Salama, 'La Colonie de Rusguniae d'après les inscriptions', in *Revue Africaine* 94 (1955), 5–52, esp. 34–47, has connected Lepidus to the founding of the colony of Rusguniae (Cap Matifou, near Algiers) because the full name of the colony contained the word *Pontif[icensis]* or *Pontif[icalis]*. Teutsch, *Städtewesen*, 199–200, says that Salama suggested that Lepidus was the founder of the colony, but this is a misinterpretation. Salama dates the founding to 33–27 and ties Lepidus in as commander of Legio VIIII Gemella, whose veterans Octavian was settling in Rusguniae. Salama (44–7) hypothesizes that the colony's name contained references to the legion, the pontifex maximus Lepidus, its former commander, and to Octavian's clemency. Lepidus could be the founder of Rusguniae and the 'Pontif.' in the original name seems to support that, but the colony is much farther west than the others associated with Lepidus. I prefer to see the 'CL' as a reference to 'classis,' since Rusguniae is a port city, rather than to Octavian's 'clementia' and I do not believe Octavian would have tolerated naming a colony after Lepidus after 36, even in an indirect reference to his pontifical status. If Lepidus founded it, it must have taken place by 36 BC. Paul MacKendrick, *The North African Stones Speak* (Chapel Hill, 1980), 205, calls Rusguniae 'a colony of Augustus' obscure and cruel colleague Lepidus,' but he cites no source. His bibliography includes the Salama article and Paul-Albert Fevrier's entry on Rusguniae in *Princeton Encyclopedia of Classical Sites* (Princeton, 1976), 776, which says the colony was founded 'perhaps by Lepidus.'

71 App. *BC* 5.67–8; Dio 48.34–5.

72 App. *BC* 5.71.

73 Ibid., 69–74; Dio 48.36–8; Broughton, *Magistrates* II, 386–7.

74 App. *BC* 5.78–92; Dio 48.45.4–49.1; Broughton, *Magistrates* II, 390–1.

75 App. *BC* 5.93–5; Dio 48.49.2 and 54; Broughton, *Magistrates* II, 396.

76 Dio 49.1.1; App. *BC* 5.97. On the Sicilian war of 36 BC, see the detailed comparison of the accounts of Appian and Dio Cassius in Gowing, 'The Triumviral Period', esp. 187–92; see also Léonie Hayne, 'The Defeat of Lepidus in 36 B.C.,' *Acta Classica* 17 (1974), 59–65; J. Melber, 'Dio Cassius über die letzten Kämpfe gegen Sext. Pompejus, 36 v.Chr.', in *Abhandlungen aus dem Gebiet der klassischen Altertums-Wissenschaft – Wilhelm von Christ zum sechzigsten Geburtstag* (Munich, 1891), 211–36. On the reasons for identifying Appian's Plenius as L. Plinius Rufus, see H. Dessau, *Inscriptiones Latinne Selectae* (3 vols in 5, Berlin, 1892–1916) 8891; Broughton, *Magistrates* II, 405; Badian, 'M. Lepidus,' 11, n.13.

77 App. *BC* 5.98.

78 Vell. Pat. 2.80.1.

79 App. *BC* 5.98; Dio 49.8.1–2; on his ancestor's defense of Lilybaeum, see Livy 21.49–51.

80 App. *BC* 5.98–102; Dio 49.1.3–5.

81 App. *BC* 5.103–4.

82 Dio 49.2–8.2; App. *BC* 5.105–12.

83 App. *BC* 5.116–17; Dio 49.8.3.

84 Dio 49.8.3–4; Zonaras 10.25.
85 Dio 49.8.5–11.1; App. *BC* 5.118–22. See Moses Hadas, *Sextus Pompey* (New York, 1930); Huzar, *Mark Antony*, 144–6; Shelley C. Stone, 'Sextus Pompey, Octavian and Sicily,' *American Journal of Archaeology* 87 (1983), 11–22; and Catherine Rubincam, 'The Chronology of the Punishment and Reconstruction of Sicily by Octavian/Augustus', *American Journal of Archaeology* 89 (1985), 521–2.
86 App. *BC* 5.122; for another example of the dissent caused by the integration of defeated enemy troops, see Nic. Dam. 19 (63). See also F.A. Wright, *Marcus Agrippa: Organizer of Victory* (New York, 1937), 79.
87 Dio 49.11.2.
88 On the number of Lepidus' legions, see App. *BC* 5.123 and P.A. Brunt, *Italian Manpower* (Oxford, 1971), 499, 688, 699.
89 App. *BC* 5.123; Dio 49.11.2–4; Zon. 10.25; Vell. Pat. 2.80.1–3; Suet. *Aug.* 16.4; Livy *Per.* 129; Oros. 6.18. See Badian, 'M. Lepidus', esp. 10–13.
90 App. *BC* 5.123.
91 Vell. Pat. 2.80.3–4.
92 See Jean-Michel Roddaz, *Marcus Agrippa* (Rome, 1984), 132–3 on Dio's account.
93 App. *BC* 5.124–6.
94 Dio 49.11.3–4 and 12.1–3.
95 Oros. 5.18.
96 Palmer, 'Octavian's First Attempt,' 319 and n. 25; see also Dessau, *Inscriptiones Latinae Selectae* (3 vols, Berlin, 1892–1916), vol. I, 30. 108. *CIL* IX.4192, X.8375; Degrassi, *I.I.* 13.1, 86, 569 and 13.2, 279–80, 505–6; Broughton, *Magistrates* II, 400.
97 Cic. *Att.* 16.8.
98 App. *BC* 5.127–8; Suet. *Div. Iul.* 69–70; see P. Jal, 'Le "soldat des Guerres Civiles" à Rome à la fin de la République et au debut de l'Empire,' *Pallas* 11 (1962), 7–27, esp. 13–16 and the numerous examples he cites of desertions; William Stuart Messer, 'Mutiny in the Roman Army: The Republic,' *Classical Philology* 15 (1920), 158–75, esp. 173 and notes; Heribert Aigner, *Die Soldaten als Machtfaktor in der Ausgehenden römischen Republik* (Innsbruck, 1974), esp. 71–87 and endnotes. See Vell. Pat. 2.25.2–3 on the consul Scipio Asiaticus' army deserting to Sulla in 83 BC and Jal, 'Soldat des Guerres Civiles,' n. 79, for several cases in Caesar's *Civil Wars*.
99 App. *BC* 5.126; Dio 49.12.4; Oros. 5.18; Vell. Pat. 2.80.4; Livy *Per.* 129; Suet. *Aug.* 16.4; Plut. *Ant.* 55.1–2; see R.A. Bauman, 'The Abdication of Collatinus,' *Acta Classica* 9 (1966), 129–41, on the legal points involving the abrogation of Lepidus' *imperium* and on his resignation to avoid criminal prosecution and loss of his priesthood. See also the account of E. Badian in 'M. Lepidus,' esp. 13–14. It is not why Badian (p.13) says that Octavian 'did not allow him [Lepidus] to live in Italy' because Circeii was clearly a place of exile.
100 Plut. *Ant.* 55.1–2; Dio 50.1.3 and 20.2–3. See Scott, 'Political Propaganda,' 38–9.

8 EXILE AND DEATH: ON THE OUTSIDE
LOOKING IN

1 Aug. *Res Gestae* 10; App. *BC* 5.131; Dio 49.15.3 and 54.15.8; Suet. *Aug.* 31.1. See my article, 'Augustus' Relations with the Aemilii Lepidi – Persecution and Patronage,' *Rheinisches Museum für Philologie* 128 (1985), 180–91.

2 Dio 54.15.5; Livy 40.51.2; see *AL*, 84.

3 Dio 49.12.4 and 50.20.3.

4 Vell. Pat. 2.88.1–3; App. *BC* 4.50; Livy *Per.* 133; Seneca *De Clem.* 1.9.5–6 and *Brev. Vit.* 4.5; Suet. *Aug.* 19.1; Dio 54.15.4; see Richard Bauman, *The Crimen Maiestatis in the Roman Republic and Augustan Principate* (Johannesburg, 1970), 180; Ernst Hohl, 'Ein Strafgericht Oktavians und ein Gnadenakt des Augustus,' *Wurzbürger Jahrbücher für die Altertumswissenschaft* 3 (1948), 107–16; D.A. Malcolm, 'Horace *Odes* iii.4,' *Classical Review* 5 (1955), 242–4. Sir Ronald Syme in *The Augustan Aristocracy* (Oxford, 1986), 35, dates the conspiracy to the autumn of 30.

5 Vell. Pat. 2.88.3.

6 See John Carter, *The Battle of Actium* (New York, 1970), 228, and F. Münzer, *Römische Adelsparteien und Adelsfamilien* (Stuttgart, 1920), 354, 370.

7 Cic. *Att.* 6.1. On Junia, see L. Hayne, 'M. Lepidus and his Wife,' *Latomus* 33 (1974), 76–9. Hayne, 79 and n. 20, makes an excellent point about Lepidus' loyalty to Junia.

8 Cic. *Phil.* 13.4.8.

9 Syme, *Augustan Aristocracy*, 112, see also 35.

10 App. *BC* 4.50. See Alain Gowing, 'The Triumviral Period in Appian and Cassius Dio' (Diss., Bryn Mawr, 1988), 183–4. On Balbinus, see Alfred Nagl, 'L. Saenius' (2) in Pauly–Wissowa, *Realencyclopädie* 1A, 2 (Stuttgart, 1920), 2, 1722; Bruno Schor, *Beiträge zur Geschichte des Sextus Pompeius* (Stuttgart, 1978), 98; T.R.S. Broughton, *The Magistrates of the Roman Republic* (3 vols, New York, 1951–2, Atlanta, 1986 Supplement), vol. III, 184.

11 Dio 54.15.4–6. See also my article, 'Augustus' Relations,' esp. 181–2.

12 Dio 54.15.7–8; Suet. *Aug.* 54. On Antistius Labeo, see Paul Jors, 'M. Antistius Labeo' (34) in Pauly–Wissowa, *Realencyclopädie* 1.2 (Stuttgart, 1894) 2548–557. See also Syme, *Augustan Aristocracy*, 79–80.

13 Richard D. Draper, 'The Role of the Pontifex Maximus and its Influence in Roman Religion and Politics' (Diss., Brigham Young University, 1988), 348–51 and 355, n. 1, claims that Lepidus did not function as pontifex maximus after 36, but cites no reasons or sources supporting this position.

14 See my article 'Augustus' Relations,' 183–5, and *AL*, 268–84, esp. 278–80, for my reasons for labeling the consul of 21 as the son of M. Lepidus, the consul of 66, rather than as the younger son of the triumvir.

15 App. *BC* 4.37.

16 See *AL*, 284–313; Syme, *Augustan Aristocracy*, 110–40.

17 Dio 54.27.2 and 56.38.2; Suet. *Aug.* 31.1; Sen. *De Clem.* 1.10.1–2; Aug. *Res Gestae* 10; *CIL* I, p. 387 and XIV.2963; Paul von Rohden 'Aemilius 73' in Pauly–Wissowa, *Realencyclopädie* 1a (Stuttgart, 1893), 560; Draper, 'Role,' 354–6.

18 Syme, *Augustan Aristocracy*, 109. On this point, see also my article 'Augustus' Relations.'

19 Tac. *Ann.* 1.9; App. *BC* 3.84 and 5.124; Dio 48.4.1, 13.4, and 49.12.1; von Rohden, 'Aemilius 73,' 561.

20 Cic. *De Oratore* 2.287 (Loeb translation by E.W. Sutton and H. Rackham). In 1.40 Cicero refers to the consul of 137 as M. Aemilius Porcina. In 2.287 he calls the censor of 179 *censor Lepidus*. A simple reference to M. Lepidus would not bring to mind Porcina unless perhaps that man's weight problems were common knowledge (Diod. Sic. 33.27). On Porcina, see *AL*, 103–17.

21 Lepidus' coin portraits are illustrated in Michael Crawford, *Roman Republican Coinage* (Cambridge, 1974), plates LVIII (nos 492/2, 494/1, 494/4), LIX (nos. 494/7b, 494/10, 494/13), and LX (no. 495/2a); and Edward A. Sydenham, *The Coinage of the Roman Republic* (London, 1952), plates 29 (no. 1161) and 30 (no. 1323); and Theodore V. Buttrey, Jr, *The Triumviral Portrait Gold of the Quattuorviri Monetales of 42 B.C.* (ANS Numismatic Notes and Monographs no. 137, New York, 1956), plates I–IV and VII (types 38, 41, 44, 47, and 50). See also above ch. 7, n. 67. On alleged portrait busts, see Ludwig Curtis, 'Ikonographische Beiträge zum Porträt der Rämischen Republik und der Julisch-Claudischen Familie,' *Mitteilungen des Deutschen Archäologischen Instituts (Römische Abteilung)* (1932), 202–68, esp. 264–8; Johann J. Bernoulli, *Römische Ikonographie* 1.1 (Stuttgart, 1882–4), 220–4; G. Monaco, 'L'iconografia imperiale nell'Ara Pacis Augustae', *Bullettino della Commissione Archeologia Comunale di Roma* 61 (1934), 17–40, esp. 24 and tables; Vagn Poulsen, *Les Portraits Romains*, vol. I (Copenhagen, 1962), 16–17; Olof Vessberg, *Studien zur Kunstgeschichte der römischen Republik* (Lund, 1941), 161–3; and R.P. Hinks, 'Recent Works on Roman Portrait-Sculpture,' *Journal of Roman Studies* 25 (1935), 88–95, esp. 91, and especially Günter Grimm, 'Die Porträts der Triumvirn C. Octavius, M. Antonius und M. Aemilius Lepidus,' *Mitteilungen des Deutschen Archäologischen Instituts (Römische Abteilung)* 96 (1989), 347–64 and plates 81–93. Busts identified as Lepidus can also be seen in Gérard Walter, *Brutus et la fin de la République* (Paris, 1938), 161, and Eleanor G. Huzar, *Mark Antony: A Biography* (Minneapolis 1978), among plates following p. 149.

9 NACHLEBEN: LEPIDUS IN HISTORY AND FICTION

1 Cic. *Phil.* 13.40 (Loeb translation by W.C.A. Ker); see also Vell. Pat. 2.64.3; Eleanor G. Huzar, *Mark Antony: A Biography* (Minneapolis, 1978), 108 and 233–52 (ch. 14, 'My Fame is Shrewdly Gored').

2 Cic. *Ad Brut.* 3.1, 22.1, 23.2, 24.9–10. For similar invective used *against* Cicero, see Christian Habicht, *Cicero the Politician* (Baltimore, 1990), 57 and n. 17, citing Ps.-Sallust.

3 Dec. Brut. in Cic. *Fam.* 11.9.1. On the associations with this 'label', see A.-M. Guillemin, 'Un cliché de la poésie élégiaque et de la langue politique' in *Mélanges Paul Thomas* (Bruges, 1930), 394–406.

4 Vell. Pat. 2.63.1, 80.1, 3.

5 Huzar, *Mark Antony*, 236.

6 Suet. *Aug.* 85.1; Aug. *Res Gest.* 2.10; see E.S. Ramage, *The Nature and Prospect of Augustus' 'Res Gestae'* (Stuttgart, 1987) and Zwi Yavetz, 'The *Res Gestae* and Augustus' Public Image' in Fergus Millar and Erich Segal, eds, *Caesar Augustus: Seven Aspects* (Oxford, 1984), 1–36.

7 Nic. Dam. 72, 103. On this author, see the translation and commentary by Jane Bellemore, *Nicolaus of Damascus, Life of Augustus* (Bristol, 1984), and Ben Zion Wacholder, *Nicolaus of Damascus* (Berkeley, 1962).

8 Livy *Per.* 119, 125, 129; see also Obs. 68 on an omen portending Lepidus' 'turpem infamiam.' R.G. Tanner has suggested (in 'Some Problems in Aeneid 7–12', *Proceedings of the Virgil Society* 10 (1970–1), 37–44, esp. 42) that the character of Latinus in Vergil's *Aeneid* is an allegorical representation for Lepidus (and also for P. Servilius Isauricus), but there is nothing definitive that makes Latinus recall Lepidus more than other priestly public figures.

9 Vell. Pat. 2.63.1. See also A.J. Woodman, *Velleius Paterculus: The Caesarian and Augustan Narrative* (Cambridge, 1983), esp. 136–249.

10 Vell. Pat. 2.63–7, 80.

11 Tac. *Ann.* 1.9.

12 It may also have resulted from confusion between Lepidus and his ancestor M. Aemilius Lepidus Porcina. See Cic. *De Oratore* 2.287; see also Diod. Sic. 33.27. Taken out of context (a discussion of famous orators), Cicero's statement could easily have been interpreted as a reference to the triumvir. On Porcina, see above, ch. 3, p. 11 and ch. 8, n. 19.

13 Tac. *Ann.* 1.10; see also Sen. *Suas.* 7.6 and Alain Gowing, 'The Triumviral Period in Appian and Cassius Dio' (Diss., Bryn Mawr, 1988), 192.

14 Plut. *Ant.* 19.2.

15 Plut. *Cic.* 46.2, 4.

16 Plut. *Mor.* 319E.

17 Suet. *Aug.* 16.4; see Livy *Per.* 129 and also Vell. Pat. 2.80.

18 Suet. *Aug.* 27.1–2.

19 Flor. 2.6, 2.8.

20 See the excellent comparison of these two historians in Gowing, esp. the section on Lepidus, pp. 171–94.

21 App. *BC.* 2.118, 130–2.

22 Ibid., 2.124.

23 Ibid. 3.4; Gowing, 'Triumviral Period,' 175.

24 App. *BC.* 3.83–4. Gowing, 'Triumviral Period' (p. 182) points out correctly that Appian focuses on military activities and on Antony and therefore includes Lepidus only when he touches these themes.

25 App. *BC.* 3.96, 4.2–3, 7–30.

26 Ibid., 4.2; Dio 46.55.4.

27 App. *BC* 3.83, 5.124.

28 Ibid., 4.12, 37; Gowing, 'Triumviral Period', 184.

29 App. *BC* 4.50; Gowing, 'Triumviral Period', 183–4.

30 Dio 41.18.2–3, 41.36.1.

31 Dio 42.15–16, 43.1; Hirt. in Caes. *Bell. Alex.* 48–64. See ch. 4, pp. 27–9 above.

32 Dio 44.22.2, 34.5–6. See also 44.28.2 where Dio has Cicero mention the failed rebellion of 78 BC and Lepidus' father as an example of what to avoid in the crisis of 44 BC.

33 Dio 44.53.6–7; see also Gowing, 'Triumviral Period,' 172–3.

34 Dio 46.38.3–7, 50–3.

35 Dio 46.55.4, 47.6–8.1, 49.15.4; see Gowing, 'Triumviral Period,' 184.

36 Dio 48.1–2, 20. 4–23, 49.1, 8–12.

37 Dio 49.12.1–3; Gowing, 'Triumviral Period,' 190–2. For a discussion of Dio's portrait of Octavian, see Gowing, 'Triumviral Period'; J. Drew Harrington, 'Cassius Dio: A Reexamination' (Diss., Lexington, Kentucky, 1970), 93–106; Bernd Manuwald, *Cassius Dio und Augustus* (Wiesbaden, 1979); Fergus Millar, *A Study of Cassius Dio* (Oxford, 1964), 83–102; M. Reinhold and P.M. Swan, 'Cassius Dio's Assessment of Augustus' in Kurt A. Raaflaub and Mark Toher, eds, *Between Republic and Empire* (Berkeley, 1990), 155–73.

38 Dio 54.15.4–8.

39 Eutrop. 6.23.1, 7.2–3, 8.

40 Rut. Nam. 1.299–302.

41 Oros. 6.18.

42 John the Lydian, *De Magistratibus* 1.38.13, 2.3.3–3.8, edited and translated by T.F. Carney (Lawrence, Kansas, 1971).

43 For example, the account of Zonaras follows pretty closely that of Cassius Dio. See Zon. 10.12, 15–17, 21–2, 25–7, 32, 34. Ranulph Higden's massive *Polychronicon* mentions (3.43) Lepidus as *magister equitum*, but in the context of his aiding Antony after Mutina and the subsequent agreement with Octavian. See the edition by Joseph Rawson Lumby, vol. IV (London, 1872) or reprint; (Neudeln, Liechtenstein, 1964), 222–5.

44 G. Boccaccio, *The Fates of Illustrious Men*, Book VI, translated by Louis R. Hall (New York, 1965), 168–70.

45 *Lydgate's Fall of Princes*, Book VI, edited by Henry Bergen (London, 1924), part III, 769–73. The reversal of Lepidus' fortune also caught the attention of Jonathan Swift (1667–1745) in 'Of Mean and Great Figures Made by Several Persons' in *The Prose Writings*, vol. V, edited by Herbert Davis (Oxford, 1962), 85.

46 Leon Battista Alberti, *Dinner Pieces*, translated with an introduction by David Marsh (Binghamton, New York, 1987); see also Joan Gadol, *Leon Battista Alberti: Universal Man of the Early Renaissance* (Chicago, 1973); Giovanni Ponte, '*Lepidus e Libripeta,*' *Rinascimento* 12 (1972), 237–65.

47 Poggio Bracciolini, *Opera Omnia* (4 vols, Turin, 1963–9), vol. I, 401.

48 Erasmus, 'Parallels' in *The Collected Works of Erasmus*, edited by Craig R. Thompson, vol. 23 (Toronto, 1978), 277; Pliny *NH* 35.121.

49 The medal is no longer extant, but was described in a volume published in 1553. See J.R. Jones, 'A Lost Renaissance Medal of Cicero and the Triumvirs,' *Numismatic Circular* 76 (1968), 264–65.

50 See my forthcoming article, 'Roman History and the Age of Enlightenment: The Dassier Medals.'

51 Hubert Goltz, *C. Iulius Caesar sive Historiae Imperatorum Caesarumque Romanorum ex Antiquis Numismatibus Restitutae*, vol. I (Bruges, 1563), 64D, 88D, 92B, 110D, 142C, 147D, 165D, 174–7, 183, 187–8, and plates 24–35.

52 Cesare Caporali, *'Vita di Mecenate,'* part 4 in *Rime*, edited by Gennaro Monti (Lanciano, 1916), 54–65; quote translated by Thomas Blackwell in *Memoirs of the Court of Augustus*, vol. II (London, 1764), 453.

53 Jean Ehrmann, 'Massacre and Persecution Pictures in Sixteenth Century France,' *Journal of the Warburg and Courtauld Institutes* 8 (1945), 195–9 and plates 46–9; Jean Adhémar, 'Antoine Caron's Massacre Paintings,' *Journal of the Warburg and Courtauld Institutes* 12 (1949), 199–200; J. Ehrmann, *Antoine Caron: Peintre à la cour des Valois* (Lille, 1955), esp. 16–20 and plates IV–VII; Anthony Blunt, *Art and Architecture in France 1500 to 1700* (London, 1953), 152–4, 420 n. 58; Howard D. Winebrot, *Augustus Caesar in 'Augustan' England* (Princeton, 1978), 59–60.

54 See n. 49 above and Pierre Quarré, 'Les bas-reliefs des triumvirs à Dijon,' *Annales de Bourgogne (Dijon)* 20 (1948), 132–6. César de Nostredame (1555–1629) also featured the 'bloody and barbaric proscription' in his account of the 'horrible triumvirate' in his *Histoire et chronique de Provence* (Lyons, 1614, reprinted Marseilles, 1971), 28. In addition, the author incorrectly assigned Provence to Antony in the initial division of provinces.

55 Jean Bodin, *The Six Bookes of a Commonweale*, edited by Kenneth McRae (Cambridge, 1962), 199 and ns. C9–10. There are additional references to Lepidus on 409 and 419. In his *Colloquium of the Seven about Secrets of the Sublime*, IV, 116, translated by Marion Leathers Daniels Kuntz (Princeton, 1975), 149, Bodin refers to Lepidus as having been 'toppled from the triumvirate.'

56 Montaigne, *Essais* (ed.) Maurice Rat, vol. II (Edition Garnier, Paris, 1962), 438 and n. 891.

57 Innocent Gentillet, *Anti-Machiavel (Discours sur les moyens de bien gouverner)*, edited by C. Edward Rathe (Geneva, 1968), 557.

58 D. P. Gent, *Severall Politique and Militarie Observations* (London, 1648), 11, 58, 71, 89.

59 D. Diderot, *'Politique des souverains'* 137 in *Œuvres politiques*, edited by Paul Vernière (Paris, 1963), 186.

60 See Plut. *Caes.* 67.2 and C.F. Tucker Brooke, ed., *Shakespeare's Plutarch* (New York, 1966), 103, where Plutarch refers to Antony and Lepidus as 'two of Caesar's chiefest friends.'

61 Shakespeare, *Julius Caesar*, Act III, scene 1; Plut. *Caes.* 67.2; App. *BC* 2.117; Dio 44.19.1.

62 Shakespeare, *Julius Caesar*, Act IV, scene 1; Plut. *Ant.* 19.2–3, *Cic.* 46.4. Shakespeare apparently got confused and transformed Antony's uncle, Lucius Caesar, into this otherwise unknown nephew Publius: see the notes on this scene in the variorum edition of Horace Howard Furness (Philadelphia, 1913), 189–195. On the treatment of Lepidus in *Julius Caesar*, see also Blanche Coles, *Shakespeare Studies: Julius Caesar* (New

York, 1940), 228–33; Augusto Guidi, '"Creature" in Shakespeare,' *Notes and Queries* 197 (1952), 443–4; M.W. MacCallum, *Shakespeare's Roman Plays and Their Background* (New York, 1967), 297; Derek Traversi, *Shakespeare: The Roman Plays* (Stanford, California, 1963), 58–9; John W. Velz, 'Orator and Imperator in Julius Caesar: Style and the Process of Roman History,' *Shakespeare Studies* 15 (1982) 55–75.

63 Shakespeare, *Julius Caesar*, Act IV, scene 1, lines 15–31.

64 Ibid., lines 34–35.

65 *Antony and Cleopatra*, edited by Marvin Spevack (MLA, New York, 1990), 708–9. For additional discussion of Lepidus' role and this play, see J. Leeds Barroll, 'Shakespeare and Roman History,' *Modern Language Review* 53 (1958), 327–43; Lawrence E. Bowling, 'Duality in the Minor Characters in *Antony and Cleopatra*,' *College English* 18 (1957), 251–5; Reuben A. Brower, *Hero and Saint: Shakespeare and the Graeco-Roman Heroic Tradition* (Oxford, 1971), 317–53; Paul A. Cantor, *Shakespeare's Rome: Republic and Empire* (Ithaca, New York, 1976), 127–225; David Cecil, *Poets and Story-tellers* (New York, 1949), 3–24; Martin Ellehauge, 'The Use of his Sources Made by Shakespeare in "Julius Caesar" and "Antony and Cleopatra",' *Englische Studien* 65 (1930–1), 197–210; Friedrich Gundolf, 'Shakespeares *Antonius und Cleopatra*', *Shakespeare Jahrbuch* 62 (1926), 7–35; Alexander Leggatt, *Shakespeare's Political Drama* (London, 1988), 161–88; MacCallum, *Shakespeare's Roman Plays*, 368–77; Julian Markels, *The Pillar of the World* (Columbus, Ohio, 1968), 31–3; Robert S. Miola, *Shakespeare's Rome* (Cambridge, 1983), 128–35; Gordon Ross Smith, 'The Melting of Authority in "Antony and Cleopatra"', *College Literature* I (1974), 1–18; Paul Stapfer, *Shakespeare and Classical Antiquity*, translated by Emily J. Carey (New York, 1970), esp. 412–17; Vivian Thomas, *Shakespeare's Roman Worlds* (London, 1989), 93–153; Traversi, *Shakespeare*, 79–203, esp. 98–117.

66 *Antony and Cleopatra* ed. Spevack, 137–21, lines 1380–4. Simon Goulart (1543–1628)'s *Life of Octavius Caesar Augustus* may have influenced Shakespeare, but the work is essentially a patchwork of Appian, Suetonius, Plutarch, and other imperial historians and adds nothing to the traditions surrounding Lepidus. Goulart's piece, attributed to a mysterious Aemilius Probus, is translated by Thomas North and included with North's translation of Plutarch, *The Lives of the Noble Grecians and Romans* (London, 1603); see esp. 51–9. See also excerpts in *Antony and Cleopatra*, ed. Spevack, 459–66, and Geoffrey Bullough, ed., *Narrative and Dramatic Sources of Shakespeare* (8 vols, New York, 1957–1975) vol. V, 321–3.

67 *Antony and Cleopatra*, ed. Spevack, 170, lines 1730–7, 1785 (Act III, scenes 5–6).

68 Shakespeare, *Antony and Cleopatra*, Act III, scene 5, lines 1–15 in *The Riverside Shakespeare*, edited by G. Blakemore Evans (Boston, 1974), 1366.

69 See John A. Garraty and Peter Gay, *Columbia History of the World* (New York, 1972), 199–200, where Lepidus is described as retiring 'to the priesthood and to drink,' and Victorien Sardou (1831–98)'s play *Cléopatre* in his *Theatre Complet*, vol. IV (Paris, 1935), where the dramatist has Antony refer to Lepidus as a drunkard ('ivrogne').

70 See William Alexander, *The Tragedie of Julius Caesar* (London, 1607), Act IV, scene 1; Robert Garnier, *The Tragedie of Antonie*, translated by Mary Herbert (Sidney), Countess of Pembroke (London, 1595), Act III; Orlando Pescetti, *Il Cesare* (Verona, 1594), Acts III, V, in Bullough, *Narrative and Dramatic Sources* V, 174–94, esp. 187, 194; Alexander Boecker, *A Probable Italian Source of Shakespeare's 'Julius Caesar'* (New York, 1913, reprint 1971), 21, 85.

71 Friedrich Gundelfinger, *Caesar in der deutschen Literatur* (Berlin, 1904), 51–9; W. Scherer, 'Brülow' in *Allgemeine Deutsche Biographie* (ed.) Rochus Freiherr von Liliencon, vol. 3 (Berlin, 1876), 420–1.

72 K. Brülow, *Cajus Julius Caesar Tragoedia* (Strasburg, 1616).

73 Georges de Scudéry, *La Mort de César*, Act II, scene 1 (Paris, 1636, reprinted New York, 1930), 38.

74 Pierre Corneille, *Mort de Pompée*, in *Théatre Complet*, edited by Maurice Rat, vol. II (Paris, 1960), 77–142, esp. 121 (Act III, scene 4, lines 1068–70). In H.T. Barnwell's notes to his edition of this play (Oxford, 1971), 60–1, he says that both Antony and Lepidus 'according to all historians' were with Caesar at Pharsalus. Antony certainly was, because he commanded the left wing, but Lepidus was in Spain and neither one joined Caesar in Egypt, as Corneille has them doing. See Plut. *Ant.* 8.3 and Huzar, *Mark Antony*, 61–3. See above, ch. 4, n. 35, for another example of confusion about Lepidus at Pharsalus.

75 Corneille, *Cinna or the Mercy of Augustus*, Act I, scene 3, Act II, scene 1, Act V, scene 2, in *Six Plays by Corneille and Racine*, ed. Paul Landis (New York, 1931), 74, 86, 119.

76 Samuel De Broé, *Histoire du triumvirat d'Auguste, Marc Antoine et Lepidus*, 2 vols, in 1 (Paris, 1694), I, 225, II, 15–18, 37, 44, 189–90.

77 Gustave Dulong, *L'Abbé de Saint-Réal* (Paris, 1921, reprinted Geneva, 1980), 304–23, esp. 305 and n. 2. *Fragmens sur Lépide* is published in *Œuvres de Mr. L'Abbé de Saint-Réal*, vol. 2 (Paris, 1722), 257–75 (=vol. 3, 126–40, of 1745 edition).

78 *Fragmens*, 257–8.

79 Ibid., 265–7.

80 Ibid., 266, 269–70.

81 Montesquieu, *Considérations sur les causes de la grandeur des Romains et de leur décadence*, edited by Gonzague Truc (Paris, 1954), 68, 193 n. 132.

82 Ibid., 63, 67. Translation by David Lowenthal, in Montesquieu, *The Greatness of the Romans and their Decline* (New York, 1965), 119. See above, ch.1, p.2. On Montesquieu's admiration for Cicero, see M.P.M. Martin, 'Montesquieu, panégyriste de Cicéron' in R. Chevallier, ed., *Présence de Cicéron* (Paris, 1984), 207–28.

83 Montesquieu, *De l'ésprit des lois*, Bk 12, ch.18 in *Œuvres complètes*, (ed.) Roger Caillois, vol. II (Paris, 1849), 448.

84 Laurence Echard, *The Roman History from the Building of the City, to the Perfect Settlement of the Empire by Augustus Caesar* (London, 1699), 331, 357, 370, 375, 384–5, 389, 395–6, 406, 410–11.

85 *The Works of John Sheffield*, vol. I (London, 1753), 309.

86 Sheffield, *Works* II, 151; Howard D. Weinbrot, *Augustus Caesar in 'Augustan' England* (Princeton, 1978), 80–2.

87 William Guthrie and John Gray, *A General History of the World from the Creation to the Present Time* (13 vols, London, 1764–7), vol. IV, 276–7, 280–3, 293–4. An earlier world history by Johannis Cluver (1593–1633) had shown Lepidus in a bad light, mentioning his proscription of his brother and quoting negative statements about him from the imperial historians: see *Historiarum Totius Mundi Epitome* (Lyons, 1657), 201a–203b (225b–228b).

88 John Blair, *The Chronology and History of the World from the Creation to the Year of Christ, 1753* (London, 1754), Table no. 20 (first century).

89 Abbé de Vertot, *The History of the Revolutions that Happened in the Government of the Roman Republic*, translated by John Ozell, vol. II (London, 1732), 335. See also the French version, *Histoire des révolutions de la république romaine*, vol. III (Paris, 1819), 333.

90 Vertot, *History* II, 340–1, *Histoire* III, 342–3, see also Vertot, *Three Dissertations* (London, 1740), 11. The commentary accompanying the 181 illustrations of Roman Republican history by Silvestre D. Mirys (*c.*1700–93) omits Lepidus from its discussion of the Lupercalia episode, follows Plutarch's account of Antony and Lepidus fleeing for cover following Caesar's assassination, and refers to the triumvirs as 'trois brigands' and to Lepidus as 'faible et méprisable' (weak and despicable), echoing Diderot and Montesquieu.

91 Charles Rollin, *The Roman History from the Foundation of Rome to the Battle of Actium*, vol. IX (London, 1768), 431, see other references on 364, 366, 383, 431, 442–3, 459, 487–8, 492, 509, 515.

92 Rollin, *Roman History* X, 152–8, 301–2.

93 Oliver Goldsmith, *The History of Rome* (London, 1828), 289–98.

94 Ibid., 299–300.

95 Ibid., 314–16.

96 Frank M. Turner, 'British Politics and the Demise of the Roman Republic: 1700–1939,' *The Historical Journal* 29 (1986), 577–99.

97 Ibid., 580.

98 Conyers Middleton, *The History of the Life of Marcus Tullius Cicero* (London, 1839), 290, see other references on 224–5, 250, 263–91, 305–8.

99 Ibid., 290; see also the commentary on Middleton in Colley Cibber, *The Character and Conduct of Cicero Considered* (London, 1747), 217, 219, 230, 239–42, 262–3, 271–3. Cibber (p. 263) calls Lepidus 'but a nose of wax.'

100 Turner, 'British Politics,' 581.

101 Blackwell, *Memoirs of the Court of Augustus* (3 vols, London, 1763–4), vol. I, 376.

102 Ibid., 376–7. On the influence of Cicero, and particularly his *Offices*, on early eighteenth-century British attitudes, see Reed Browning, *Political and Constitutional Ideas of the Court Whigs* (Baton Rouge, 1982), esp. 210–56.

103 Blackwell, *Memoirs* I, 220, 362–3, 367, II, 452, III, 360. See Howard Erskine-Hill, *The Augustan Idea in English Literature* (London, 1983), 251–4.

104 Turner, 'British Politics,' 582.

105 Ibid., 582–3.

106 Nathaniel Hooke, *The Roman History from the Building of Rome to the Ruin of the Commonwealth*, vol. XI (London, 1818), 68–70, 120–4, 140–58, 174–97, 271, 318–21.

107 Turner, 'British Politics,' 584.

108 Adam Ferguson, *The History of the Progress and Termination of the Roman Republic* (New York, 1852), 434.

109 Ibid., 275.

110 *The Fair Triumvirate at War* (London, 1742), title page.

111 Ibid., 11–13. The comment about imposing upon and working Lepidus to the purposes of Antony and Octavian recalls Shakespeare's 'slight, unmeritable man' speech.

112 John Adams, *History of Rome* (2 vols, Dublin 1792), vol. II, 123, see 120–1 on Caesar.

113 Ibid., 127.

114 Ibid., 133–4.

115 Ibid., 156–7, see other references on 135–38, 152–5, 158, 161.

116 Prosper Jolyot de Crébillon, *Le Triumvirat, ou la mort de Cicéron*, in *Œuvres de Crébillon* ed. M. Parelle, vol. II (Paris, 1828), Act I, scene 3, lines 350–1. On Crébillon, see Eleanor F. Jourdain, *Dramatic Theory and Practice in France, 1690–1808* (New York, 1968), 105–16.

117 Crébillon, *Le Triumvirat*, Act I, scene 4, lines 351–7.

118 Voltaire, *Le Triumvirat*, in *Œuvres complètes de Voltaire*, vol. V (Paris, 1877), Act I, scene 3, lines 189–90 and 190 n. 1, see also 226–7, 246–7.

119 Voltaire, *La Mort de César* (Lyons, 1794), 18.

120 Voltaire, *Letter* 9174 in *Œuvres complètes de Voltaire*, vol. XVII (Paris, 1882), 74–5.

121 Marie-Joseph de Chénier, *Brutus et Cassius ou les derniers romains*, in *Œuvres de J.F. Ducis suivies des œuvres de M.J. de Chénier* (Paris, 1859), 531–45, esp. 538 (Act II, scene 1).

122 E.Q. Visconti, *Iconographie romaine*, vol. I (Paris, 1817), 181 n. 1.

123 Ibid., 181–2.

124 Ibid., 182.

125 Ibid., 182–4 and 183 n. 1.

126 Ibid., 184 and n. 2.

127 Ibid., 186.

128 Turner, 'British Politics,' 588.

129 Thomas Arnold, *History of the Later Roman Commonwealth* (New York, 1846), 335, 361. Arnold (p. 414) credits not Lepidus but the soldiers sent to murder Paullus with Paullus' escape, claiming that they either 'respected . . . the brother of their general, or perhaps were shocked at the unnatural wickedness of that general, in commanding the murder of so near a relation.'

130 Vell. Pat. 2.63.1; Arnold, *History*, 335, 374.

131 Arnold, *History*, 359, 399, 409, 414, 420.

132 Ibid., 383.

133 Turner, 'British Politics,' 590.

134 Charles Merivale, *History of the Romans under the Empire* (8 vols, New York, 1904), vol. II, 173. See Dio 43.1.1–3 and above, ch. 4, 27–9 and n. 36.

135 Merivale, *History* II, 340, 417.

136 Ibid., III, 197.

137 Ibid., 181, 269.

138 Charles Merivale, ed., *An Account of the Life and Letters of Cicero* (London, 1854), 423, 452.

139 Charles Merivale, *The Roman Triumvirates* (New York, 1887), 201, see also 137–9, 150, 197, 199, 202, 205, 217.

140 Ibid., 219.

141 Henry G. Liddell, *A History of Rome* (New York, 1860), 704, 710, see also 678, 712, 720, 722, 724; Turner, 'British Politics,' 592.

142 J. A. Froude, *Caesar: A Sketch* (London, 1899), 454, 459; Turner, 'British Politics,' 593.

143 Samuel Eliot, *History of Liberty, Part I: The Ancient Romans*, vol. II (Boston, 1853), 384, see also 372–3, 376–7, 379, 381.

144 William Smith, *Dictionary of Greek and Roman Biography and Mythology*, vol. II (London, 1849), 768.

145 Anthony Trollope, *The Life of Cicero*, vol. II (London, 1880), 252, 266, 278, see also 271, 275–7, 287–92.

146 George Long, *The Decline of the Roman Republic*, vol. V (London, 1874), 287–9, 452, 454–6, 460.

147 T.M. Taylor, *A Constitutional and Political History of Rome: From the Earliest Times to the Reign of Domitian* (London, 1899, reprinted in 1923), 399, see also 357, 379–82, 388, 390, 392–8.

148 H.F. Pelham, *Outlines of Roman History* (London, 1893, reprinted in 1949), 326–32, 337, 344–6.

149 Gilbert Abbott à Beckett, *The Comic History of Rome* (London, 1852), 301.

150 John Bonner, *A Child's History of Rome*, vol. II (New York, 1856), 37.

151 Ibid., 44.

152 E.M. Sewell, *The Child's First History of Rome* (New York, 1867), 176, 184, 186.

153 William F. Allen, *A Short History of the Roman People* (Boston, 1890), 228. Hutton Webster's view (*Ancient History*, Boston, 1913, 429) more than echoed Allen's: 'the incompetent Lepidus was set aside by his stronger colleagues.'

154 Arthur Gilman, *The Story of Rome* (New York, 1896), 266–7, see also 243, 251, 256, 261.

155 Pierre-Charles Levesque, *Histoire critique de la république romaine*, vol. III (Paris, 1807), 358–9, 420 (translation mine).

156 Ibid., 352–3.

157 Ibid., 352, 359, 419.

158 A.E. Egger, *Examen critique des historiens anciens de la vie et du regne d'Auguste* (Paris, 1844), 2 (translation mine), see also 252–3, 257–8, 304–5.

159 Victor Duruy, *History of Rome and of the Roman People*, (8 vols, Boston, 1883), vol. III, 434, 442, 534–5, 542, 553–6, 572–6, 584–6, 597, 601, 617, 619, 622, 625, 630, 632, 634–5, 637–8, and vol. IV, 87. On Duruy's life, see Sandra Horvath-Peterson, *Victor Duruy and French Education* (Baton Rouge, 1984), 11–23, 241–6.

160 Jules Michelet, *History of the Roman Republic*, translated by William Hazlitt (London, 1863), 378–9.

161 Ibid., 374–6, 380.

162 Ibid., 375–7, 379, 386, 389.

163 P. Deschamps, *Essai bibliographique sur M.T. Cicéron* (Paris, 1863), pp. xxvii–xxviii (translation mine).

164 B.G. Niebuhr, *The History of Rome*, edited by Leonhard Schmitz, vol. V, (London, 1844), 107–8. The German version is *Historische und philologische Vorträge*, vol. III.1 (Berlin, 1848), esp. 89, see also 87, 91, 104, 109, 117.

165 Niebuhr, *History*, 125, 131.

166 W. Drumann and P. Groebe, *Geschichte Roms*, vol. I (Berlin, 1899), 16–17.

167 Karl Wilhelm Nitzsch, *Geschichte der römischen Republik*, vol. II (Leipzig, 1885), 271–91.

168 Theodor Mommsen, *Gesammelte Schriften*, vol. IV (Berlin, 1906), 162, 261; Benedictus Niese, *Grundriss der Römischen Geschichte nebst Quellenkunde*, revised by E. Hohl (Munich, 1923), 257–70, esp. 260.

169 Ludwig Lange, *Römische Alterthümer*, vol. III (Berlin, 1876), 486–586, esp. 563.

170 Carl Peter, *Geschichte Roms*, vol. II (Halle, 1881), 431–2, 439, see also, in general, 381–4, 429–77.

171 Vell. Pat. 2.63; Felix Brueggemann, *De Marci Aemilii Lepidi vita et rebus gestis* (Diss., Münster, 1887), 8, 72.

172 Viktor Gardthausen, *Augustus und seine Zeit* (Leipzig, 1891) vol. I.1, 28, see also 35, 107–9, 132, 276–8 (translation mine).

173 Paul von Rohden, 'Aemilius 73' in Pauly–Wissowa, *Realencyclopädie* (Stuttgart, 1893) 1.1 556.

174 Ibid., 557.

175 Ibid., 558.

176 Cic. *Phil.* 13.8; von Rohden, 'Aemilius 73,' 561.

177 William Forsyth, *Life of Marcus Tullius Cicero* (2 vols, New York, 1887) vol. II, 15, 132, 239, 260, 277, 291, 295–301, 311–13; J.L. Strachan–Davidson, *Cicero and the Fall of the Roman Republic* (London, 1894), 381–2, 408–9, 419–23.

178 Gaston Boissier, *Cicero and his Friends*, translated by Adnah David Jones (New York, 1897), 346; Gaston Delayen, *Cicero*, translated by Farrell Symons (London, 1931), 249, see also 242, 248, 257.

179 Torsten Petersson, *Cicero: A Biography* (Berkeley, 1920), 598, see also 671–4. In addition, see E.G. Sihler, *Cicero of Arpinum* (New York, 1933), 448.

180 G.C. Richards, *Cicero: A Study* (London, 1935), 200.

181 R.E. Smith, *Cicero the Statesman* (Cambridge, 1966), 252–3.

182 D.R. Shackleton Bailey, *Cicero* (New York, 1971); Elizabeth Rawson, *Cicero: A Portrait* (London, 1975); W. K. Lacey, *Cicero and the End of the Roman Republic* (London, 1978); Richard Mitchell, *Cicero: The Senior Statesman* (New Haven, 1991).

183 Max Radin, *Marcus Brutus* (London, 1939), 159, 161.

184 Ibid., 163.

185 M.L. Clarke, *The Noblest Roman: Marcus Brutus and His Reputation* (London, 1981), 39; G. Walter, *Brutus* (Paris, 1938).

186 John B. Firth, *Augustus Caesar and the Organization of the Empire of Rome* (London, 1902), 49, 62–3, 81, 83; see also Turner, 'British Politics,' 596–7.

187 Firth, *Augustus Caesar*, 97.

188 Ibid., 117–19, 124–5.

189 E.S. Shuckburgh, *Augustus* (London, 1903), 106–7.

190 René Francis, *Augustus: His Life and His Work* (London, 1914), 73, 84–6.

191 John Buchan, *Augustus* (Boston, 1937), 49.

192 Ibid., 69.

193 Ibid., 72, 82, 93.

194 Dietmar Kienast, *Augustus: Prinzeps und Monarch* (Darmstadt, 1982).

195 Arthur Weigall, *The Life and Times of Marc Antony* (Garden City, New York, 1931); Jack Lindsay, *Marc Antony* (New York, 1937); Hermann Bengtson, *Marcus Antonius* (Munich, 1977); Eleanor G. Huzar, *Mark Antony: A Biography* (Minneapolis, 1978); Alan Roberts, *Mark Antony* (Upton upon Severn, 1988); François Chamoux, *Marc Antoine* (Paris, 1986).

196 Huzar, *Mark Antony*, 146.

197 W.E. Heitland, *The Roman Republic* (3 vols, Cambridge, 1909), vol. III 404, 420.

198 Tenney Frank, *History of Rome* (New York, 1923), 301; Holmes, *The Roman Republic*, vol. III (Oxford, 1923); André Piganiol, *Histoire de Rome* (Paris, 1939).

199 H.G. Wells, *The Outline of History*, vol. I (New York, 1921), 514.

200 Henry Smith Williams, *The Historians' History of the World*, vol. V (New York, 1926), 616.

201 *Cambridge Ancient History*, vol. X (Cambridge, 1934), 63.

202 Ibid., 62.

203 Ibid., 17–18.

204 Frank B. Marsh, *A History of the Roman World from 146 to 30 B.C.* (2nd edition, London, 1953), 273.

205 Ibid., 294.

206 Ernst Hohl, 'Das Angebot des Diadems an Cäsar,' *Klio* 47 (1941), 92–117, esp. 107.

207 Michael Grant, *The Twelve Caesars* (New York, 1975), 40; Erich Gruen, *The Last Generation of the Roman Republic* (Berkeley, 1974), 103; Paul MacKendrick, *The North African Stones Speak* (Chapel Hill, 1980), 205.

208 Christian Meier, 'Lepidus' in *Lexicon der alten Welt*, ed. Carl Anderson (Zurich and Stuttgart, 1965), 1712; Alfred Heuss, *Römische Geschichte* (Braunschweig, 1976), 223; Ernst Kornemann, *Römische Geschichte*, vol. II (3rd edition, Stuttgart, 1954), 85, 91; N.A. Maschkin, *Zwischen Republik und Kaiserreich* (Leipzig, 1954); Helga Botermann, *Die Soldaten und die römische Politik in der Zeit von Caesars Tod bis zur Begründung des zweiten Triumvirats* (Munich, 1968); Joseph Vogt, *Die römische Republik* (6th edition, Munich, 1973); Peter Wallmann, *Triumviri Rei Publicae Constituendae* (Frankfurt, 1989).

209 Ronald Syme, *The Roman Revolution* (Oxford, 1939), 109, 163, 166, 180, 230; see also 69.

210 Ibid., 180.

211 Ronald Syme, 'A Roman Post-Mortem,' in *Roman Papers*, ed. Ernst Badian, vol. I (Oxford, 1979), 214.

212 Ronald Syme, *Sallust* (Berkeley, 1964), 123, 220.

213 Ibid., 220.

214 Ronald Syme, *Tacitus* (2 vols, Oxford, 1958), vol. I, 150, 355; vol. II, 569.

215 Syme, 'Livy and Augustus,' in *Roman Papers* I, 436.

216 Ronald Syme, *The Augustan Aristocracy* (Oxford, 1986), 108. See above, ch. 8, p. 99.

217 Ronald Syme, 'Paullus the Censor,' *Athenaeum* 65 (1987), 8.

218 Orville Prescott's review in *New York Times* (August 13, 1958), 25.

219 Alfred Duggan, *Three's Company* (New York, 1958), 182. For additional, especially negative passages, see 25–8, 36–8, 53, 106, 119, 205, 210.

220 W.G. Hardy, *The Scarlet Mantle* (Toronto, 1978), 195, 340–1; *The Bloodied Toga* (Toronto, 1979), 381, 407–8, 416–17, 440, 443–6, 466, 480.

221 Hardy, *Bloodied Toga*, 464. Hardy mistakenly allocates Narbonese Gaul to Antony in the initial division of provinces.

222 Ibid., 466–8.

223 Thornton Wilder, *The Ides of March* (New York, 1948), 244, see also 239.

224 Phyllis Bentley, *Freedom, Farewell!* (New York, 1936), 406.

225 Ibid., 464.

226 Ibid., 466.

227 Dyke Williams, *Twilight at Janiculum* (Roslyn Heights, New York, 1975), 56–62.

228 Alan K. Massie, *Let the Emperor Speak* (Garden City, New York, 1987), 31.

229 Ibid., 59.

230 Ibid., 64.

231 Ibid., 67.

232 Ibid.

233 Ibid., 108–16.

234 See Jon Solomon, *The Ancient World in the Cinema* (London, 1978), 40–1.

235 Russell Baker, 'Three Men on an Eagle,' *New York Times* (March 12, 1988), 13.

236 Walter Goodman's review, *New York Times* (October 27, 1986), C19; John Willis, *Theatre World*, vol. 43 (1986–7 Season) (New York, 1988), 71.

237 Léonie Hayne, 'Lepidus' Role after the Ides of March,' *Acta Classica* 14 (1971), 116–17.

238 Cic. *Fam.* 11.9; Léonie Hayne, 'M. Lepidus and his Wife,' *Latomus* 33 (1974), 76–9.

239 Léonie Hayne, 'The Defeat of Lepidus in 36 B.C.,' *Acta Classica* 17 (1974), 59–65.

240 Hermann Bengtson, 'Untersuchungen zum mutinensischen Krieg' in *Kleine Schriften zur alten Geschichte* (Munich, 1974), 479–531, esp. 520–31.

241 J. Guey and A. Pernette, 'Lépide à Thàbraca,' *Karthago* 9 (1958), 78–89;

J. Guey, 'Dedicace à Lépide,' *Bulletin de la Societé Nationale des Antiquaires de France* (1957) [1959], 186–7 and plate XV, 1.

242 François Bertrandy, 'Thibilis (Announa), de Juba Ier au Triumvir M. Aemilius Lepidus,' *Karthago* 19 (1977–8), [1980] 87–106, esp. 103–6 and n. 71.

243 Gowing, 'The Triumviral Period' esp. 171–94; 'Lepidus' Role in the Proscriptions of 43/42 BC' (paper presented by Gowing at the annual meeting of the American Philological Association in 1990).

244 Richard D. Weigel, 'The Coins Issued by Lepidus as *Triumvir Monetalis*,' *SAN* (Society for Ancient Numismatics Journal) 5 (1973–4), 51–2; 'Lepidus Reconsidered,' *Acta Classica* 17 (1974), 67–73; 'The Career of L. Paullus, cos. 50,' *Latomus* 38 (1979), 637–46; 'Augustus' Relations with the Aemilii Lepidi – Persecution and Patronage,' *Rheinisches Museum für Philologie* 128 (1985), 180–91; 'A Reevaluation of Lepidus' "Basilica Aemilia" Denarius' in Ian Carradice, ed., *Proceedings of the 10th International Congress of Numismatics* (London, 1990), 147–52.

245 Some of the concluding statements in this section are repeated from my article 'Lepidus Reconsidered.'

SELECT BIBLIOGRAPHY

Badian, Ernst, 'M. Lepidus and the Second Triumvirate,' *Arctos* 25 (1991), 5–16.

Bengtson, Hermann, 'Untersuchungen zum mutinensischen Krieg,' *Kleine Schriften zur alten Geschichte* (Munich, 1974), 479–531.

Bengtson, Hermann, *Zu den Proskriptionen der Triumvirn* (Munich, 1972).

Bertrandy, François, 'Thibilis (Announa), de Juba Iᵉʳ au Triumvir M. Aemilius Lepidus,' *Karthago* 19 (1977–8 [1980]), 87–106.

Botermann, Helga, *Die Soldaten und die römische Politik in der Zeit von Caesars Tod bis zur Begründung des zweiten Triumvirats* (Munich, 1968).

Bringmann, Klaus, 'Das Zweite Triumvirat' in Peter Kneissl and Volker Losemann, eds, *Alte Geschichte und Wissenschaftsgeschichte* (Darmstadt, 1988), 22–38.

Brueggemann, Felix, 'De Marci Aemilii Lepidi vita et rebus gestis' (Diss., Münster, 1887).

Buttrey, Theodore V., Jr, *The Triumviral Portrait Gold of the Quattuorviri Monetales of 42 B.C.* (New York, 1956).

Criniti, Nicola, 'M. Aimilius Q.f.M.n. Lepidus, "*ut ignis in stipula*",' *Memorie – Istituto Lombardo Accademia di Scienze e Lettere* 30 (1969), 319–460.

Draper, Richard D., 'The Role of the Pontifex Maximus and its Influence in Roman Religion and Politics' (Diss., Brigham Young University, 1988).

Gabba, Emilio, 'The Perusine War and Triumviral Italy,' *Harvard Studies in Classical Philology* 75 (1971), 139–60.

Galve-Izquierdo, Mária Pilar, *Lépido en España – Testimonios* (Zaragoza, 1974).

Gowing, Alain M., 'The Triumviral Period in Appian and Cassius Dio' (Diss., Bryn Mawr, 1988).

Grimm, Gunter, 'Die Porträts der Triumvirn C. Octavius, M. Antonius und M. Aemilius Lepidus,' *Mitteilungen des Deutschen Archäologischen Instituts, Römische Abteilung* 96 (1989), 347–64 and plates 81–93.

Guey, J., 'Dedicace à Lépide,' *Bulletin de la Société Nationale des Antiquaires de France* (1957) [1959], 186–7 and plate XV, 1.

Guey, J., and Pernette, A., 'Lépide à Thàbraca,' *Karthago* 9 (1958), 78–89.

Hayne, Léonie, 'Lepidus' Role after the Ides of March,' *Acta Classica* 14 (1971), 109–17.

Hayne, Léonie, 'L. Paullus and his Attitude toward Pompey,' *L'Antiquité Classique* 41 (1972), 148–55.

Hayne, Léonie, 'M. Lepidus (cos. 78): A Reappraisal,' *Historia* 21 (1972), 661–8.

Hayne, Léonie, 'The Defeat of Lepidus in 36 B.C.,' *Acta Classica* 17 (1974), 59–65.

Hayne, Léonie, 'M. Lepidus and his Wife,' *Latomus* 33 (1974), 76–9.

Hinard, François, *Les Proscriptions de la Rome républicaine* (Rome, 1985).

Huzar, Eleanor Goltz, *Mark Antony: A Biography* (Minneapolis, 1978).

Labruna, L., *Il 'console sovversivo'* (Naples, 1975).

Münzer, F., *Römische Adelsparteien und Adelsfamilien* (Stuttgart, 1920).

Syme, Ronald, *The Roman Revolution* (Oxford, 1939).

Syme, Ronald, *The Augustan Aristocracy* (Oxford, 1986).

Taylor, Lily Ross, 'Caesar's Colleagues in the Pontifical College,' *American Journal of Philology* 63 (1942), 385–412.

Taylor, Lily Ross, 'The Election of the Pontifex Maximus in the Late Republic,' *Classical Philology* 37 (1942), 421–4.

von Rohden, Paul, 'Aemilius 73' in Pauly–Wissowa, *Realencyclopädie der classischen Altertumswissenschaft* Ia (Stuttgart, 1893), 556–61.

Wallmann, Peter, *Triumviri rei publicae constituendae* (Frankfurt am Main, 1989).

Weigel, Richard, 'The Coins Issued by Lepidus as *Triumvir Monetalis*,' *SAN* (Society for Ancient Numismatics Journal) 5 (1973–4), 51–2.

Weigel, Richard, 'Lepidus Reconsidered,' *Acta Classica* 17 (1974), 67–73.

Weigel, Richard, 'The Career of L. Paullus, cos. 50,' *Latomus* 38 (1979), 637–46.

Weigel, Richard, 'Augustus' Relations with the Aemilii Lepidi – Persecution and Patronage,' *Rheinisches Museum für Philologie* 128 (1985), 180–91.

Weigel, Richard, 'A Reevaluation of Lepidus' "Basilica Aemilia" Denarius' in Ian Carradice, ed., *Proceedings of the 10th International Congress of Numismatics* (London, 1990), 147–52.

GENERAL INDEX

NACHLEBEN INDEX

Note: Classical writers have been included in the General index. Although not all post-classical commentators have been included in the *Nachleben* chapter, an attempt has been made to incorporate those who represented different periods of time or distinctive points of view.